*Cheap Eats in Italy*

# CHEAP EATS IN ITALY

**SECOND EDITION**
The Savvy Traveler's Guide to
the Best Meals at the Best
Prices.

**SANDRA A. GUSTAFSON**

**CHRONICLE BOOKS**
SAN FRANCISCO

Printed in the United States of America.

Second Edition
ISBN 0-8118-1070-4
ISSN 1074-5084

Cover design: Robin Weiss
Cover photograph: Debra Lande
Book design: Words & Deeds
Original maps: Françoise Humbert


Distributed in Canada by Raincoast Books,
8680 Cambie Street, Vancouver, B.C. V6P 6M9


10 9 8 7 6 5 4 3 2 1


Chronicle Books
275 Fifth Street
San Francisco, CA 94103

**For Mr. L**

*Con Amore*

*e*

*tante grazie per tanti ricordi*

# Contents

# To the Reader

**In Florence you think, in Rome you pray, and in Venice you love. In all three, you eat.**

*—Italian proverb*

Italians have been trendsetters at the table ever since the Middle Ages. They were the first to use a fork, the first to wash their hands before a meal, and one of the first to make a point of preparing their food using the freshest of ingredients. When it comes to cuisine, few countries in the Western world have given so much to so many. Just think of all the foods you love and no doubt a majority of them will be Italian: pasta, pizza, balsamic vinegar, Parmesan cheese, sundried tomatoes, porcini mushrooms, polenta, osso buco, prosciutto, minestrone—the list is endless. When we want satisfaction, comfort, or pure enjoyment, we eat Italian.

To Italians, life is meant to be lived fully. Food is not considered mere sustenance, but it is a work of art to be enjoyed and relished at every meal. If you overindulge, a shot of the strong herbal mix Fernet-Branca, available in most bars, will set you straight in no time.

In the last thirty-five years, Italy has gone through a complete economic transformation and is now the world's fifth-largest industrial power. As a result, prices have skyrocketed, the dollar goes up and down like a yo-yo, and inflation is rampant. *Nothing* is cheap in Italy, and certainly not the food. Today it costs almost $1.50 to buy and send a postcard back to the States, even modest restaurants charge $25 to $30 for a meal, and you can easily spend $10 or more on a mediocre sandwich and warm beer if you don't know where to eat. If you want a *cheap* Italian meal, you had better stay home and go to your local pizza or pasta parlor. It will not be as good as the wood-fired pizza you will eat at Pizzeria da Baffetto in Rome, or the robust pasta you will have at Taverna San Trovaso in Venice, but I can assure you it will be cheaper.

Here is where *Cheap Eats in Italy* comes to your rescue. Before you read on, however, *please* be aware that this book is *not* a listing of the cheapest places to eat in Florence, Rome, and Venice. It is, instead, your reliable guide in each city to good quality food with a realistic cost-to-value ratio. This book will lead you to good meals in all price ranges, from Big Splurges to picnics on the piazza. It will help you plan your dining according to the constraints of your budget—you will know just where to go to get the maximum value for the minimum outlay. Just as important is that you will be dining where the natives do, not where the tour buses stop.

When it comes to research, other guide books may send only a questionnaire or have someone stop by a random selection of entries. I do not do that. I am personally responsible for every entry in this book, and

I have been to every address listed. Updates are frequent. In doing the research for *Cheap Eats in Italy,* I spend months in Italy, walking hundreds of miles in every type of weather, checked on countless addresses, and ate meals that ranged from terrible and indifferent to delightful and gourmet. The result is this edition of *Cheap Eats in Italy,* which lists more than two hundred dining establishments. In the write-ups, I describe the atmosphere and decor; the other diners; how the food is prepared, presented, and tastes; and what it all costs. I recommend dishes to give you an idea of what the restaurant does best. Because most menus in these three cities reflect four seasons of the year, it is possible that many of the dishes I describe may not be served when you visit. The subject of the many fine Italian wines is one I do not cover . . . That would necessitate another book. I do comment on some of the house wines and tell you if they are drinkable.

Whether you are traveling for business or pleasure, I urge you to travel with an open mind. When you leave home, don't expect to encounter your way of life or your favorite soul food. Enjoy where you are, the people, the sights, the sounds, and even the smells. Sample a wide variety of foods, and try to roll with the punches, since travel is rarely trouble-free. If you can see the humor in a difficult situation, you will come home a more knowledgeable person, with a lifetime of happy memories.

By using this edition of *Cheap Eats in Italy,* I hope you will return with some of the best memories of all: those of good meals in wonderful settings, enjoyed all the more because they cost less. If I have been able to help you do this, I will consider my job well done. I want to hear from all of you . . . Until then, *buona fortuna* and *buon appetito!*

# *How to Use*
# Cheap Eats in Italy

Each listing in *Cheap Eats in Italy* includes the following information: the name and address of the establishment; the area of the city in which it is located; the telephone number; the days it is open and closed; annual closing dates; hours of service; whether reservations are necessary; credit cards accepted; the average price of a three-course à la carte meal without beverages; the price of the *menù turistico* (set-price meal); what the cover and service charges are; and whether or not English is spoken.

The following abbreviations are used to indicate which credit cards are accepted:

| | |
|---|---|
| American Express | AMEX |
| Diners Club | DC |
| MasterCard or Access | MC |
| Visa | V |

At the end of the restaurant listings, you will find a glossary of words, phrases, and menu and food terms as well as an address where you can send me any comments you may have.

# Twelve Tips for Enjoying Cheap Eats in Italy

**The President could solve all the country's problems by having a big plate of spaghetti once a week. Congress can supply the meatballs.**

*—Will Rogers*

1. When dining out, remember where you are when you are ordering and stay within the limits of the chef's abilities. Do not expect gourmet fare in a snack bar, and do not go to a fancy restaurant and order only a salad and a glass of wine.

2. Always read the menu posted outside before going in. This prevents you from being seated before finding out that you do not like what is being served, or worse, that the prices are too high.

3. Consider ordering the daily specials and the house specialties. You can be sure these will be the best the chef has to offer and will usually consist of seasonally fresh foods.

4. Drink tap water (*acqua naturale*) and stick to the house wine.

5. Don't sit down! Drink your morning cappuccino and eat your snack or lunch while standing. If you sit down in a *caffè*, you will be charged up to twice as much for the privilege than if you consume your food on foot. If you sit at an outside table, the tab could be even more. The benefit of sitting is that you acquire something akin to "squatter's rights" and can linger at your table without being bothered.

6. For the Cheapest Eat, consider the *menù turistico* (set-price meal). Even though the choices may be boring and limited, it is usually a good buy because it includes at least two courses and the cover and services charges. Some also include dessert and/or beverage.

7. To keep the tab lower on an à la carte meal, skip the antipasto course and head for the pastas and main dishes. Keep in mind that most main courses on an à la carte menu are not garnished, and orders of vegetables and salads will be extra. Also beware of dishes on the à la carte menu (such as fresh fish or Florentine beef steaks) marked *S.Q.* or *L 4,000 hg*. *S.Q.* means that you will be charged according to the total weight of the food ordered. For example, *L 4,000 hg* means you will pay L 4,000 *per* hectogram (3.5 ounces). These hectograms can add up in a big hurry.

8. By law, restaurants must indicate when frozen food is used. Most often you will find that if anything is frozen, it will be the fish. If there is an asterisk (*) by any menu item, it is *congelato* (frozen). Make sure what you are ordering is *fresco* (fresh).

9. The cover charge is *per person* and the service charge is a percentage of the total bill. The good news is that *the service charge is the tip*. You do not have to pay one lira more unless you feel the service has been out of the ordinary. If you are having a coffee at the bar, leave the bartender L 200. If the restaurant does not include or add the service charge themselves, leave 12 to 15 percent of the total bill as a tip.

10. Every restaurant in Italy is required to give you a formal bill, which you are legally required to carry with you when you leave. Before leaving, compare the bill with the prices on the menu and add up the figures. Do not hesitate to question anything you do not understand. Mistakes are rampant.

11. If you see a headwaiter standing in the doorway, tour buses parked outside, or an empty restaurant during prime time, keep going.

12. If you are thirty years old or younger, invest in a Rolling Venice Card (*carta Giovani*). This bargain to end all bargains entitles the holder to discounts at restaurants, hotels, shops, and certain museums. It costs L 5,000 and requires the bearer to produce a photo ID and a photo to use on the issued card. Cards are available only in Venice at the following locations:

   **Corte Contanina, 1529 (San Marco)**
   Telephone: 27-07-650
   Open: Mon–Fri 9:30 A.M.–1 P.M., Tues, Thur also 3–5 P.M.

   **Calle Loredan, 4127 (San Marco)**
   Telephone: 52-39-666
   Open: Tues–Fri 3:30–7 P.M., Sat 9:30 A.M.–12:30 P.M.

   **Railroad Station**
   Summer Only

# General Information about Italian Dining

**Everything you see I owe to spaghetti.**
—Sophia Loren

## WHEN TO EAT

### Breakfast (*La Colazione* or *La Prima Colazione*)

Hotels and *pensione* usually serve a Continental breakfast that consists of coffee, tea, or hot chocolate, fresh rolls, butter, and preserves. Sometimes juice and cheese are included. Cheap Eaters should try to get their hotel to deduct this cost—which can be as much as $15 per person—from their bill and eat their breakfast at a bar or *caffè*. It will cost half of what a hotel will charge, and the coffee will be better, the pastry fresher, and the local scene far more interesting. Remember: If you sit down, the price will increase by 50 to 250 percent *more* per person than if you stand at the bar with all the other Italians.

### Lunch (*Pranzo* or *Colazione*)

Lunch usually starts at 12:30 P.M. and lasts anywhere from thirty minutes (stand up) to three hours. Last order is supposed to be the time the restaurants lists as closing, but more often the last order will be taken about thirty minutes *before* closing. Lunch can be anything from a quick sandwich eaten standing at the corner bar to a full-blown four- or five-course meal ending with a strong coffee under the umbrellas on a busy piazza . . . which has to be one of the true pleasures of eating in Italy. Time, cost, calories, location, and hunger are the factors that will help you decide what to do for lunch. Sandwiches are available in a *paninoteca,* a bar selling sandwiches either made to order or ready made and found displayed under napkins in a case. If you are staying in one place for a few days, it is fun to become a "local" by eating your lunch each day in the same small restaurant or trattoria. The first day you will be treated with politeness. The second, your waiter will be pleased to see you back, and on the third, you will be treated as a "regular" and your waiter will already know what type of wine you like. Try it . . . you will be surprised. In most places, the menus for lunch and dinner are the same, and there is no price break offered at lunch.

### Dinner (*La Cena*)

Dinner is usually served from 7:30 P.M. on. If you want to eat with other foreigners, reserve a table for 7:30. If you want a more Italian experience, dine at 8:30 or later.

## WHERE TO EAT

At one time there was a distinct difference between a trattoria and a *ristorante,* based on the type of clientele and the prices charged. Now they are virtually interchangeable. A trattoria is generally a family-run affair with Mamma or Papà in the kitchen, and children helping out wherever needed. The decor and the menu are simple and the prices only *slightly* less than in a *ristorante.*

Fast-food *italiano* is a boon to all Cheap Eaters, and I am not talking McDonalds, where a burger, fries, and shake can cost upwards of $12. Besides, who wants a Big Mac in Italy? Inexpensive meals can be found in stand-up snack bars that feature the *tavola calda,* which means "hot table." Usually frequented for lunch, these places feature a series of hot and cold dishes either to eat there or take out. *Rosticcerie* are also places that offer hot and cold dishes to eat in or take out. At either the *tavola calda* or *rosticceria,* items are priced by the portion. You choose your food, pay the cashier, get a receipt, and give that to the person behind the counter, who will dish up your food. Snack counters in bars sell ready-made sandwiches and so do *paninotece,* which are actual sandwich bars. You will also encounter pizzerias (very often open only in the evening, especially in Rome and Florence) and places called *pizza a taglio* or *pizza rustica.* These are hole-in-the-wall shops selling ready-made pizza by the slice. The pizza is cut to order and sold by weight. It is fun to try several small pieces. Alcoholic beverages are usually not served, but soft drinks and bottled mineral water will be. Seating is virtually nonexistent.

Other places for a quick bite or a simple meal include a *latteria,* which sells cheese, yogurt, and other dairy products; a *gelateria,* which serves ice cream; or a *pasticceria,* where you can go for a fresh pastry any time of the morning or afternoon. At *il forno* you can buy bread, and at an *alimentari, salumeria,* or *gastronomia* you can buy cold cuts, cheese, wine, bread, mineral water, and other foods to put together a picnic in the piazza or back in your hotel room. For a glass or two of wine and a light meal or snack, go to an *enoteca,* or wine bar. *Osterias* are also wine bars, but more the blue-collar type.

An Italian *caffè,* or bar, is much more than a place to drink coffee or alcoholic beverages. Here you can eat breakfast, have a snack, buy a sandwich, make phone calls, use the toilet, read the newspaper, listen to or watch sporting events, meet your neighbor or lover, and argue over politics. If there is a black-and-white "T" (for tobacco) displayed outside, you can also buy cigarettes, matches, some toiletries, stamps, and bus tickets. No wonder there are more than five thousand such places in central Rome alone.

What kind of coffee should you order in a *caffè?* The possibilities can be confusing to many Americans. This is a list of the most popular caffeine-laden drinks.

| | |
|---|---|
| *caffè* | A small cup of very strong coffee, i.e., espresso |
| *caffè Americano* | American-style coffee, but stronger |

| | |
|---|---|
| *caffè corretto* | Coffee "corrected" with a shot of grappa, cognac, or other spirit |
| *caffè freddo* | Iced coffee |
| *caffè Hag* | Decaffeinated coffee |
| *caffè latte* | Hot milk mixed with coffee and served in a glass for breakfast |
| *caffè macchiato* | Espresso "stained" with a drop of steamed milk. A small version of a cappuccino |
| *cappuccino* | Espresso infused with steamed milk and drunk in the morning, but never, never after lunch or dinner |
| *granitadi di caffè con panne* | Iced coffee with whipped cream |

Like the French, Italians never drink coffee or tea *with* any meal except breakfast. Coffee (*caffè*) is often ordered after a meal. Tea is only considered a morning or between-meal beverage or one to be used for medicinal purposes. It is the unknowing tourist who orders a cappuccino in a restaurant after lunch or dinner. When ordering your after-dinner coffee, do not ask for an espresso, ask for a *caffè, per favore.*

## HOW TO EAT ITALIAN-STYLE

**No man is lonely while eating spaghetti; it requires too much attention.**

*—Christopher Morley*

Italians believe that God keeps an Italian kitchen, and so everyone should enjoy *la cucina italiana*. The following advice will help you do it in style.

Dealing with Italian waiters is similar to crossing Italian streets: you can do it if you are brazen enough, showing skill and courage and looking all the time as though you own the place. A good waiter should explain the dishes on the menu and help you select the wine. But if you order coffee or tea during the meal, ask for the ketchup bottle, or request a doggie bag . . . watch out, you will be in big trouble.

Cocktails before dinner are not popular and are associated negatively with Americans and the three-martini lunch. However, an apéritif, such as a flute of sparkling wine to sip as you are deciding what to order, is often served.

You do not have to order all of the courses in an Italian meal, but you will be expected to have more than a pasta and salad in a nice place. When you add the cover and service charges, fine dining will not be a Cheap Eat. If you want a true Cheap Eat, go to a cafeteria, snack bar, or dine al fresco with a picnic you have put together yourself.

A guiding principle in Italian dining is that you eat one food at a time and that every food has its place. If you order a light supper of pasta and salad at an informal trattoria, you will be served the pasta first and the salad after. If you want to start your meal with a salad, the key word is *come*, as in *come antipasto, vorrei un insalata mista* (as an antipasto, I would like a mixed salad), or *comme secondo, vorrei un contorno* (as a second course, I would like a vegetable).

If the waiter does not bring the Parmesan cheese, it probably does not go with what you are eating. Parmesan is never used on pasta with fish or lots of garlic, but it is offered with many types of soup.

Bread is served with all Italian meals and is part of the *pane e coperto* charge. Butter is seldom served except with breakfast.

The container of olive oil on the table is for more than sprinkling on your salad. A plain broiled or grilled fish is enhanced with a few drops of *olio,* and maybe some lemon.

Don't order fish on Sunday, when the markets are closed: the fish will be at least one day old. In Venice, extend this to Monday, since the Rialto Fish market is closed that day as well.

Coffee is served *after* a meal, never with it. For further coffee information and etiquette, see page 16.

Most places do not require men to wear a tie, but Italians do dress with casual elegance when they eat out, and they do not consider athletic shoes of any type to be acceptable with street clothes.

Taking children to restaurants in Italy is not the problem it can be in France. You can ask for a high chair (*seggiola* or *sediolina*) and for half portions (*mezze portione*).

Solo diners may be relegated to poor table locations. To avoid this as much as possible, reserve a table for two. Upon arrival, say your dining companion had to cancel at the last minute, and tell the waiter how sad this makes you. It usually works.

## THE ITALIAN MENU

**One cannot think well, love well, or sleep well, if one has not dined well.**

*—Virginia Woolf*

The most important thing about eating in Italy is not to let the length of the menu frighten you, and order according to the establishment. If you are in a simple trattoria, you probably will not be expected to order every course. But the better the restaurant, the more you will be expected to order.

Some restaurants and trattorias offer a *menù turistico* at an all-inclusive price. Do not let the name turn you off . . . it is only a fixed-price menu that at the very least includes pasta, an entrée, and either a vegetable or a salad. It may also include dessert and beverage. *Pane e coperto* (bread and cover charge per person) and *servizio* (service charge) are almost always included, so there will be no additional expenses tacked onto your final bill. While this is the Cheap Eat way to go, the quality and quantity might not be up to the standard of an à la carte meal. You cannot expect the finest beef, soft-shell crabs, or the chef's best dishes. You will get a filling if slightly boring meal.

Finally, it cannot be said enough: double-check your bill before you pay, and ask questions if you think something is incorrect. Mistakes unfortunately happen with great regularity.

**IMPORTANT NOTE:** If you are handed the English menu, it may not list the daily specials. Always ask to see the Italian menu along with the English one. Otherwise you may miss out on the best dishes at the best prices.

For a complete list of menu terms, and for phrases to help you while ordering, please see the glossary.

## CHIUSO (CLOSED)

All eating and drinking establishments have a regular *giorno de chiusura*: the one or two days a week they are closed. Due to holidays, local customs, the ever-present threat of strikes (*scioperi*), yearly vacations, restoration and remodeling, and much more than the non-Italian can never fathom, the one place you really want to try may be closed. Though *Cheap Eats in Italy* listings include each establishment's days and hours of operations, be sure to call ahead to double-check, especially if you do not have a backup nearby or it is important that you eat at a particular place.

Bakery, fruit and vegetable, and other food shops are closed all day Sunday and one afternoon per week. Their hours are generally 8:30 A.M. to 1 P.M. and 3:30 to 7:30 P.M. Open-air markets are open Monday through Saturday from 8 A.M. to 1 P.M.

## HOLIDAYS

Very few restaurants in Italy are open 365 days a year. Most are closed at least one day a week and for an annual vacation of up to one month. Many close on some or all of the holidays listed below, and those closings depend on the economy at the moment as well as the whims of the owner. You can also count on most places being closed at least a few days between Christmas and the New Year. Because of these constantly changing policies, please call ahead to check if your visit falls during these holiday times or in the months of December, January, July, or August.

| | |
|---|---|
| New Year's Day (*Capo d'anno*) | January 1 |
| Epiphany (*La Befana*) | varies; early in January |
| Good Friday | varies |
| Easter (*Pasqual*) | varies |
| Easter Monday (*Lunedi Pasqua*) | varies |

| | |
|---|---|
| Liberation Day (*Venticinque Aprile*) | April 25 |
| Labor Day, May Day (*Primo Maggio*) | May 1 |
| Assumption Day (*Ferragosto*) | August 15 |
| All Saints' Day (*Tutti Santi*) | November 1 |
| Day of Immaculate Conception (*Festa dell'Immacolata*) | December 8 |
| Christmas Day (*Natale*) | December 25 |
| Day after Christmas (*Santo Stefano*) | December 26 |

To Honor Patron Saints:

| | |
|---|---|
| Florence: St. John the Baptist | June 24 |
| Rome: St. Peter's Day | June 29 |
| Venice: St. Mark's Day | April 25 |

## SMOKING

Italian smokers outdo puffers in almost every other country in Europe. There is no Italian campaign saluting the health benefits of a smoke-free environment . . . or any hint of one in the future. During peak hours, especially in bars, *caffès,* and smaller restaurants and trattorias, the haze gets thick. If a restaurant listed in *Cheap Eats in Italy* is one of the few places where smoking is prohibited or that has a special nonsmoking section, it is noted. Otherwise . . . *buona fortuna!*

## RESERVATIONS

Every *Cheap Eats in Italy* listing states the establishment's reservation policy. If reservations are advised, please make them. It is always better to arrive with reservations than to wish you had. If you feel uncomfortable calling yourself, ask your hotel to do it for you. They may even be able to get you a better table. Only a few places that are very busy do not honor their reservation times. However, you should arrive on time, and if you will be unable to keep your reservation, call to cancel.

Italian telephone numbers are crazy. In Rome, some phone numbers have only five or six digits, although seven-figure numbers are the most common. If you have difficulties, try calling Operator 12. Operator assistance offers no guarantees, but it is worth a try.

## PAYING THE BILL

Italian restaurant bills can be confusing. With the following information, you will be better able to avoid the pitfalls of being overcharged or confused when *il contro* (the bill) is presented.

In two out of three small eating establishments, especially bars, *caffès,* bakeries, and snack bars, cash is king and plastic money (credit) is out.

Italian law requires that all establishments give a bill to the customer and that the customer carry the bill out of the restaurant. Who knows if anyone ever checks, but it is a protection for the consumer—you must get a proper bill for your money spent.

And finally, always remember to add up the bill yourself and question any discrepancies. There are too many mistakes.

### Prices

All *Cheap Eats in Italy* listings give the prices for à la carte meals and the *menù turistico* (fixed-price meal) if there is one available. Almost every *menù turistico* includes at least two courses and the cover and the service charges. À la carte prices rarely include the cover; sometimes the service is included. All printed menus are required to list whether or not there is a cover and/or a service charge and the amount. The à la carte prices quoted in this book represent the *average* cost of a three-course meal only. The prices quoted *do not include* the cover or service charge if there is one or (unless otherwise noted) any beverages. In determining the average price of a meal, the cheapest and the most expensive foods were avoided. Thus, you could spend more, or less, depending on what you decide to eat and drink. In using *Cheap Eats in Italy,* you should expect a margin of labor costs, and the owner's view of the economy.

#### Cover Charge (*Pane e Coperto*)

*Pane e coperto* (bread and cover) is not to be confused with the service charge. Almost every restaurant and trattoria in Italy charges the à la carte customer for bread, even if it is never touched, and for cover, which includes the table settings, flowers, and everything else the owner wants to toss into this catch-all charge. All menus *must* clearly state the cost of the cover charge, which is levied *per person,* listed separately in the bill, and added to the total on which you will pay service. If you order the *menù turistico,* or eat standing at a bar counter, you will avoid the cover charge.

#### Service Charge (*Servizio*)

*Servizio incluso* or *servizio compreso* means the service charge is included in the price of the meal, and no further tip is necessary nor will there be another charge added to your bill. *Servizio non-incluso* or *servizio non-compreso* means that the service charge has not been added, and you will be expected to pay an additional amount of 10 to 15 percent of the total bill, including the cover. Sometimes the service is not included but the restaurant will automatically add the service to your bill, and this will appear as a separate charge. All of the listings in *Cheap Eats in Italy* describe how the service charge is handled: they say either "service included," "service not included," or "12% service added" (though the percentages will vary).

Please remember that *the service charge is the tip,* and you are not required to leave anything more unless the service has been especially good and you are feeling generous. For service above and beyond, consider the ultimate tip: informing the person's employer by writing a letter of praise.

# Restaurants

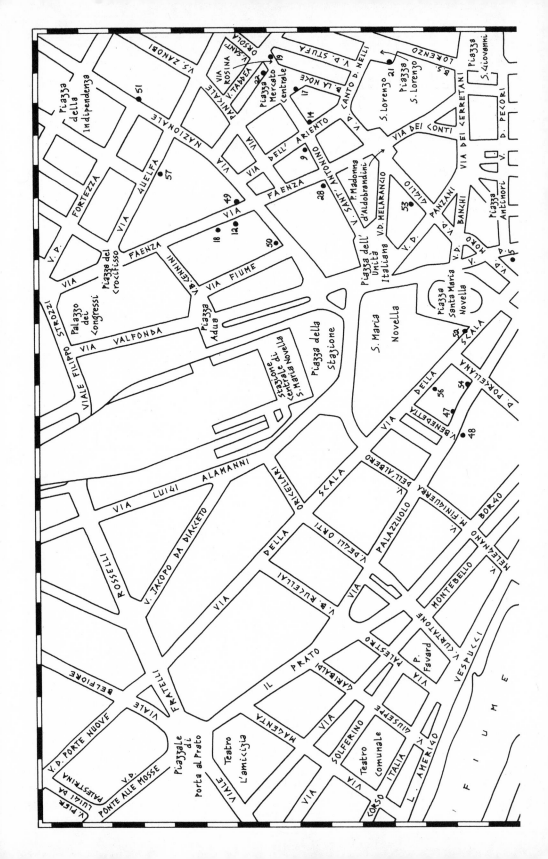

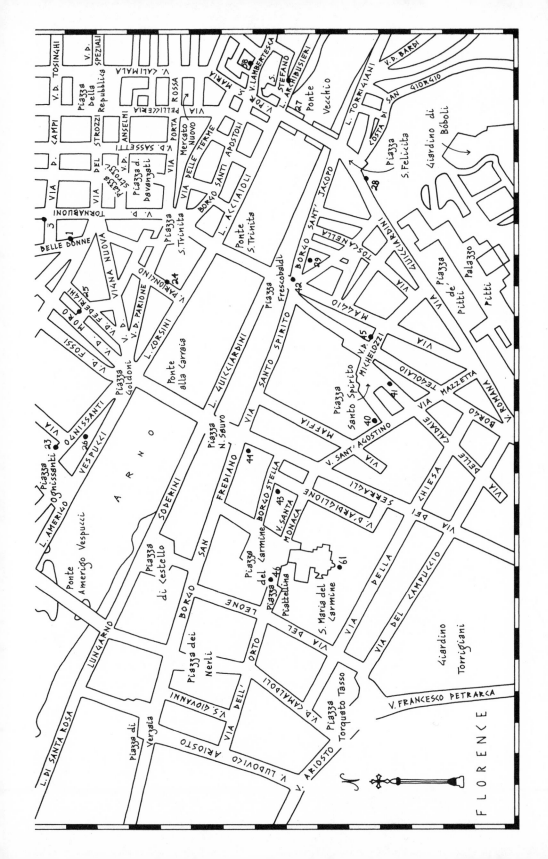

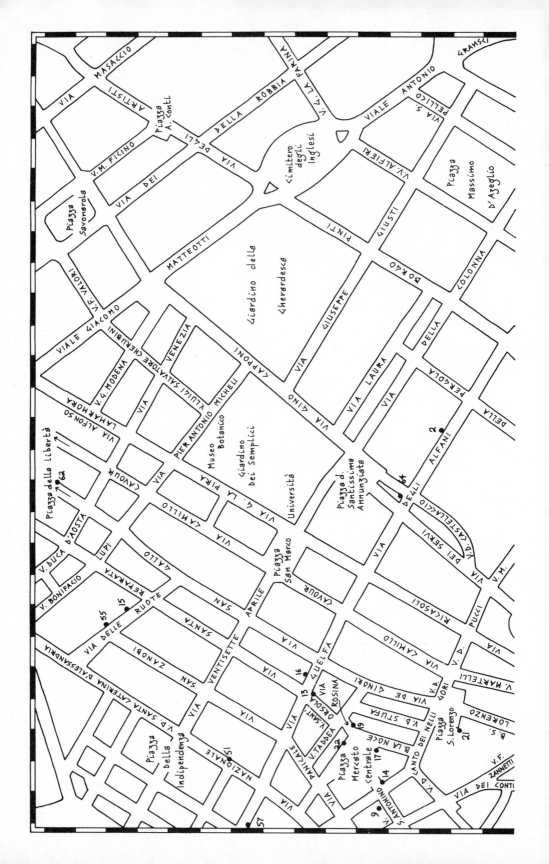

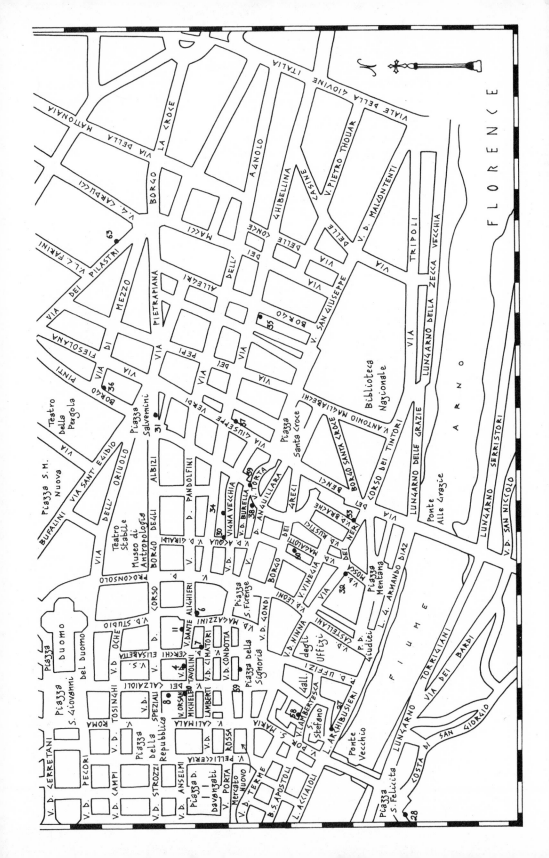

# Florence

Their smiles and laughter are due to their habit of thinking pleasurably about the pleasures of life.
> —*Peter Nichols,* Italia, Italia, *1973*

Whichever way you turn, you are struck with picturesque beauty and faded splendors.
> —*William Hazlitt,* Notes of a Journey Through France and Italy, *1826*

For nearly three centuries, from Giotto's time to Michelangelo's, Florence was the cultural center of Europe, producing countless art treasures and generating ideas that formed the cornerstone of twentieth-century thought. Five centuries after the Renaissance was born here, Florence has become a victim of her own beauty and is in danger of being consumed by traffic, pollution, and crowds from the four corners of the planet. Streets designed to accommodate horse-drawn carriages and pedestrians now cope with cars, trucks, and hundreds of smog-inducing tour buses. Despite this, visitors continue to flock to Florence to immerse themselves in the art, literature, and soft Tuscan light of this beautiful city. The home of Dante and *David,* Machiavelli, the Medicis, and Guccis, Florence is still the perfect place to fall in love all over again.

The food in Florence is simple and hearty, without rich sauces or elaborate spices. The cuisine reflects the Tuscan emphasis on bread, beans, deep-green extra-virgin olive oil, wild game, free-range poultry, and grilled and roasted meats. Most of Florence's restaurants are not gourmet, but many regional dishes are prepared so well that the food is considered to be some of the best in Italy. Because of the influx of more than one million visitors a year, the good-value restaurants are known to visitors and natives alike. To avoid eating with your fellow compatriots, plan to eat dinner when the Italians do, after 8:30 or 9 P.M.

In Florence you will probably eat more bread than you will pasta. Most of the bread is baked without salt, which seems odd at first, but once you develop a taste for it, the plain unsalted bread is almost addictive. Stale bread goes into some of the best dishes. *Crostini* (toasted bread spread with pâté) is a delicious antipasto or light snack. *Ribollita,* a hearty vegetable soup with beans and black cabbage, reheated and poured over a thick slice of bread, is a favorite first course. In the summer, *panzanella,* a salad of torn bread tossed with tomatoes and onion in red wine and virgin olive oil is a light and refreshing lunch. The meat courses are a delight to all carnivores, especially the *bistecca alla fiorentina,* a two- to three-inch slab of Chianti beef, salted and coated with olive oil and served juicy rare. Chianti wine is always a fit accompaniment for any meal. For an even better wine, look for Chianti Classico, with the *gallo nero,* or black rooster, label on the neck.

Dessert is not the main focus of the meal. It is usually a piece of fresh fruit or a glass of *vin santo,* a sweet wine made from dried grapes. *Cantuccini di Prato* (also called *biscotti di Prato*), which are hard almond cookies, are usually dipped in the wine. It is a nice finish to any Tuscan meal.

**NOTE:** The street numbers of commercial establishments (stores, restaurants, and businesses) are indicated by a red "r" following the numerical number of the address (i.e., 34r). A blue or black "b" means the address is a hotel or private residence. To add to the fun, addresses are seldom in sequence as we think they should be. Instead, they are in sequence according to the "r" or the "b" numbers, but they are not necessarily next to one another, which can create confusion for the unknowing foreigner.

## RESTAURANTS IN FLORENCE
### Near Il Duomo

| | | |
|---|---|---|
| (1) | Belle Donne | 31 |
| (2) | Buffet Freddo | 31 |
| (3) | Cantinetta Antinori* | 32 |
| (4) | Cantinetta dei Verrazzano | 32 |
| (5) | Croce al Trebbio | 33 |
| (6) | Da Pennello | 33 |
| (7) | I Fratellini | 34 |
| (8) | Il Granduca | 34 |
| (9) | Palle d'Oro | 35 |
| (10) | Perchè Nò! | 35 |
| (11) | Tripe Stand | 36 |

### Near Mercato Centrale and Piazza Indipendenza

| | | |
|---|---|---|
| (12) | Antichi Cancelli | 36 |
| (13) | Cafaggi* | 37 |
| (14) | Focaccine | 38 |
| (15) | Il Vegetariano | 38 |
| (16) | I' Toscano | 39 |
| (17) | Nerbone | 39 |
| (18) | Trattoria Enzo e Piero | 40 |
| (19) | Trattoria Mario | 40 |
| (20) | Trattoria San Zanobi | 41 |
| (21) | Trattoria da Sergio e Gozzi | 41 |
| (22) | Trattoria Zàzà | 42 |

### Near Piazza Goldoni

| | | |
|---|---|---|
| (23) | Armando | 42 |
| (24) | Coco Lezzone | 43 |
| (25) | Il Latini* | 44 |
| (26) | Pepolino | 44 |

\* Restaurants marked with an asterisk (\*) are considered Big Splurges.

## Restaurants near Il Duomo

### (1) BELLE DONNE
### via delle Belle Donne, 16r

There is no sign or menu outside Belle Donne, only a cluster of Florentines waiting for a vacant seat. The inside is overpowered by massive fruit and vegetable displays and a forest of green plants. The closely spaced tables, set for two or four with red napkins and green drinking glasses, are always filled to capacity. The menu is written on a blackboard and is seldom the same two days in a row. You can eat lightly and order only one course or go full tilt and have several courses if you are starved. If available, do not pass up the cream of chestnut soup or the avocado and zucchini salad. For a main course, look for the chicken in lemon, carpaccio with *rucola* (thinly sliced raw beef filet served with a salad of bitter greens), or if you are up to it, the tripe. If you are having a vegetable, watch for anything au gratin, but for dessert, do yourself a favor and go elsewhere for *gelato*. The service can be rushed and borders on the rude, especially during the peak lunch hour. Don't let this deter you . . . it doesn't the locals.

**AREA**
Il Duomo
**TELEPHONE**
23-82-609
**OPEN**
Mon–Fri
**CLOSED**
Sat, Sun, Aug
**HOURS**
Lunch 12:30–2:30 P.M., dinner 7:30–9:30 P.M.
**RESERVATIONS**
Advised
**CREDIT CARDS**
None
**À LA CARTE**
L 25,000, beverage extra
**MENÙ TURISTICO**
None
**COVER & SERVICE CHARGES**
Cover L 1,000, service included
**ENGLISH**
None

### (2) BUFFET FREDDO
### via degli Alfani, 70r

When I see an eating place that is SRO every time I pass by, no matter what time of the day or evening, I know they are dishing out good food at prices the locals appreciate. The lively clientele at Buffet Freddo is drawn from both the university and blue-collar ranks, who gather to meet, greet, and eat at the five, shared marble-topped tables. And eat well they do. A daily blue-plate

**AREA**
Il Duomo
**TELEPHONE**
None
**OPEN**
Mon–Sat
**CLOSED**
Sun, Aug
**HOURS**
8:30 A.M.–8:30 P.M., continuous service; hot lunch noon–2:30 P.M.

special, two to three pastas, a soup, and enormous custom-made sandwiches filled with every combination of meat, cheese, and vegetable known to the civilized world are consumed in great quantities until 8:30 P.M. every day but Sunday.

### (3) CANTINETTA ANTINORI
**Palazzo Antinori, piazza Antinori, 3r**

Many years ago, owners of large estates around Florence kept small cellars in their palaces, and from little windows on the street they sold products from these estates. Following this long-standing tradition, the Antinori family has established the Cantinetta in their fifteenth-century Renaissance Palazzo Antinori in the heart of Florence. Without question, this is a magnificent showplace for the vintages of the oldest and most distinguished wine producer in Tuscany. The dark-paneled bar and restaurant are filled with beautifully clad Florentines who have made this the most popular wine bar in their city. All of the food comes from the family estates, which are known especially for their rich extra-virgin olive oil, outstanding cheeses, and fine wines. Full meals can run into the Big Splurge category and are worth every delicious bite. If you want to spend less and still enjoy this memorable experience, order an appetizer, a salad, or a plate of assorted cheeses along with a glass or two of their excellent wines. If you sit at the bar, you will save both the cover and service charges.

### (4) CANTINETTA DEI VERRAZZANO
**via dei Tavolini, 18–20r**

On one of my early morning walks, I found this elegant *caffè* that is also a bakery, wine shop, and elegant teatime rendezvous. Starting at 8 A.M., the bakers send out heaping trays of breakfast goodies along with loaves of brown, white, olive, or wine-flavored breads. I would stop in after walking, order a glass of freshly squeezed orange juice, a *cornetto,* and a double cappuccino to enjoy while glancing through the morning paper. The gleaming glass display cases are filled with a colorful assortment of individual tarts, marvelous cakes that are sold whole or by the slice, beautiful piles of *biscotti,* and sandwiches made with salmon, cucumber, thinly sliced beef, or ham. By noon, the wood-burning oven along the back is in full force, turning out individual pizzas or focaccia bread that is split in half while still hot and layered with your choice of fillings. Later in the day, it is a good place for a glorious Italian pastry treat to either eat here or have packaged to go; and anytime after noon until 8 P.M., it is a nice place to sip a glass of wine while contemplating your next shopping, sightseeing, or walking destination.

**CREDIT CARDS**
AMEX

**À LA CARTE**
From L 2,500, beverage extra

**MENÙ TURISTICO**
None

**COVER & SERVICE CHARGES**
None

**ENGLISH**
Limited

## (5) CROCE AL TREBBIO
### via delle Belle Donne, 49r

A meal at Croce al Trebbio is pleasant and unhurried, with good service and food to match. The interior is upmarket rustic, with beams, bountiful food displays, and two walls papered with foreign money. The downstairs basement features a hundred-year-old arched brick ceiling and rough stone walls. If romance is on your agenda, this is a more intimate place to dine, especially in the evening when the lights are low.

Newcomers and old-timers alike go for either the *menù turistico* or the daily specials. The à la carte choices are broader, but they are only borderline bargains. The meal gets off to a stunning start if you order the *breasola rucola e parmigiano*—dried beef with arugula and paper-thin slices of fresh Parmesan cheese. First-course standouts include a *tortellini panne e prosciutto* (tortellini with cream and ham), *risotto al quatro formaggi* (rice with four cheeses), and an especially worthy *ribollita* (the famed Florentine reboiled soup). *Osso buco* with peas, roast beef with potatoes, and the ever-present tripe are three *piatti pronti*—ready-to-serve main courses. Taking a little more time, and definitely worth the wait, are any of the veal dishes, especially the scaloppine with lemon or mushrooms. Desserts are rather limited, but if it's on, the *tiramisù* is worth the calorie splurge.

**AREA**
Il Duomo and piazza Santa Maria Novella

**TELEPHONE**
28-70-89

**OPEN**
Tues–Sun

**CLOSED**
Mon, Feb (dates vary)

**HOURS**
Lunch noon–2:30 P.M., dinner 7–10 P.M.

**RESERVATIONS**
Advised for dinner

**CREDIT CARDS**
AMEX, DC, MC, V

**À LA CARTE**
L 34,000, beverage extra

**MENÙ TURISTICO**
L 20,000, 3 courses, cover and service included, beverage extra

**COVER & SERVICE CHARGES**
Cover L 2,000, service included

**ENGLISH**
Yes, and English menu

## (6) DA PENNELLO
### via Dante Alighieri, 4r

Da Pennello has been discovered, but never mind. The brightly lit restaurant with its pretty garden for summer dining is deservedly popular with everyone who visits or lives in Florence. It is located on a narrow street near Dante's house, about a five-minute stroll from Il Duomo in the direction of the Uffizi Gallery and the

**AREA**
Il Duomo

**TELEPHONE**
29-48-48

**OPEN**
Tues–Sat; Sun lunch only

**CLOSED**
Mon, Aug, Dec 25–Jan 2

**HOURS**
Lunch noon–2:30 P.M., dinner
7–10 P.M.

**RESERVATIONS**
Definitely

**CREDIT CARDS**
AMEX, DC, MC, V

**À LA CARTE**
L 30,000, beverage extra

**MENÙ TURISTICO**
L 25,000, 3 courses, cover and
service included, beverage extra

**COVER & SERVICE CHARGES**
Cover L 2,000, service included

**ENGLISH**
Yes

Arno River. The kitchen is known for producing an impressive variety of outstanding antipasti, and if you wish, you can make an entire meal out of these wonderful appetizers.

The *menù turistico* offers good Cheap Eating. There is a choice of *primi piatti* (first courses) of several pastas or the soup of the day. The *secondi piatti* (second course) usually lists a roast, veal scaloppine, and an omelette of some sort, along with vegetables or a salad and dessert. Wine is extra. If you want to take advantage of the groaning antipasti table, yet need something more, you can order an à la carte pasta and a dessert to round out your meal. The restaurant is always packed to the walls, so if you arrive without a reservation, especially during prime lunch time, be prepared to wait up to an hour.

### (7) I FRATELLINI
### via dei Cimatori, 38r

**AREA**
Il Duomo

**TELEPHONE**
23-96-096

**OPEN**
Mon–Sat

**CLOSED**
Sun, Aug (2 weeks)

**HOURS**
8 A.M.–8 P.M. continuous service

**RESERVATIONS**
Not accepted

**CREDIT CARDS**
None

**À LA CARTE**
sandwiches from L 3,000

**MENÙ TURISTICO**
None

**COVER & SERVICE CHARGES**
None

**ENGLISH**
Very limited

One of the best ways to cut food costs and have a good Cheap Eat in the bargain is to have lunch at a snack bar. Here you will be joined by savvy Italians who know they can order the blue-plate special, or a meaty sandwich and a glass of wine, for a mere fraction of a restaurant meal. Further savings are possible if the meal is eaten while standing rather than seated at a table. Only you can decide how far you want to pinch your lire on that score.

This brings me to I Fratellini, a stand-up wine bar and sandwich counter run by two brothers. You can order your freshly made sandwiches to eat here or to go. They serve a variety of twenty to twenty-five sandwiches, and specialize in those made with *prosciutto crudo* (air-dried, salt-cured ham) and homemade chicken liver pâté spread on thinly sliced bread. To round out the repast, order a glass of their Chianti Classico . . . but be careful. If you ask for the large, it will be served in a tall water tumbler.

### (8) IL GRANDUCA
### via dei Calzaiuoli, 57r

**AREA**
Il Duomo

**TELEPHONE**
29-81-12

**OPEN**
Thur–Tues

**CLOSED**
Wed, Dec, Jan

**HOURS**
11 A.M.–midnight, continuous
service

For the scoop on some of the best *gelati* in Florence, don't forget Il Granduca near Il Duomo and Piazza della Repubblica. Here you will have some difficult decisions: fresh kiwi, strawberry, melon, pineapple, papaya, blackberry, coffee custard, cream caramel, amaretto, rice . . . and more, depending on the season. In winter they make *semifreddo,* the heavenly *gelato* fluffed with cream to a mousselike texture and topped with a cloud of whipped cream to gild the lily. For dieters, there are a few sugar-free flavors and some frozen yogurts. For kids of all ages, cones come plain, chocolate, and nut-dipped. Prices start at L 2,000 for a scoop in a cone and go on to L 17,000 for a gargantuan blitz.

### (9) PALLE D'ORO
**via Sant'Antonio, 43/45r**

Sooner or later all Cheap Eaters in Florence learn about Palle d'Oro, which sits on an interesting shopping street midway between Il Duomo and the big central market. For lunch, join well-dressed Florentines ordering freshly crafted sandwiches up front or quick and easy hot dishes in the back. In the evening, take a seat and order a brimming bowl of soup or pasta, a fragrantly roasted chicken with a green salad, or a piece of grilled fish seasoned with fresh lemon and a splash of olive oil.

This antiseptically clean spot is slightly surgical in decor, reminding me of a coffee shop in a motel. Don't let this discourage you, because for over a hundred years this family-run jewel has been providing dependable, good, fast food *alla italiano*.

### (10) PERCHÈ NÒ!
**via dei Tavolini, 19r (angle via Calzaioli)**

Perchè Nò! opened its doors in 1939 and is recognized today as the oldest *gelateria* in Florence. In addition to its longevity, it has an impressive history. During World War II, it supplied the American troops stationed in Florence with ice cream. When the city's electrical supply was shut off, officers ordered soldiers to reconnect the electrical supply that served Perchè Nò! and the surrounding area. After the war, the owners installed the first counter showcase for ice cream, which has become a model for all others in the area.

From the beginning, they have been known for their varieties of *semifreddo,* that illegally rich and creamy ice cream that has untold fat grams and tastes like a gift from heaven. Be sure you sample their white chocolate,

**RESERVATIONS**
Not accepted
**CREDIT CARDS**
None
**À LA CARTE**
From L 2,000
**MENÙ TURISTICO**
None
**COVER & SERVICE CHARGES**
None
**ENGLISH**
Enough

**AREA**
Il Duomo and piazza Mercato Centrale
**TELEPHONE**
28–83–83
**OPEN**
Mon–Sat
**CLOSED**
Sun, Aug (3 weeks)
**HOURS**
Lunch noon–2:30 P.M., dinner 6:30–10 P.M.
**RESERVATIONS**
Not accepted
**CREDIT CARDS**
AMEX, MC, V
**À LA CARTE**
L 30,000, sandwiches from L 4,000, beverage extra
**MENÙ TURISTICO**
L 16,000, 3 courses, cover and service included, beverage extra
**COVER & SERVICE CHARGES**
Cover L 2,000, service included
**ENGLISH**
Limited

**AREA**
Il Duomo, near piazza Signoria
**TELEPHONE**
23-98-969
**OPEN**
Daily in summer; Tues–Sun in winter
**CLOSED**
Mon in winter; Nov
**HOURS**
Summer 8 A.M.–midnight, winter 8 A.M.–8:30 P.M.
**RESERVATIONS**
Not accepted
**CREDIT CARDS**
None
**À LA CARTE**
From L 2,000

rum crunch, hazelnut mousse, or coffee mousse. In the summer, the green apple *sorbetto* is refreshing change of pace. You can have your *gelato* in a cone or a cup and dipped in a flurry of chocolate pieces or nuts—or just plain if you are dieting.

### (11) TRIPE STAND
### via Dante Alighieri, 22r

Almost all American visitors to Florence eventually find themselves in one of the two American Express offices in the city. If you go to the office on via Dante Alighieri around lunchtime, a portable food cart with a blue-and-white awning will be sitting out in front. There will be a line, and the busy man behind the cart won't miss a beat as he serves his hungry customers. What is he selling at this prime pit stop? Tripe.

Wait a minute . . . it isn't *that* bad, and here it is really quite good. Big pieces of tripe are pulled from two steaming pots, sliced thinly onto fresh rolls, dipped into the juice (optional), served with salt, pepper, and green salsa, and rolled in wax paper. Afraid to go whole hog on a sandwich? Then order a small helping of just the tripe, served again on waxed paper and accompanied by toothpicks. If you are cooking in, you can buy fresh tripe from this stand at L 950 for 100 grams. What to drink with your repast? Remember this *is* Italy, so you can purchase a chilled minibottle of wine, a more pedestrian soda, or a beer to complement your meal.

## *Restaurants near Mercato Centrale and Piazza Indipendenza*

### (12) ANTICHI CANCELLI
### via Faenza, 73r

Trattoria Antichi Cancelli, which means "the old gate," is under the same ownership as Trattoria Guelfa (see page 61). With its hanging peppers and garlic braids, potted plants, and tiny paper-covered marble-topped tables set under a brick ceiling, it looks like something from a movie. The difference, of course, is that the great food and jovial ambience is real. It does not take newcomers long to blend in and to quickly catch the mood of the place. As with Trattoria Guelfa, do not even *think* of arriving without reservations, and even then you can count on having to wedge yourself into the crowd and wait for a table.

It is important that you come prepared to eat. Management takes a dim view of dieters or anyone else not ordering at least a pasta, main course, and dessert. The daily menu is based on what is best at the market during each season. The dishes of Tuscany are well prepared, and everything from the antipasti and pasta to the sauces and desserts is made here. The filling portions promise that no one will be thinking about the next meal for a long time.

## (13) CAFAGGI
### via Guelfa, 35r

One of the best ways to find out about good places to eat is to ask the natives where they go. The top contender on via Guelfa, between piazza della Indipendenza and piazza San Marco off via Cavour, is Cafaggi. This plain-Jane restaurant has been in the same family for six decades. It consists of two rooms done in boring beige. The second room off the kitchen is slightly more appealing due to a few plants scattered about and some flowers on the tables. So come prepared to dine, not to lounge in magnificent surroundings. After you have been served and tasted the fine food, you will quickly forget all about the dull atmosphere.

Cheat Eaters *must* stay with one of the set-priced menus. The good value, three-course *menù turistico* includes a first and second course, vegetable garnish, dessert, and beverage. For the quality, it is a great deal. The *menù leggero,* the dieter's menu, and the *menù vegetariano,* for vegetarians, have limited selections and only two courses, but do include either wine or mineral water. If you stray into the à la carte selections, you will no longer be having a Cheap Eat.

The chef prides himself on turning out carefully prepared dishes using the freshest seasonal ingredients. He is a wizard with fresh fish and veal, especially the veal served in a buttery asparagus sauce. The desserts are all made here and are beautiful, especially the *millefoglie alla crema,* layers of flaky pastry filled with whipped cream. The house wine is adequate, so there is no need to splurge on anything else.

**RESERVATIONS**
Absolutely essential
**CREDIT CARDS**
AMEX, DC, MC, V
**À LA CARTE**
L 30,000–35,000, beverage extra
**MENÙ TURISTICO**
L 20,000, 3 courses, cover and service included, beverage included
**COVER & SERVICE CHARGES**
Cover L 2,000, 10% service added
**ENGLISH**
Yes, and *Menù Turistico* in English

**AREA**
Mercato Centrale
**TELEPHONE**
29-49-89
**OPEN**
Mon–Sat
**CLOSED**
Sun, mid-July to Aug (dates vary)
**HOURS**
Lunch noon–2:30 P.M., dinner 7–10:30 P.M.
**RESERVATIONS**
Advised, especially weekends and holidays
**CREDIT CARDS**
AMEX, MC, V
**À LA CARTE**
L 35,000–45,000, beverage extra
**MENÙ TURISTICO**
L 30,000 for 3 courses, L 25,000 for 2 courses, cover and service included, beverage included
**COVER & SERVICE CHARGES**
Cover L 2,500, 12% service added
**ENGLISH**
Yes, and English menu

## (14) FOCACCINE
### via dell Ariento, 85r

**AREA**
Mercato Centrale

**TELEPHONE**
28-73-90

**OPEN**
Tues–Sun

**CLOSED**
Mon, Aug

**HOURS**
Lunch noon–3 P.M., dinner
7–10 P.M.

**RESERVATIONS**
Not accepted

**CREDIT CARDS**
None

**À LA CARTE**
Sandwiches from L 3,000

**MENÙ TURISTICO**
None

**COVER & SERVICE CHARGES**
None

**ENGLISH**
Usually

Strawberry pizza? Yes! Trust me, it is a knockout, and the cooks can barely keep up with the demand. This delightful indulgence consists of a crisp cookie crust layered with custard cream and topped with fresh strawberries and a dusting of sugar. I wish I lived close enough to run by for a *big* slice of this whenever the spirit moved me.

What else is there to eat in this fast food stop only a few minutes walk from the San Lorenzo Market? Lots of good things. In addition to the regular pizzas, you will find warm triangles of homemade focaccia bread, split and filled with combinations of mushrooms, eggplant, tomatoes, salmon, roast beef, melted cheese, and prosciutto. When you arrive, go directly to the counter to order. When served, take your meal to one of the eight picnic tables that line the walls. Remember to order your dessert strawberry pizza upon arrival . . . it goes like wildfire.

## (15) IL VEGETARIANO
### via delle Ruote, 30r

**AREA**
piazza Indipendenza

**TELEPHONE**
47-50-30

**OPEN**
Tues–Fri; Sat dinner only

**CLOSED**
Sun, Aug

**HOURS**
Lunch 12:30–2:30 P.M., dinner
7:30–10:30 P.M.

**RESERVATIONS**
Not accepted

**CREDIT CARDS**
None

**À LA CARTE**
L 20,000, beverage extra

**MENÙ TURISTICO**
None

**COVER & SERVICE CHARGES**
Cover L 2,000, service included

**ENGLISH**
Yes

Exceptional vegetarian food, served in a warm, friendly atmosphere, is dished out cafeteria style to faithful diners, many of whom eat here with great regularity. Murals of Tuscany, fresh flowers on the tables, and a summer garden create an appealing natural setting.

The menu changes daily and varies with the seasons. Once you enter the restaurant, check the printed blackboard, decide what you want, write it down on the form provided, and take it to the cashier to pay. The dishes for each course are priced the same, thus allowing you to add up your total easily. After paying, take your menu form to the cafeteria counter to be served. You can eat at communal tables, either in the smoking or nonsmoking section. The varied selection of food usually includes rice and pastas, casseroles made from beans and legumes, quiches, soufflés, vegan and macrobiotic choices, and lots of salads. Desserts are in the lead-ball category. I recommend skipping them.

**NOTE:** There is no sign outside the restaurant. Look for the round sign with a red telephone receiver hanging above the entrance at via delle Ruote, 30r. This is it.

## (16) I' TOSCANO
### via Guelfa, 70r

The chef at i' Toscano displays his varied skills with dishes of fresh, flavorful food attractively presented in two rather formal rooms. Formal by Florence standards, that is. A bouquet of flowers adds one of the only spots of color in the brightly lit, stark white surroundings. The properly set tables are well-spaced enough to prevent being a part of your neighbor's conversation, and the waiters are friendly and make an effort to explain any dish you are not sure about.

The food has just enough creativity and imagination to lift it out of the ordinary and place it into the near-gourmet category. For something unusual, start with a plate of cold slices of wild boar, deer, and other game meats, or try something typically Florentine, toasted bread topped with black cabbage, garlic, and olive oil. The spinach ravioli is a satisfying first course, as is the gnocchi in a truffle cream sauce. For the main dish, if you are here on Friday, by all means order the stockfish served with a fresh tomato sauce. On other days, it is a toss up between the veal scaloppine with white wine or the savory beef stew. For your vegetable, please order the *"gobbi" alla fiorentina,* a thistlelike plant with the leaves and stalks eaten like celery and served here lightly braised in a butter sauce. Saving room for dessert takes some willpower, but at least share a slice of the lemon cake or try the *semifreddo alla arancio,* a creamy orange ice cream that slides down refreshingly.

**AREA**
Mercato Centrale

**TELEPHONE**
21-54-75

**OPEN**
Wed–Mon

**CLOSED**
Tues, Aug

**HOURS**
Lunch noon–2:30 P.M., dinner 7:30–11:30 P.M.

**RESERVATIONS**
Advised

**CREDIT CARDS**
AMEX, DC, MC, V

**À LA CARTE**
L 35,000, beverage extra

**MENÙ TURISTICO**
L 25,000, 3 courses, cover and service included, beverage included

**COVER & SERVICE CHARGES**
Cover L 3,000, service included

**ENGLISH**
Yes, and English menu

## (17) NERBONE
### Stand #292, Mercato di San Lorenzo, piazza del Mercato Centrale (next to the San Lorenzo Church)

Since 1872, hot meat sandwiches have been the major drawing card at Nerbone, Stand #292, at the Mercato di San Lorenzo in Florence. This huge indoor market is the main source of food for a region that takes food very seriously, and it's without peer for its wide variety and enormous selection. Be sure you allow yourself enough time to appreciate the magnificent displays of food, which serve as a quick study course in the fine points and ingredients of Italian cooking.

Nerbone, which is under the same ownership as Alla Vecchia Bettola (see page 63), appeals to those with hearty appetites who don't mind a noisy, no-frills setting. The menu lists bowls of beans, mashed potatoes,

**AREA**
Inside the Mercato Centrale

**TELEPHONE**
None

**OPEN**
Mon–Sat lunch only

**CLOSED**
Sun, Aug (dates vary)

**HOURS**
7 A.M.–2 P.M.

**RESERVATIONS**
Not accepted

**CREDIT CARDS**
None

**À LA CARTE**
From L 3,500

MENÙ TURISTICO
None

COVER & SERVICE CHARGES
None

ENGLISH
None

tripe, and pastas. Never mind any of these. The standard order here is a sandwich of boiled beef (*bollito*), sliced onto a crusty roll and then dipped into the meat juices (*bagnato*). After you are handed your food, take it to the tables across the way, or stand at the bar with a beer, and enjoy!

## (18) TRATTORIA ENZO E PIERO
### via Faenza, 105r

AREA
piazza Mercato Centrale

TELEPHONE
21-49-01

OPEN
Mon–Fri in Feb, Mar, July, and Aug; Mon–Sat in Jan, April–June, Sept–Dec

CLOSED
Sun, Aug (3 weeks)

HOURS
Lunch noon–3 P.M., dinner 7–10 P.M.

RESERVATIONS
Advised for dinner

CREDIT CARDS
AMEX, DC, MC, V

À LA CARTE
L 30,000, beverage extra

MENÙ TURISTICO
L 18,000, 3 courses, cover and service included, beverage extra

COVER & SERVICE CHARGES
Cover L 3,000, service included

ENGLISH
Yes

Enzo and Piero's trattoria is very simple, with rough stuccoed walls and lots of well-fed habitués sitting at the red-linen-clad tables. On each table is a bottle of Chianti wine vinegar and one of good olive oil, so you can dress your own salad or, as the Italians do, sprinkle olive oil on just about everything but dessert.

Both Enzo and Piero are on hand each day to ensure that all runs well. They greet their guests at the table, suggest what is best to order, and check back periodically to see that everyone has everything needed for a good meal. They also keep an eagle eye on the kitchen, where their high standards ensure absolutely fresh ingredients prepared with care. If you are here on a Friday, do try the *baccalà alla livornese,* salt cod cooked in a nippy red sauce with liberal doses of garlic. Other flavorful options are the *tortellini alla cardinale* (with cream, tomatoes, and ham), the veal stew, or the stuffed and baked breast of turkey and ham. The *menù turistico* is a Cheap Eat if there ever was one, even though it does not include a beverage. For a few lire more, you can add a quarter or a half carafe and still get away for under L 28,000 per person.

## (19) TRATTORIA MARIO
### via Rosina, 2r

AREA
Mercato Centrale

TELEPHONE
21-85-50

OPEN
Mon–Sat bar and lunch only

CLOSED
Sun, Aug

HOURS
7 A.M.–5 P.M., lunch noon–3 P.M.

RESERVATIONS
Not accepted

CREDIT CARDS
None

Mario's boasts many avid regulars, all of whom seem to be on a first-name basis. Consequently, there is a great deal of good cheer and camaraderie, with everyone swapping tall tales and telling jokes. They all know to arrive early and order a glass or two of the house red while waiting for the lunch service to begin. Latecomers will have to wait, or worse yet, they won't get their favorite dish, since the kitchen often runs out early.

The daily menu is posted on a board by the open kitchen. Friday is fish day, and on Thursday gnocchi is the dish to order. On any day smart choices include the vegetable soup, stewed tripe, or a slab of roast veal or beef. You don't need to save room for dessert because all they serve is fresh fruit or a glass of sweet wine with those wonderful, hard, almond-flavored dipping cookies called *biscotti*. No coffee is served, either, but there are dozens of bars around the market. It is fun to merge in and stand at the bar for an after-lunch espresso that will recharge your batteries for the rest of the afternoon.

## (20) TRATTORIA SAN ZANOBI
### via San Zanobi, 33A/r

It's a simple trattoria . . . red tile floors, original brick archways, and wood-framed windows with a pleasant couple, Dante and his wife, Mariengela, running the show. The *menù turistico* should appeal to every committed Cheap Eater in Florence, not only for the price-to-quality ratio but for the portions, which more than satisfy. The printed à la carte menu covers the bases, but as usual, prime plates are those the chef recommends that day. You will see this neatly written on a small sheet of paper fastened to the inside of the menu. The kitchen produces uncomplicated interpretations of *ribollita, pasta e fagioli, tagliatelle* with duck, roast lamb with potatoes, and breaded lamb chops garnished with fried artichokes. Homemade *tiramisù* and *panna cotta* add just the right sweet finishing notes to a typical meal Florentines survive on.

## (21) TRATTORIA DA SERGIO E GOZZI
### piazza San Lorenzo, 8r

When in Florence, under no circumstances should you miss a trip to the Mercato Centrale de San Lorenzo, a landmark, nineteenth-century cast-iron building housing one of the largest and most interesting markets in Europe. Surrounding the market are hundreds of stalls with sellers hawking more than enough treasures to fill up that extra suitcase. For even the least committed Cheap Chic shopper, it is definitely worth a look, even though the prices are not always the bargains the setting suggests.

There are many places to eat around the market, some very good and others appallingly bad. One of the most authentic and tourist-free is this trattoria, a true worker's hangout, where you can taste hearty Tuscan food in two old-fashioned rooms filled with burly market men and

**À LA CARTE**
L 18,000, beverage extra

**MENÙ TURISTICO**
None

**COVER & SERVICE CHARGES**
Cover L 1,000, service included

**ENGLISH**
Yes

**AREA**
Mercato Centrale

**TELEPHONE**
47-52-86

**OPEN**
Mon–Sat

**CLOSED**
Sun, Aug (one week)

**HOURS**
Lunch noon–2:30 P.M., dinner 7–10:30 P.M.

**RESERVATIONS**
Advised for dinner

**CREDIT CARDS**
AMEX, MC, V

**À LA CARTE**
L 28,000, beverage extra

**MENÙ TURISTICO**
L 20,000, 3 courses, cover and service included, beverage included

**COVER & SERVICE CHARGES**
Cover L 2,500, service included

**ENGLISH**
Yes

**AREA**
Mercato Centrale

**TELEPHONE**
28-19-41

**OPEN**
Mon–Sat lunch only

**CLOSED**
Sun, Aug

**HOURS**
Noon–4 P.M.

**RESERVATIONS**
Not accepted

**CREDIT CARDS**
None

**À LA CARTE**
L 25,000–30,000, beverage extra

**MENÙ TURISTICO**
None

COVER & SERVICE CHARGES
Cover L 1,500, service included
ENGLISH
Some

women. The only menu is posted outside. When you are seated, the waiter will tell you what's cooking. You are expected to order a full meal—just a salad and a glass of wine is *out*. You can count on chunky minestrone and bean soups, roasted meats, and sturdy boiled brisket. Good country bread and creamy desserts add to your pleasure. Follow the lead of fellow diners and order a bottle of the house Chianti while enjoying the friendly service and a lunch that will leave some lire in your pocket.

## (22) TRATTORIA ZÀZÀ

**piazza Mercato Centrale, 26r (on corner of via Rosina)**

AREA
Mercato Centrale
TELEPHONE
21-54-11
OPEN
Mon–Sat
CLOSED
Sun
HOURS
Lunch noon–3 P.M., dinner
7–11 P.M.
RESERVATIONS
Advised
CREDIT CARDS
AMEX, DC, MC, V
À LA CARTE
L 30,000–35,000, beverage
extra
MENÙ TURISTICO
L 20,000, 3 courses, cover and
service included, beverage extra
COVER & SERVICE CHARGES
Cover L 2,000, service included
ENGLISH
Usually

Trattoria Zàzà, on the piazza Mercato Centrale, offers a winning mix of accommodating service, atmosphere, and hearty Tuscan food. Wooden picnic tables with long benches and hard stools line both the upstairs and downstairs dining rooms. The walls are papered with framed newspaper clippings of famous trotting horses and with film posters of Jimmy Cagney and of Ingrid Bergman and Humphrey Bogart in the famous farewell scene in *Casablanca.* Overhead are three rows of shelves stacked high with the Chianti you will be drinking with your meal.

The wide-ranging menu offers a multitude of choices for every course. To start, order the trio of their best soups, which includes a bowl of *ribollita, pomodoro fresca* (fresh tomato), and *passato di fagioli con faro* (bean soup). The roast chicken or veal scaloppine are good entrées. Lighter eaters will appreciate their *insalate giganti*—six huge salads that are meals in themselves. They seem to appeal to just about everyone. The de rigueur dessert is Zàzà's own *torta di mele alla Zàzà,* an upside-down apple tart similar to the French *tarte Tatin.*

## *Restaurants near Piazza Goldoni*

## (23) ARMANDO

**borgo Ognissanti, 140r**

AREA
piazza Goldoni
TELEPHONE
21-62-19
OPEN
Mon, Thur–Sun; Tues lunch only

Armando, on my short list of best-value restaurants in Florence, offers cooking that will not only please but nourish very well. Handed down from father to son, this typically Tuscan trattoria is as authentic as the cuisine, with friendly service provided by family and long-term staff in an ever-crowded and cheerful atmosphere. As the evening wears on, it can get loud, but that is part of the fun of eating here. Keep in mind that Italians dine late; in fact, at 9:30 P.M. they are still milling about waiting for a table to clear.

The Oscar for the best pasta dish goes to their *ravioli al burro e salvia,* homemade ravioli stuffed with ricotta cheese and sage and lightly covered in a buttery sauce. Throw cholesterol and fat counting to the wind just once and treat yourself to this. Another hands-down favorite in the pasta category goes to the *spaghetti alla carriettiera,* pasta topped with a spicy sauce made from garlic, fresh basil, tomato, and red pepper. This dish will wake up your taste buds in a hurry. Even if you have spent a lifetime turning up your nose at liver, please consider it here and try the *fegato alla salvia,* calves' liver broiled just to the tender pink stage. In the dessert department, nothing is a particular standout, so opt for an assortment of local cheeses, a scoop of cool *gelato,* or save these calories for a better opportunity.

**CLOSED**
Wed, Aug (dates vary)

**HOURS**
Lunch 12:30–2:30 P.M., dinner 7:30–10 P.M.

**RESERVATIONS**
Advised, especially for dinner

**CREDIT CARDS**
MC, V

**À LA CARTE**
L 35,000, beverage extra

**MENÙ TURISTICO**
None

**COVER & SERVICE CHARGES**
Cover L 2,500, 10% service added

**ENGLISH**
Yes

## (24) COCO LEZZONE
### via del Parioncino, 26r

In Italian, the name of this trattoria translates into "the crazy cook." Let me assure you there is nothing crazy about this beloved trattoria. There is no sign outside, but that does not mean that this century-old spot has not been found by everyone from Florentine workers and blue bloods to Prince Charles and Luciano Pavarotti. The inside has barely changed since it opened. It still has plain white-tiled walls and elbow-to-elbow seating along narrow tables. The hearty, traditional cooking is prepared with only high quality, fresh ingredients.

Diners are expected to order full meals, to eat them with zeal, and to drink plenty of wine in the process. That is very easy to do, especially if you start out with a light *primo piatto* (first plate) of *pappa al pomodoro* or the *farfalle con porcini* (pasta with mushrooms). For the *secondo piatto,* beef eaters can really dig into the Florentine steaks, cooked rare and literally overflowing the plate. I like the roast pork, served with a side order of seasonal vegetables, or the richly satisfying *osso buco*. If you have been working up the courage to try tripe, here is your chance. Served in a tomato sauce with freshly grated Parmesan cheese, it is perfectly tender and delicious. Desserts are all made here and depend on the season and mood of the chef.

**AREA**
piazza Goldoni

**TELEPHONE**
28-71-78

**OPEN**
Mon–Sat

**CLOSED**
Sun, July–Aug (5 weeks), Dec 22–Jan 7

**HOURS**
Lunch noon–2:30 P.M., dinner 7–10:30 P.M.

**RESERVATIONS**
Not accepted

**CREDIT CARDS**
None

**À LA CARTE**
L 30,000, beverage extra

**MENÙ TURISTICO**
None

**COVER & SERVICE CHARGES**
Cover L 3,500, service not included

**ENGLISH**
Yes

## (25) IL LATINI
### via dei Palchetti, 6r

**AREA**
piazza Goldoni

**TELEPHONE**
21-09-16

**OPEN**
Tues–Sun

**CLOSED**
Mon, Aug (dates vary)

**HOURS**
Lunch 12:30–2:30 P.M., dinner
7:30–10:30 P.M.

**RESERVATIONS**
Advised for large parties

**CREDIT CARDS**
AMEX, DC, MC, V

**À LA CARTE**
L 40,000, beverage extra

**MENÙ TURISTICO**
None

**COVER & SERVICE CHARGES**
Cover L 2,500, service included

**ENGLISH**
Yes, and English menu

Narciso Latini opened Il Latini around the turn of the century as a *fiaschetteria,* or wine shop. In the fifties, his nephew took over, expanded the shop, and began to serve sandwiches and hot food prepared by his wife, first in her own kitchen at home and later on in the restaurant. Now the popular trattoria is synonymous with good food, good wine, and good cheer. It is everything one expects and hopes for, from the interior festooned with hanging hams and trestle tables to the big servings of typical Tuscan food dished up with plenty of their own bottles of wine and extra-virgin olive oil.

A good opening course is their signature soup, *zuppa di fagioli con farro,* made with wild grain and puréed kidney beans and seasoned with garlic and rosemary. For the meat dish, you have a wide choice, ranging from saddle of pork, leg of lamb, herb-scented squabs, and roasted veal to the red meat blowout to end them all—the *piatto misto,* a mixed plate made up of a piece of all of their meats. To end, you must have either their silky rendition of *tiramisù* or their own plum cake topped with ice cream.

## (26) PEPOLINO
### via Borgognissanti, 1r

**AREA**
piazza Goldoni

**TELEPHONE**
29-09-78, 28-75-18

**OPEN**
Mon–Sat dinner only

**CLOSED**
Sun, Aug

**HOURS**
7–11:30 P.M.

**RESERVATIONS**
Advised

**CREDIT CARDS**
AMEX, DC, MC, V

**À LA CARTE**
L 45,000–55,000, beverage
extra

**MENÙ TURISTICO**
None

**COVER & SERVICE CHARGES**
No cover, service included

**ENGLISH**
Yes, and English menu

Great taste and a hint of elegance. If this does not describe your dining companion(s), at least it can describe your dinner at Pepolino.

The restaurant occupies two small rooms, a few steps below the street level just down the street from the Hotel Excelsior. The minimalistic interior is highlighted by orange banquette seating along one wall and an assortment of traditionally upholstered chairs around white linen–covered tables. Casually clad waiters wear cords or jeans with shirts and V-neck sweaters in the winter. Contemporary music wafts over it all.

The imaginative food presentations are not only bright, colorful, and bold but well prepared and correctly served. The seasonal menu changes monthly and offers *nouvo* twists on old Italian favorites. There are, however, a few dishes you can always count on. The light cauliflower soufflé, garnished with tiny vegetables, a sprig of dill, and a wedge of lemon, is a delightful beginning. Red beet *tagliatelle* topped with asparagus points in a rosé cream sauce, and the veal *saltimbocca* with truffle sauce are two of the other all-time menu standards. Otherwise, you might see carpaccio punctuated with pine nuts and black olives; chickpeas folded into an omelette garnished with shrimp; gnocchi served with a truffle fondue; roasted salmon with a pretty watercress sauce; or beef stew served with mashed turnips. The boring side orders of mixed salads are the only disappointments I found on the otherwise near-perfect menu. For the final touch, beautiful desserts include a poached pear surrounded by a white and dark chocolate sauce, accompanied by a glass of sweet dessert wine. The well-priced wine list, offering vintages from every region, should add even more to your enjoyment of this Big Splurge.

## Restaurants near the Ponte Vecchio

### (27) BUCA DELL'ORAFO
### volta dei Girolami, 28r (near the Ponte Vecchio)

Hidden under an archway near the Ponte Vecchio is the Buca dell'Orafo, a favorite for years with Florentines and visitors for its good value and authentic cuisine. The two owners are on tap every day to run the kitchen and serve the guests. Everyone seems to know one another, particularly at lunch when there is lots of laughing and talking going on between the tables. If you go for lunch or after 9 P.M., you will likely share your dining experience with Italians. If you go for an early dinner, you will hear mostly English spoken and probably run into your cousin's neighbor from Detroit.

The regulars know to come on the specific days their favorite dishes are served. Friday it is always fresh cod fish. Thursday, Friday, and Saturday, *ribollita* headlines the openers. Every day you can count on finding a special, such as *stracotto e fagioli,* braised beef with beans in a sauce with garlic, onions, and sage. A favorite in the spring is the *tortino di carciofi,* an artichoke omelette that will change your mind about what can be done with an artichoke. The dessert to melt your heart and your willpower is the house special *dolce,* a sponge cake with cream layers and meringue and almonds on top. It will be one of the best desserts you have on your entire trip.

**AREA**
Ponte Vecchio

**TELEPHONE**
21-36-19

**OPEN**
Tues–Sat

**CLOSED**
Sun, Mon, Aug

**HOURS**
Lunch 12:30–2:30 P.M., dinner 7:30–10:30 P.M.

**RESERVATIONS**
Essential as far in advance as possible

**CREDIT CARDS**
None

**À LA CARTE**
L 40,000, beverage extra

**MENÙ TURISTICO**
None

**COVER & SERVICE CHARGES**
Cover L 3,000, service included

**ENGLISH**
Yes

## (28) IL FORNAIO
### Ponte Vecchio location: via Guicciardini, 3r
### piazza Mercato Centrale location: via Sant'Antonio and via Faenza

**TELEPHONE**
None at either location
**OPEN**
Mon–Tues, Thur–Sat; Wed morning only
**CLOSED**
Sun
**HOURS**
8 A.M.–2 P.M., 4:30–7:30 P.M.
**RESERVATIONS**
Not accepted
**CREDIT CARDS**
None
**À LA CARTE**
From L 1,500, beverage not available
**MENÙ TURISTICO**
None
**COVER & SERVICE CHARGES**
None
**ENGLISH**
Depends on server

For a sandwich on the run or a pastry to go, you cannot beat Il Fornaio, a chain of bakeries with several locations in Florence. They open at 8 A.M. selling trays of hot *cornetti* (croissants), *brioche,* and other early morning treats and temptations. The lunch lines are legion, proving that when you have good food at decent prices the world will beat a path to your door. All the food is to go, and the service is frenetic during the crazy lunch scene. If, however, you go about noon, or wait until after 1:30 P.M., when admittedly the selection will be diminished, you will at least be able to place your order without a long wait.

## (29) OSTERIA DEL CINGHIALE BIANCO
### borgo San Jacopo, 43r

**AREA**
Ponte Vecchio
**TELEPHONE**
21-57-06
**OPEN**
Mon, Thur–Sun
**CLOSED**
Tues, Wed, July (3 weeks)
**HOURS**
Lunch noon–2:30 P.M., dinner 7–10:30 P.M.
**RESERVATIONS**
Essential
**CREDIT CARDS**
None
**À LA CARTE**
L 40,000–45,000, beverage extra
**MENÙ TURISTICO**
None
**COVER & SERVICE CHARGES**
Cover L 2,000, service included
**ENGLISH**
Yes

Massimo Masselli along with his wife and son represent the third generation of well-known restaurateurs in Florence. Their popular restaurant, set in a fourteenth-century tower close to the Ponte Vecchio, specializes in wild boar. This delicacy is best made into sausage, salami, or ham and served as an antipasto or stewed with red wine and vegetables and served with polenta as a main course.

Headlining the Tuscan dishes on the menu are *pappa al pomodoro* (a filling bread soup made with tomatoes, garlic, and olive oil) and *ribollita,* a hearty, long-simmered soup made with beans, vegetables, and bread. These age-old recipes date back to the times when peasants did not have much to eat and had to make do with what few ingredients they could find. Another wonderful dish is the *strozzapreti al burro,* boiled spinach pasta dumplings filled with cheese and drizzled with butter. Delicately crafted desserts include a *crema di Mascarpone* served with cookies and a *tiramisù* made with ricotta cheese that turns out to be light and less sweet than the regular, heavier versions.

Please keep in mind that reservations are essential for lunch and dinner, and that the romantic mezzanine table must be booked several days in advance.

# Restaurants near Santa Croce Church

## (30) ACQUA AL 2
### via della Vecchia, 40r (angle via dell' Acqua)

Everyone loves Acqua al 2, one of the most firmly established and well-known eating establishments in Florence. It consists of three rooms with stone walls, arched brick ceilings, wooden banquettes, and hard wooden chairs and benches. Tables are set with fresh flowers and paper placemats. The animated diners come from all walks of life and every corner of the globe.

The menu doesn't leave much to chance, with thirty pastas, hamburger fixed five ways, at least ten variations of veal, and a dozen salads. House specialties offer some particular treats, especially the *assaggio di primi,* your choice of any five pastas, or a gooey, rich serving of focaccia bread, split, stuffed, and then baked. Desserts don't sparkle.

**AREA**
Between piazza Santa Croce and piazza Signoria
**TELEPHONE**
28-41-70
**OPEN**
Tues–Sun dinner only
**CLOSED**
Mon, Aug (dates vary)
**HOURS**
Dinner 7:20 P.M.–1 A.M.
**RESERVATIONS**
Advised
**CREDIT CARDS**
MC, V
**À LA CARTE**
L 40,000, beverage extra
**MENÙ TURISTICO**
None
**COVER & SERVICE CHARGES**
Cover L 2,000, 10% service added
**ENGLISH**
Yes

## (31) ANTICO NOÈ
### volta di San Piero, 6r

Ask any student in Florence where to go for the best sandwiches and the answer will be Antico Noè, a real hole-in-the-wall where good food and good cheer have been served since 1520. To say it is hidden is an understatement—even though it is not too far from the Santa Croce Church. The best directions if you are coming from the church are to walk north along via Giuseppe Verdi to piazza Salvermini; on your left you will see a covered passageway (volta di San Piero) that usually has a man selling flowers right in front. Antico Noè is in the passageway with a crowd of students standing in front eating and drinking.

Except for a few bar stools, there is no seating, but no one minds standing up to eat their overstuffed made-to-order sandwiches. Prices begin around L 2,500 for a plain meat sandwich; each addition (i.e., tomato, lettuce, cheese, etc.) costs an additional L 500. The best sandwiches are the spiced rolled roast beef or the turkey washed down with a beer or glass of wine. House wine is cheap, but spend a few hundred lire more and enjoy a glass of their Chianti Classico. For dessert, stroll over to Vivoli (see page 52) and enjoy a cone or a cup of their famous *gelato*.

**AREA**
Santa Croce Church
**TELEPHONE**
23-40-838
**OPEN**
Mon–Fri, Sun
**CLOSED**
Sat, Aug (2 weeks)
**HOURS**
10:30 A.M.–10:30 P.M.
**RESERVATIONS**
Not accepted
**CREDIT CARDS**
None
**À LA CARTE**
Sandwiches from L 2,500
**MENÙ TURISTICO**
None
**COVER & SERVICE CHARGES**
None
**ENGLISH**
Yes

## (32) DA BENVENUTO
### via Mosca, 16r (angle via de' Neri, 47r)

**AREA**
Santa Croce
**TELEPHONE**
21-48-33
**OPEN**
Mon–Tues, Thur–Sat
**CLOSED**
Sun, Wed, Aug
**HOURS**
Lunch 12:30–3 P.M., dinner
7:30–10 P.M.
**RESERVATIONS**
Advised
**CREDIT CARDS**
None
**À LA CARTE**
L 25,000, beverage extra
**MENÙ TURISTICO**
None
**COVER & SERVICE CHARGES**
Cover L 2,000, service included
**ENGLISH**
Yes

For more than two decades, Gabriella Pallini has been greeting the guests, making espresso, serving dessert, and tending the cash register, while her husband, Loriano, has been busy at work in his kitchen turning out the type of Tuscan fare that natives rave about. Frankly, this is exactly the type of place that, once found, people hate to divulge for fear it will change or fill up with loud tourists and never be the same again.

The three-room trattoria is very casual, with benches and tables placed close together, creating a high-decibel noise level, especially at lunch when people stand in the aisles waiting to be seated. When I go, I try to sit at one of the tables along the window in the large room; I avoid the stuffy anteroom next to the kitchen with three little tables squeezed into it. When ordering, select something simple or one of the daily specials. Be sure to include a salad or vegetable, as all the produce comes from the Pallini's own garden. For the first course, the rich and flavorful *pasta e fagioli* is always good and so are any of the ravioli dishes. For the second course, try the house goulash or the *bollito misto e sottaceti*—boiled meats garnished with pickled vegetables. The only dessert made here is an irresistibly good seasonal fruit tart.

## (33) FIASCHETTERIA AL PANINO
### via de' Neri, 2r

**AREA**
piazza Santa Croce
**TELEPHONE**
21-68-87
**OPEN**
Mon–Sat bar and lunch only
**CLOSED**
Sun, Aug (dates vary)
**HOURS**
Bar 9 A.M.–9 P.M., lunch
12:30–3 P.M.
**RESERVATIONS**
Not accepted
**CREDIT CARDS**
None
**À LA CARTE**
Sandwiches from L 4,000,
2 courses for L 10,000–15,000,
beverage extra
**MENÙ TURISTICO**
None

Smart Italian Cheap Eaters eat their lunches in snack bars that serve a hot noon meal. One of the best of these around the Santa Croce Church is the Fiaschetteria al Panino. You won't be able to miss its corner location . . . just look for the hungry crowd standing outside patiently waiting for the food rewards inside. This is a fast-paced place where dallying over long conversations is not part of the acceptable game plan. Everyone eats quickly at the bar, or sits on a stool at the marble counters circling the windows.

The food is guaranteed to do wonders for your well-being. Following the Italian tradition of preparing a special dish each day, the chef has *pappa al pomodoro* on Monday and *zuppa di faro* on Tuesday. Wednesday he makes *tagliatelle,* and on Thursday, cannelloni stuffed with spinach and ricotta cheese. Friday is fish day, and the pasta has a clam sauce. Every day you can count on lasagna, an assortment of *frittatas,* and warm foccacia bread, split and filled with meat or cheese. For dessert, abandon all diet worries and try the chocolate mousse torte, a rich pie that chocoholics will dream of for years to come. The other dessert, fried doughnut holes, are forgettable. They are heavy lumps that sit like wet laundry in the pit of your stomach for days.

**COVER & SERVICE CHARGES**
No cover, service included

**ENGLISH**
No

**MISCELLANEOUS**
Coffee is not served

## (34) IL BARROCCIO
### via Vigna Vecchia, 31r

For Sunday lunch, Il Barroccio is a full house, with a good mix of Italian families, area regulars, and tourists visiting the Santa Croce Church. The closely spaced tables are set with white and red linen cloths, nice silver, china, and fresh flowers. The smoke-yellowed walls have appealing Tuscan watercolors crowding almost every inch of space. The service is generally good, but it can be distracted when the tables are full and the two waiters are stretched to the limit.

The menu has all the Tuscan standbys plus a selection of seasonal and daily specials. All the pasta, sauces, and desserts are made here and are free of preservatives and additives. You can actually taste the potatoes in the gnocchi with its fresh basil and tomato sauce. The *ravioli alle noci*, ravioli with nuts in a cream sauce, is a very interesting first course. Main courses to rely on include the *carpaccio Parmigiano e rucola*—thin slices of raw beef served with fresh Parmesan cheese and bitter greens. Veal is fixed several ways, and there are always grilled meats. Desserts are limited to *panna cotta*, a pudding, *tiramisù*, or *biscotti con vin santo*.

**AREA**
Santa Croce Church

**TELEPHONE**
21-15-03

**OPEN**
Mon, Tues, Thur–Sun

**CLOSED**
Wed

**HOURS**
Lunch noon–2:30 P.M., dinner 7:15–10:30 P.M.

**RESERVATIONS**
Advised for Sun lunch

**CREDIT CARDS**
AMEX, DC, MC, V

**À LA CARTE**
L 30,000, beverage extra

**MENÙ TURISTICO**
None

**COVER & SERVICE CHARGES**
Cover L 3,000, service included

**ENGLISH**
Yes

## (35) LA BARAONDA
### via Ghibellina, 67r

*La baraonda* means "hubbub," and that is an apt description at noon when the prices are lower and every seat is occupied. The trattoria is owned by Duccio Magni and his wife, Elena, who is responsible for the kitchen. Florentine regulars flock here for the wholesome yet imaginative food prepared with only seasonally grown produce. The three-room interior consists of pure white tiles halfway up the walls, beamed ceilings, a bar with a few antique prints of boxing matches, and Villeroy and Bosch china placed on white linen–clad tables.

Lighter, Cheap Eater–friendly lunches keep everyone coming back for more, especially on the days their favorite dishes are on the menu. Tuesday you will find

**AREA**
Santa Croce

**TELEPHONE**
23-41-171

**OPEN**
Tues–Sat; Mon dinner only

**CLOSED**
Sun, Aug

**HOURS**
Lunch 12:45–2:30 P.M., dinner 8–10:30 P.M.

**RESERVATIONS**
Advised

**CREDIT CARDS**
AMEX, DC

**À LA CARTE**
Lunch L 25,000; dinner
L 45,000; beverage extra

**MENÙ TURISTICO**
None

**COVER & SERVICE CHARGES**
Lunch cover L 3,000; dinner
cover L 5,000; service included

**ENGLISH**
Yes

kidneys; Wednesday, pigeon; Thursday, rabbit; Friday, codfish; and Saturday, oxtail. Every day you'll find veal meatloaf covered in fresh tomato sauce, which always sells out, and the vegetable soufflés, which are actually more like a quiche than an airy soufflé.

At dinnertime, there is no printed menu, and each course has only one price. The meal begins with complimentary appetizers served with a basket of homemade bread and a crock of black olive pâté. I like the risotto baked with greens and the penne tossed with lots of garlic and broccoli as sturdy first courses. If I don't have one of the daily specials or the veal meatloaf, then I might order the braised beef in a lemon sauce or the leg of pork. All main courses are garnished, saving the extra expense of a side order of vegetables or a salad. The house dessert is billed an apple torte, but it is more like a thin pancake piled high with lightly cooked apples. A glass of Italian grappa, vin Santo, or Amaretto liqueur along with a piece of candy finalizes the excellent meal.

### (36) LA GIOSTRA CLUB
### On Borgo Pinti (on the right) a block past the intersection of via dell' Oriulo

**AREA**
Between Il Duomo and Santa
Croce

**TELEPHONE**
24-13-41

**OPEN**
Daily

**CLOSED**
Never

**HOURS**
Lunch 12:30–2:30 P.M., dinner
7:30 P.M.–midnight

**RESERVATIONS**
Essential

**CREDIT CARDS**
AMEX, DC, MC, V

**À LA CARTE**
L 50,000, beverage extra

**MENÙ TURISTICO**
None

**COVER & SERVICE CHARGES**
Cover L 4,500, service included

**ENGLISH**
Yes

You will recognize the Russian owner of this local favorite when he comes out of the kitchen in full chef's garb and goes from table to table greeting his guests. He is a very dignified and well-educated man, with doctorates in both chemistry and biology. Always a lover of fine food and cooking, he was told for years by his friends, "You are such a good cook, why don't you open your own restaurant?" Several years ago he came out of retirement and opened La Giostra Club with the help of his twin sons and his daughter. The restaurant was an instant hit, and it remains fully booked for both lunch and dinner seven days a week. The name means "carousel," and you can see a picture of one to the right of the entry.

Lunchtime does not seem to be a drawn-out affair, though dinner can be. If you go when the restaurant opens, chances are the service will be more attentive. As the evening progresses, the three waiters are stretched beyond their limits, resulting in long delays between courses. Almost the minute you are seated, you are served a flute of champagne and a plate of assorted *crostini,* toast with various toppings. The menu is small but choice. All of the *primi piatti* (first courses) are good, especially the ricotta-filled crêpe or the *tagliatelle* with a flavorful sauce of *funghi porcini*. One of the most popular main courses is the *filetto di bue Lorenzo il Magnifico,* finely sliced beef topped with fresh spinach and brought to your table on a sizzling hot plate that sits on a breadboard. Another favorite is the *scamorza,* slices of ham covered with melted cheese that has been browned and bubbled under the broiler just before it arrives at your table. For dessert, forget the *torta di mele,* a dreary apple tart, and opt instead of a cool lemon sorbet or the wickedly fattening *tiramisù.* The wine list is not cheap, but vintages are happily served by the glass, thus enabling you to sample more than one without ruining the budget completely.

## (37) LA MAREMMA
### via Verdi, 16r

It was about 9 P.M. on a rainy Sunday night. I had just arrived in Florence, had settled into my flat overlooking the Santa Croce Church, and was faced with finding something nearby for dinner. Following the advice I always give to readers, I decided to check out two or three candidates in the neighborhood and select the one with the most diners. La Maremma won, and it turned out to be a reliable standby.

The menu is of the utmost simplicity, with no whistles and bells . . . just good, solid cooking, the type you look forward to coming home to. There is sliced prosciutto, *ribollita, pasta e fagioli,* gnocchi, ravioli, and *tagliatelle* with assorted sauces. Meats include a mixed grill, roast chicken, veal, and lamb chops. Sautéed veggies, a small selection of desserts (i.e., fruit salad), *biscotti,* and a tart or cake complete the selections. The house Chianti is drinkable, the service polite and timely, the ladder-back chairs comfortable, the flowers on your table fresh, and the decor, if you overlook the stuffed boar's head mounted by the kitchen, very pleasing. All in all it is a good place to fall back on.

**AREA**
Santa Croce Church

**TELEPHONE**
24-46-15

**OPEN**
Mon, Tues, Thur–Sun

**CLOSED**
Wed, Aug (several weeks, dates vary)

**HOURS**
Lunch 12:30–2:30 P.M., dinner 7:30–11 P.M.

**RESERVATIONS**
Not necessary

**CREDIT CARDS**
AMEX, MC, V

**À LA CARTE**
L 25,000–30,000, beverage extra

**MENÙ TURISTICO**
None

**COVER & SERVICE CHARGES**
Cover L 3,000, service included

**ENGLISH**
Yes

## (38) PALLOTTINO
### via Isola delle Stinche, 1r

Ask the natives living around Santa Croce Church where they eat and the unanimous reply is: Pallottino! Where else? Because it was located very close to my flat, I had the opportunity of trying it several times, and I certainly share the enthusiasm, especially for the *menù*

**AREA**
Santa Croce Church

**TELEPHONE**
28-95-73

**OPEN**
Tues–Sun

CLOSED
Mon, Aug
HOURS
Lunch 12:30–2:30 P.M., dinner
7:30–10:15 P.M.
RESERVATIONS
Accepted for dinner only
CREDIT CARDS
AMEX, DC, MC, V
À LA CARTE
Dinner only, L 35,000,
beverage extra
MENÙ TURISTICO
Lunch only, L 12,000, 2
courses, cover and service
included, beverage extra
COVER & SERVICE CHARGES
Dinner only, cover L 3,000,
10% service added
ENGLISH
Enough

turistico, served only at lunch. This is a Cheap Eat to behold. To keep the regulars interested and coming back in droves, the menu, two courses plus a vegetable, changes daily and offers three choices for each course. Whole-meal bread comes with the meal, but wine and dessert do not. No problem. The house wine is cheap, and Vivoli, one of the most famous gelaterias in Florence, is next door (see page 52).

What about dinner? The menù turistico is replaced by à la carte choices, which provide enough variety of the usual Tuscan favorites to keep everyone well-fed and happy. Naturally, the offerings are a little more sophisticated, but prices are still reasonable enough not to crash the budget.

## (39) VIVOLI
### via Isola delle Stinche, 7r

AREA
Santa Croce Church
TELEPHONE
29-23-34
OPEN
Tues–Sun
CLOSED
Mon, Jan, Aug (last 2 weeks)
HOURS
8 A.M.–1 A.M.
RESERVATIONS
Not accepted
CREDIT CARDS
None
À LA CARTE
Gelato from L 2,000–14,000
MENÙ TURISTICO
None
COVER & SERVICE CHARGES
None
ENGLISH
Depends on server

Since 1930, the largest and creamiest selections of ice cream have been scooped out at Vivoli, located across the street from Florence's only English-language movie house. It is the most active in the evening, when young Florentines strut their stuff, and on Sundays, when it becomes a family affair. At these times you will be able to witness the Italian phenomenon of the passeggiata, the see-and-be-seen stroll all Italians love.

Baskets of fresh berries, cases of bananas, and crates of oranges go into the thousand-plus quarts of ice cream made and consumed here each day. For my gelato lire, the absolute best flavor, and one of their specialties, is the orange-chocolate cream, a cloudlike mixture of chocolate, cream orange liqueur, and pieces of fresh orange. Any of the semifreddo choices are fabulous, provided you can stand the fat-gram blowout from the whipped cream–based ice cream. Dieters need not feel left out: the fruit flavors are fat free, with the exception of banana. The gelato is served only in cups, and you pay for the size of the cup, not the number of flavors you want in it. . . . Avoid the strange rice cream flavor, a bland-tasting vanilla with hard pieces of almost raw rice sprinkled throughout.

# Restaurants near Piazza Santo Spirito

## (40) ANTICA TRATTORIA ORESTE
### piazza Santo Spirito, 16r

Cheap Eat readers are great restaurant scouts, and I receive countless letters from them suggesting new places for me to check out. One such place is the Antica Trattoria Oreste, which occupies a prime corner on the piazza Santo Spirito.

Anytime you go, dining here will be a good experience from beginning to end. I think it is an especially good choice for a long, lazy Sunday lunch spent with someone special, lingering over good conversation and a nice Tuscan wine. Whether you are seated in the upstairs room under the arches or in the shade of an umbrella on the piazza, you will have a good meal, nicely served in pleasant surroundings.

The dishes on the menu have just enough of an imaginative spin to be interesting but not overworked and contrived. Their recipe for ravioli was printed by request from a reader in *Gourmet* magazine. It consists of pillows of pasta filled with a combination of nuts and ricotta and Mascarpone cheeses, all bathed in a cream sauce. I promise you it is as delicious as it is fattening. The grilled lamb chops accented with black olives or the pork with herbs are main courses I will order again. Another favorite I will repeat is the orange torte, a slice of heaven that brims with sweetness and ends the meal perfectly.

**AREA**
piazza Santo Spirito

**TELEPHONE**
23-82-383

**OPEN**
Mon, Wed–Sun

**CLOSED**
Tues

**HOURS**
Lunch 12:30–2:30 P.M., dinner 7:30–10:30 P.M.

**RESERVATIONS**
Advised, especially in summer and for Sun lunch

**CREDIT CARDS**
AMEX

**À LA CARTE**
L 45,000, beverage extra

**MENÙ TURISTICO**
None

**COVER & SERVICE CHARGES**
Cover L 3,000, service included

**ENGLISH**
Limited

## (41) BAR RICCHI
### piazza Santo Spirito, 9r

What a pleasant Cheap Eat the Bar Ricchi continues to be! I dashed in one day several years ago to avoid being drenched by a sudden rainstorm. I had planned to have a quick sandwich and regroup for the rest of the afternoon. When I saw the lunch plates being served to eager patrons, who have been returning here for years, I quickly changed my order. Every time I have been here, I have found the food to be simple yet delicious. When you go in the winter, sit in the room next to the stand-up bar area and settle into a soft banquette seat before a tiny marble-topped café table. Covering the walls here and in the bar is a fascinating display of framed photographs of the Santo Spirito Church. In the summer, enjoy your

**AREA**
piazza Santo Spirito

**TELEPHONE**
21-58-64

**OPEN**
Mon–Sat bar and lunch only

**CLOSED**
Sun, Aug (last 2 weeks)

**HOURS**
Bar 7 A.M.–8 P.M. (Summer bar hours, 6 A.M.–6 P.M.); lunch noon–3 P.M.

**RESERVATIONS**
Not accepted

**CREDIT CARDS**
AMEX, MC, V

À LA CARTE
L 8,000–16,000, beverage extra

MENÙ TURISTICO
None

COVER & SERVICE CHARGES
Cover L 2,000, service included

ENGLISH
Yes

MISCELLANEOUS
Bar Ricchi is open for lunch on the second Sunday of every month, when there is an open-air market on piazza Santo Spirito.

lunch outside on the terrace with its commanding view of the church.

The power behind the success of the kitchen is Alfonsina, the young wife of the owner of the Bar Ricchi. Her menu selections are limited, but they change every day with the exception of the roast beef and creamy mashed potatoes and the big one-plate salads. On my last visit, in addition to these two staple items, she had roast veal, chicken croquettes, and a fresh fish. This is *not* the place to skip dessert. Treat yourself and indulge in one of Alfonsina's almost illegally rich pastries, a piece of fruit-topped cheese cake, or a serving of *tiramisù*. As with most "insider" Cheap Eats, the best dishes go quickly, so plan to arrive early for your lunch.

## (42) GASTRONOMIA VERA
### piazza Frescobaldi, 3r

AREA
near piazza Santo Spirito (across the Ponte S. Trinità, en route to piazza Santo Spirito)

TELEPHONE
21-54-65

OPEN
Mon–Sat; Wed morning only

CLOSED
Sun

HOURS
8:30 A.M.–8 P.M.; Wed 3:30 A.M.–1 P.M.

RESERVATIONS
Not accepted

CREDIT CARDS
AMEX, MC, V

À LA CARTE
Sandwiches from L 4,200

MENÙ TURISTICO
None

COVER & SERVICE CHARGES
None

ENGLISH
Some

Perfect picnics begin at Vera, one of the city's best-stocked and most appealing gourmet delicatessens. In addition to the usual roast meats, hanging hams and salamis, assorted cheeses, six types of olives, wines, olive oils, vinegars, and dairy products, Vera stocks dried pastas, countless herbs and spices, and enough fancy canned and bottled delicacies to keep you eating well for weeks. Prices tend to be on the high side for almost everything, but for the unequalled quality of the food, I think it is well worth the extra outlay.

There are not tables for dining at Vera's, so plan to take whatever you order with you. This is actually a bonus because it saves the cover and service charges.

## (43) I RADDI
### via Ardiglione, 47r

AREA
Between piazza Santo Spirito and Pitti Palace

TELEPHONE
21-10-72

OPEN
Tues–Sat, Mon dinner only

CLOSED
Sun, Aug

HOURS
Lunch 12:30–2:30 P.M., dinner 7:30–11:30 P.M.

Luciano Raddi is a former European and Italian boxing champ of the fifties who has switched careers. Now, with his wife and daughter, he cooks and serves homestyle Florentine dishes in a trattoria somewhat off the usual tourist track, but it's close enough for a nice walk after lunch to the piazza Santo Spirito, with its interesting church, or to the Pitti Palace museum a few blocks farther.

Quiet, well-spaced tables are set in a rough-hewn room dominated by a heavy-beamed ceiling. The crowd at lunch is sparse, making it easy to get a good table without advance reservations. Things pick up at night, when the neighborhood pours in for an evening of conversation, fine Chianti, and generous helpings of good food. The menu does not go on forever, a sure sign that everything is fresh. Daily specials are usually the best bets, and if you are like I am and can barely think of dinner without a dessert of some sort, you will like the *dolce della casa,* either cheesecake or lemon or chocolate mousse.

**RESERVATIONS**
Advised for dinner
**CREDIT CARDS**
AMEX, MC, V
**À LA CARTE**
L 30,000–38,000, beverage extra
**MENÙ TURISTICO**
None
**COVER & SERVICE CHARGES**
Cover L 2,000, service included
**ENGLISH**
Very limited

## (44) PASTICCERIA MARINO
### piazza N. Sauro, 19r (From piazza Goldoni, cross the Arno River)

For some of the best croissants (called *cornetti* or *brioche*) in Firenze, the name to remember is Pasticceria Marino, a bar and pastry shop on the piazza N. Sauro at the end of the Ponte alla Carraia. Dozens of other pastries are also made here, but the best are these buttery croissants that come out of the oven all morning long.

The croissants are available plain or filled with chocolate or vanilla custard (called *crema*) or with marmalade. If they are temporarily out when you arrive, be patient. There is undoubtedly another batch baking in the back. To consume your treat, order a cappuccino and stand with the crowd around the bar, or sit at one of the stools placed at the counter along one wall.

**AREA**
piazza N. Sauro
**TELEPHONE**
21-26-57
**OPEN**
Tues–Sat; Sun morning only
**CLOSED**
Mon, Aug
**HOURS**
Tues–Sat 6:30 A.M.–8 P.M., Sun 6:30–11 A.M.
**RESERVATIONS**
Not accepted
**CREDIT CARDS**
None
**À LA CARTE**
*Cornetti* are L 1,200
**MENÙ TURISTICO**
None
**COVER & SERVICE CHARGES**
None
**ENGLISH**
Some

## (45) TRATTORIA LA CASALINGA
### via dei Michelozzi, 9r

If you are a collector, or just an admirer of fine furniture and antiques, be sure to walk down via Maggio and browse the many beautiful shops and boutiques selling one-of-a-kind items with prices to match. Try to time your visit to include a meal at this typical Florentine trattoria, which is extremely popular with everyone from students, families, and toothless pensioners to Japanese tourists and ladies-who-lunch.

The two rooms with knotty pine wainscoting and high ceilings have closely spaced white linen–covered tables. Service is bright and friendly. The basic menu of pastas, grills, roasts, and vegetables remains the same.

**AREA**
piazza Santo Spirito
**TELEPHONE**
21-86-24
**OPEN**
Mon–Sat
**CLOSED**
Sun, Aug (2–3 weeks)
**HOURS**
Lunch noon–2:30 P.M., dinner 7–9:30 P.M.
**RESERVATIONS**
Advised for 4 or more
**CREDIT CARDS**
None

**À LA CARTE**
L 20,000–24,000, beverage
extra
**MENÙ TURISTICO**
None
**COVER & SERVICE CHARGES**
Cover L 1,500, L 1,000 service
added
**ENGLISH**
Yes

Daily specials are handwritten, and as usual, these are the dishes to pay attention to. Because the tables are turned at least twice during each meal, service is quick, so you can count on being in and out in an hour or so, and that is something in Italy.

### (46) TRATTORIA DEL CARMINE
### piazza del Carmine, 18r

**AREA**
piazza del Carmine, near piazza
Santo Spirito
**TELEPHONE**
21-86-01
**OPEN**
Mon–Sat
**CLOSED**
Sun, Aug (1 week)
**HOURS**
Lunch noon–2:30 P.M., dinner
7–10:30 P.M.
**RESERVATIONS**
Advised for outside table
**CREDIT CARDS**
AMEX, DC, MC, V
**À LA CARTE**
L 25,000–35,000, beverage
extra
**MENÙ TURISTICO**
L 20,000, 3 courses, cover and
service included, beverage extra
**COVER & SERVICE CHARGES**
Cover L 2,000 service included
**ENGLISH**
Yes

Tucked away from the tourist glare is the appealing Trattoria del Carmine, a simple choice where everything seems to turn out. I like to go in the summertime and sit under an umbrella on the outside sidewalk terrace. During the cooler months, seating is on ladder-back chairs in two whitewashed rooms filled with attractive watercolors and leafy green plants.

The *menù turistico* is definitely the best Cheap Eat going in the neighborhood. It gives you a selection of five or six first and second courses along with a vegetable or salad and wine or water. Dessert, which could be the Florentine favorite of *vin santo con biscotti,* hard almond cookies to dip in sweet wine, or *crostata de frutta,* a fruit tart, will only add a few well-spent lire to the total bill. On the à la carte side, look for the chef's daily recommendations. Perhaps you might start with his sampler plate of several pastas and follow this with the grilled lamb chops or veal scaloppine. If you like chicken, look for the *petto di pollo alla Carmine,* a moist chicken breast with a mushroom and black olive cream sauce. The combination sounded a bit heavy to me, but I found it to be not at all overpowering.

## Restaurants near the Train Station, Piazza Santa Maria Novella, and Piazza Indipendenza

### (47) DA GIORGIO
### via Palazzuolo, 100r

**AREA**
Between train station and
piazza Santa Maria Novella
**TELEPHONE**
28-43-02
**OPEN**
Mon–Sat

If the line is too long down the street at Il Contadino, (see below), walk up to Da Giorgio, another Cheap Eat with a set-price-only menu. If I had to choose between the two, I would give the edge to Da Giorgio. In spite of the shared tables with plastic-covered linen, there are cloth napkins, green plants, a few pictures scattered on the walls, and a larger selection. Of course, there is no printed menu; you must depend on the waiter to tell you what is available that day. For starters there might be macaroni with a spicy sauce, *pasta al pesto,* risotto with peas, tomatoes, and meat, or *fettuccine al freddo.* On Thursday, there is always gnocchi. Your second course of meat, chicken, or fish is garnished with vegetables, salad, or potatoes. Wine or mineral water is included, but coffee is extra. The only dessert option is a piece of fresh fruit, which costs extra and is not worth it.

## (48) IL CONTADINO
### via Palazzuolo, 71r

You will probably have to wait in line with the Italians at lunch and the tourists at dinner if you want one of the Cheapest Eats in Florence. Il Contadino is across the street from the area's other bargain Cheap Eat, Da Giorgia (see above), and they both serve just about the same food and appeal to the same type of thrifty eater. At Il Contadino, interior decor is nonexistent: not a picture, plant, or flower of any sort graces the white-tiled rooms, which are filled with eager eaters with their sleeves rolled up and their ties loosened. The food is unimaginative but filling, and there is plenty of it. House wine or mineral water are included. For both courses, there are usually at least five selections, such as ravioli, minestrone, *pasta e fagioli,* pork, and beef, and there is fish on Wednesday and Friday. Main courses are garnished with either a salad, vegetable, fries, or beans. Coffee and fresh fruit are extra.

## (49) IL TRIANGOLO DELLE BERMUDE
### via Nazionale, 61r

Rose whiskey, peanut, licorice, After-Eight mint, Amaretto-strawberry, coffee crunch, trifle, and fat-free *sorbettos* are just a few of the unusual *gelati* flavors dished out daily at Il Triangolo delle Bermude. Do as the Florentines do and order a cup (*coppa*) or cone (*cono*). The various sizes and prices of each are prominently displayed, and you can mix and match several flavors in a single serving.

**CLOSED**
Sun, Aug (2 weeks)
**HOURS**
Lunch noon–3 P.M., dinner 6–10 P.M.
**RESERVATIONS**
Not accepted
**CREDIT CARDS**
MC, V
**À LA CARTE**
None
**MENÙ TURISTICO**
2 courses, cover and service included, beverage included
**COVER & SERVICE CHARGES**
Both included
**ENGLISH**
Yes

**AREA**
Between train station and piazza Santa Maria Novella
**TELEPHONE**
23-82-673
**OPEN**
Mon–Sat
**CLOSED**
Sun, Aug (2 weeks)
**HOURS**
Lunch noon–2:30 P.M., dinner 6:30–9:30 P.M.
**RESERVATIONS**
Not accepted
**CREDIT CARDS**
None
**À LA CARTE**
None
**MENÙ TURISTICO**
Lunch L 15,000; dinner L 16,000; 2 courses, cover and service included, beverage included
**COVER & SERVICE CHARGES**
Both included
**ENGLISH**
Yes

**AREA**
Train station
**TELEPHONE**
28-74-90
**OPEN**
Daily April–Sept; Tues–Sun Oct–March
**CLOSED**
Sun in winter, Jan
**HOURS**
11:30 A.M.–midnight

RESERVATIONS
Not accepted
CREDIT CARDS
None
À LA CARTE
*Gelati* from L 2,000
MENÙ TURISTICO
None
COVER & SERVICE CHARGES
None
ENGLISH
Some

If you would like to sample a flavor before ordering, ask for an *assaggio,* or a taste, and you will be given one on a plastic spoon. If you won't want a cone or a cup, consider the chocolate yo-yo, an ice cream sandwich with cream in the middle of two cookies.

### (50) IL GIARDINO DI BARBANO
**piazza Indipendenza, 3/4r**

AREA
Train station and piazza
Indipendenza
TELEPHONE
48-67-52
OPEN
Mon, Tues, Thur–Sun dinner
only
CLOSED
Wed
HOURS
5 P.M.–1 A.M.
RESERVATIONS
Not necessary
CREDIT CARDS
AMEX, DC, MC, V
À LA CARTE
L 21,000, beverage extra; pizzas
from L 6,000
MENÙ TURISTICO
None
COVER & SERVICE CHARGES
Cover L 1,000, service included
ENGLISH
Yes, and English menu

Handsome Gian Carlo, who has been running his successful restaurant for over twelve years, told me, "I was born in Florence, my entire family lives here, and I will die here." He has definitely captured the essence of being Florentine. From 5 P.M. until 1 A.M. every night but Wednesday, most of the restaurant's 120 seats are filled with a happy crowd that ranges from tourists and tradesmen to fashionable men and women. In the summer, the table to request is one in the back garden; in winter, ask for a booth in front. The specialty is *pappardelle al cinghiale,* wide, flat noodles sauced with wild boar meat. If that doesn't speak to you, perhaps one of the thirty-three pastas will. Pasta doesn't sound good? Then order one of the twenty-nine pizzas. There are also salads, appetizers, and a host of desserts, including the house version of profiteroles, all guaranteed to keep you fully contented for some time.

### (51) LA LAMPARA
**via Nazionale, 36r**

AREA
Train station
TELEPHONE
21-51-64
OPEN
Daily in summer, Mon, Wed–
Sun in winter
CLOSED
Tues in winter, Dec (last 2 weeks)
HOURS
Noon–11 P.M., continuous
service
RESERVATIONS
Not necessary
CREDIT CARDS
AMEX, DC, MC, V
À LA CARTE
L 30,000–35,000, beverage
extra; pizza from L 6,000

For a pizza, a bowl of pasta, or a complete meal anytime from noon until 11 P.M. (to midnight in the summer), La Lampara on via Nazionale, close to the train station, is a handy address to remember.

The interior would have pleased P. T. Barnum, with seating for 240 diners, a long curved bar where every drink imaginable is poured, a beautiful brass espresso machine dispensing strong coffees, and an interior garden. There is a take-out counter up front or, past the wood-burning pizza ovens, seating in the back, with service by formally clad waiters. There will be something for everyone on the five-page menu, plus mimeographed specials, all of which are mercifully translated into English. While prices are not dirt cheap, with care you will be able to enjoy a good meal at an acceptable price.

## (52) L'ANGOLO DEL GELATO
### via della Scala, 2r

Italians are addicted to *gelato,* and nowhere is this more evident than in Florence, where *gelaterias* seem to be a dime a dozen. For the best ice cream near Santa Maria Novella, drop by L'Angolo del Gelato. This corner store is owned by a friendly man named Fabrizio and his mother. Everything they serve is made here from fresh ingredients and seasonal fruits. In winter, look for creamy *semifreddo* flavors; in summer, fat-free fruit *sorbettos*. The servings are generous. The most popular flavors are chocolate and, in the summer, lemon. Those in the know always ask for their *gelato* with some *panna montana* on top . . . or fresh whipped cream.

## (53) RISTORANTE DE' MEDICI
### via del Giglio, 49r–51r

If you order one of the pastas, a wood-fired pizza, or one of the succulent grilled meats—and avoid the tiny, overpriced salads–you will do just fine at this large, rather formal restaurant only fifty meters from the Medici Chapel and the Basilica of San Lorenzo. I think it is a place to remember for several reasons. First, it is open from noon until 1 A.M., and you can go in anytime for a full meal or a light snack . . . great advantages if you have children. Second, the wide selection of pastas and pizzas are offered at prices that won't send you and your budget into orbit. The grilled meats are all of the finest quality, and the house specialty is *bistecca alla fiorentina,* sold by the gram. Watch out . . . this can make your bill soar. Fine Chianti wines are featured, as are several beers that pair well with a pizza. Desserts are all made in-house.

**MENÙ TURISTICO**
None
**COVER & SERVICE CHARGES**
No cover, 12% service added
**ENGLISH**
Yes, and English menu

**AREA**
piazza Santa Maria Novella
**TELEPHONE**
21-05-26
**OPEN**
Tues–Sun
**CLOSED**
Mon
**HOURS**
Summer, 9:30 A.M.–1 A.M.; winter, 11 A.M.–midnight
**RESERVATIONS**
Not accepted
**CREDIT CARDS**
None
**À LA CARTE**
*Gelato* from L 1,500–7,000
**MENÙ TURISTICO**
None
**COVER & SERVICE CHARGES**
None
**ENGLISH**
Some

**AREA**
Train station
**TELEPHONE**
21-87-78
**OPEN**
Tues–Sun
**CLOSED**
Mon
**HOURS**
Noon–1 A.M., continuous service; pizza 6 P.M.–1 A.M.
**RESERVATIONS**
Not necessary
**CREDIT CARDS**
MC, V
**À LA CARTE**
L 20,000, beverage extra; pizza from L 5,000
**MENÙ TURISTICO**
None
**COVER & SERVICE CHARGES**
Cover L 3,000, service not included
**ENGLISH**
Yes

## (54) SOSTANZA
### via del Porcellana, 25r

**AREA**
piazza Santa Maria Novella
**TELEPHONE**
21-26-91
**OPEN**
Mon–Fri
**CLOSED**
Sat, Sun, Aug
**HOURS**
Lunch noon–2:30 P.M., dinner
seatings 7:30 P.M. and 9:30 P.M.
**RESERVATIONS**
Essential
**CREDIT CARDS**
None
**À LA CARTE**
L 35,000, beverage extra
**MENÙ TURISTICO**
None
**COVER & SERVICE CHARGES**
Cover L 3,500, 10% service
added
**ENGLISH**
Enough

Sostanza is one of the city's oldest and best-loved trattorias, frequented by the great, the near-great, and the just-plain folks. Forty places are crammed into a long room that despite its pristine plainness becomes quite hectic as the meal progresses and the diners crowd in together. Waiters wear jackets, but formality ends here. Wine is served in tumblers, bread is handed to you, and plates are passed. Lots of hugging, kissing, and waving goes on among the regulars. Reservations are essential for the two dinner seatings nightly.

The handwritten menu is easy to read. Dishes to remember are the *frittata al carciofi* (artichoke omelette) and the *bistecca alla fiorentina,* a six-hundred-gram T-bone steak geared for lumberjacks but ordered, and finished, by wafer-thin models. The only dessert made here, an orange meringue cake, is a must—you won't want to share a bite.

## (55) TAVERNA DEL BRONZINO
### via delle Ruote, 25r

**AREA**
piazza della Indipendenza
**TELEPHONE**
49-52-20
**OPEN**
Mon–Sat
**CLOSED**
Sun, Aug
**HOURS**
Lunch 12:30–2 P.M., dinner
7:30–10 P.M.
**RESERVATIONS**
Essential
**CREDIT CARDS**
AMEX, DC, MC, V
**À LA CARTE**
L 50,000–60,000, beverage
extra
**MENÙ TURISTICO**
None
**COVER & SERVICE CHARGES**
Cover L 4,000, service included
**ENGLISH**
Yes
**MISCELLANEOUS**
Coat and tie recommended

Eating at the Taverna del Bronzino is always a great pleasure. It is the perfect place for Big Splurge occasion dining, be it a birthday, an anniversary, or a romantic evening with the love of your life.

The understated and elegant interior is done in muted colors with flattering lighting. You will sit comfortably at nicely appointed tables with crisp linens, heavy silver, and fresh flowers. Formal waiters offer gracious and unobtrusive service that is always one step ahead of what you need.

You are bound to be as impressed with the food as the surroundings. It all starts with a glass of the house apéritif and a plate of tiny appetizers to enjoy while you are deciding what to order. If you ask, your waiter will make knowledgeable suggestions to help you plan your meal. The imaginative dishes are inspired by the seasonal best of the Italian harvest. Fresh pastas are blanketed under robust sauces of fresh seafood, *funghi porcini,* or black truffles. Meat, poultry, and fresh fish are perfectly cooked, gently perfumed with wines and herbs, and attractively served. Sublime desserts and a distinguished wine list round out a meal you will favorably recall long after you have forgotten many others.

## (56) TRATTORIA GIARDINO
### via della Scala, 61r

Trattoria Giardino fits the bill for a hearty Cheap Eat in the area around the train station and piazza Santa Maria Novella. The present owner, a former waiter here, bought it thirty years ago and is still on hand daily along with his attractive English-speaking daughter, who takes care of the dinner rush hour. It is a comfortable, friendly place where everyone is welcome and treated with the same degree of kindness and respect. The main room is paneled in knotty pine, and in the summer, a garden terrace in back is open for dining.

The *menù turistico* is positively philanthropic when you consider the price includes three courses, a beverage, and the cover and service charges. À la carte diners will fare well with any of the *piatti del giorno* selections neatly printed on graph paper and stuck to the regular menu. For dessert, either the chocolate cake or the *torta della nonna,* a cream-filled yellow cake, should set you on your merry way.

**AREA**
Between train station and piazza Santa Maria Novella
**TELEPHONE**
21-31-41
**OPEN**
Mon, Wed–Sun
**CLOSED**
Tues, July 15–Aug 15
**HOURS**
Lunch noon–3 P.M., dinner 7–10 P.M.
**RESERVATIONS**
Not necessary
**CREDIT CARDS**
DC, MC, V
**À LA CARTE**
L 25,000, beverage extra
**MENÙ TURISTICO**
L 18,000, 3 courses, cover and service included, beverage included
**COVER & SERVICE CHARGES**
Cover L 2,000, 10% service added
**ENGLISH**
Sometimes

## (57) TRATTORIA GUELFA
### via Guelfa, 103r

The Trattoria Guelfa is a hands-down favorite, and regulars fill it every day for lunch and dinner. Reservations are crucial, but even with them, be prepared to wait up to half an hour, especially on weekends. Service can be irritatingly slow, but when you consider that only two waiters, including hardworking Claudio, the owner, are on duty to serve the congenial crowd, it is amazing anyone gets anything, let alone to have it always arrive piping hot. Also under the same ownership is Antichi Cancelli (see page 36).

The key to success here is the wonderful back-to-basics food—all of it lovingly prepared Italian home-cooking. If you stay with the chef's specialties, or daily offerings, you cannot go wrong. Depending on the day and time of year, expect to find fat green and white tortellini stuffed with ham and mushrooms, spaghetti with fresh crab, or *cappellacci,* three big pasta tubes stuffed with cheese and spinach and served in a wild mushroom cream sauce. Other standouts include roast pork, grilled veal chops served with rosemary-roasted potatoes, and a delightful *pinzimonio di verdure crude*—a selection of seasonal raw vegetables served with oil for dipping. All the

**AREA**
Train station
**TELEPHONE**
21-33-06
**OPEN**
Mon, Tues, Thur–Sun
**CLOSED**
Wed
**HOURS**
Lunch noon–3 P.M., dinner 7–11 P.M.
**RESERVATIONS**
Essential
**CREDIT CARDS**
AMEX, MC, V
**À LA CARTE**
L 35,000, beverage extra
**MENÙ TURISTICO**
L 16,000, 3 courses, cover and service included, beverage included
**COVER & SERVICE CHARGES**
cover L 2,000, service included
**ENGLISH**
Yes

desserts remind me of home, especially the *panna cotta con cioccolato,* a cold pudding with hot chocolate poured over it.

# Restaurants near the Uffizi Gallery

## (58) CAFFÈ CARUSO
### via Lambertesca, 14–16r

**AREA**
Uffizi Gallery
**TELEPHONE**
28-19-40
**OPEN**
Mon–Sat
**CLOSED**
Sun, Aug (2 weeks)
**HOURS**
8 A.M.–8 P.M. continuous service; hot food noon–3 P.M.
**RESERVATIONS**
Not accepted
**CREDIT CARDS**
None
**À LA CARTE**
Sandwiches from L 2,000; hot dishes from L 6,000
**MENÙ TURISTICO**
L 14,000, 2 courses, beverage extra
**COVER & SERVICE CHARGES**
None
**ENGLISH**
Enough

The medieval part of Florence around the Uffizi Gallery was once a poor and unsavory section of the city. Not anymore. Now it is an energized area filled with art galleries, interesting shops, and amusing boutiques. Caffè Caruso is in the middle of it all, on via Lambertesca, the street that cuts through the Uffizi.

The beauty of Caffè Caruso is that you can eat here cheaply, cafeteria-style, or get a quick sandwich to go, either pre-prepared or made to order. Hot food is available from noon until 3 P.M., but the good dishes go quickly, so be here when the line opens for the best selection. The place is big, and you are expected to serve yourself and then take your food to a table. Nothing approaches the gourmet level, but it is a decent Cheap Eat, and a fast one to boot.

## (59) CIRCOLO PRIVATO CASTELVECCHI
### piazza della Signora, 6r (near the Uffizi Gallery)

**AREA**
piazza della Signora
**TELEPHONE**
21-19-28
**OPEN**
Mon–Sat
**CLOSED**
Sun, Aug (2 weeks)
**HOURS**
Lunch noon–3 P.M., dinner 7:30–10:30 P.M.
**RESERVATIONS**
Advised
**CREDIT CARDS**
AMEX
**À LA CARTE**
Lunch, L 16,000–20,000, beverage included; dinner, L 50,000, beverage extra
**MENÙ TURISTICO**
None

Beware: For dinner the kitchen specializes in fresh fish, and the prices are outrageous. But for lunch, this is a true Cheap Eat—you can get a good choice of first and second courses plus a vegetable and mineral water for under L 18,000. The location won't jump out at you: it is buried in a basement on the piazza della Signora, with only a signboard discreetly placed at the top of the downstairs entrance. The low ceilings, stone walls, and rambling interior make you feel as though you are dining in the caverns of an archeological dig.

Lunch starters include your choice of *ribollita* or fusilli with four different sauces. The second plate lists tripe, roast beef, oxtail, ham, liver with sage, or turkey accompanied by potatoes, beans, fennel, salad, or tomatoes. Lemon *sorbetto, tartufo bianco,* or the house dessert of the day will cap off the meal. For the location, quality of food, and interesting setting, this is a Cheap Eat steal . . . but, remember, *only* for lunch.

**COVER & SERVICE CHARGES**
No cover at lunch, cover L 3,500 at dinner; service included
**ENGLISH**
Some

### (60) I' CCHÈ C'È C'È
### via Magalotti, 11r

In Italian the name means "what you find, you find," and there is always excellent Tuscan fare and service to be found here.

Owner and chef Gino Noci is a native Florentine with long experience in the restaurant business, including time spent in a French restaurant in London. He emphasizes that his establishment is a casual, family-run place where everyone is welcomed in the same friendly way. For lunch, the long wooden tables are set with paper placemats and napkins. At night, green-and-white linen napkins replace the paper ones. Ringing the room are shelves of wine bottles and assorted paintings of varying quality.

Cheap Eaters will want to pay close attention to the *menù turistico,* which includes a first and second course and either a salad or frozen fried potatoes. When deciding what to order, always ask your waiter what Gino is cooking that day, and also take a long look at the grilled fresh fish. Everything is kept simple, using only the best olive oils and fresh ingredients. The house wine, poured from large barrels, is drinkable and recommended.

**NOTE:** If you are going to Siena, ask Gino for directions to Trattoria Mamma Rosa, which he owns there. It is at via Cassia, 32, and the telephone number is 82-49-100. It is closed on Thursday.

**AREA**
Uffizi Gallery
**TELEPHONE**
21-65-89
**OPEN**
Tues–Sun
**CLOSED**
Mon, Aug 17–Sept 10
**HOURS**
Lunch 12:30–2:30 P.M., dinner 7:30–10:30 P.M.
**RESERVATIONS**
Essential; not accepted for *menù turistico* for lunch
**CREDIT CARDS**
AMEX, MC, V
**À LA CARTE**
L 38,000, beverage extra
**MENÙ TURISTICO**
L 20,000, 2 courses, cover and service included, beverage extra
**COVER & SERVICE CHARGES**
Cover L 2,000, service included
**ENGLISH**
Yes

## *Miscellaneous Locations in Florence*

### (61) ALLA VECCHIA BETTOLA
### viale Ludovico Aristo, 32–34r

Tuscany's simplest foods tend to be its most successful, and nowhere is this more evident than at Alla Vecchia Bettola, a picturesque trattoria specializing in the region's native cuisine. Also under the same ownership is Nerbone (see page 39).

The small menu changes almost daily. A bottle of house wine is on the table for you to pour into green

**AREA**
piazza del Carmine
**TELEPHONE**
22-41-58
**OPEN**
Tues–Sat
**CLOSED**
Sun, Mon, Aug, Dec 23–Jan 2

**HOURS**
Lunch 12:30–2:30 P.M., dinner
7:30–10 P.M.
**RESERVATIONS**
Essential
**CREDIT CARDS**
None
**À LA CARTE**
L 35,000, beverage extra
**MENÙ TURISTICO**
None
**COVER & SERVICE CHARGES**
Cover L 2,000, service included
**ENGLISH**
Yes

glasses, paying for as much as you drink. Seating is at marble-topped row tables on benches along the wall or on four-legged, backless stools. Despite the rather rustic ambience, the atmosphere is upscale and so are the diners, arriving when the doors open and standing in line as the meal goes on. As you can see, management does not stress creature comforts. It does, however, definitely stress good food offered at fair prices.

If it is available, start with the *baccelli e pecorino*, a basket of raw, unshelled fava beans (similar to limas) and two slabs of smoky *pecorino* cheese. You shell the beans and pop them into your mouth with a piece of the cheese and a chunk of country bread. It is different, not heavy, and good. Move on to *topini al pomodoro*, a light gnocchi bathed in tomato sauce, and follow this with a second course of roast veal or rabbit served with crisply fried artichokes. Salads are disappointing, especially the tired spinach version, drenched in too much oil. Desserts, on the other hand, won't let you down. Try the house apple cake or the plate of assorted *biscotti*, consisting of macaroons and almond cookies for you to dip into a glass of sweet *vin santo*.

## (62) TRATTORIA DA TITO
### via San Gallo, 112r

**AREA**
piazza della Libertà
**TELEPHONE**
47-24-75
**OPEN**
Mon–Fri; Sat lunch only
**CLOSED**
Sun, Aug 10–31
**HOURS**
Lunch noon–3 P.M., dinner
7–10:30 P.M.
**RESERVATIONS**
Advised
**CREDIT CARDS**
MC, V
**À LA CARTE**
L 40,000, beverage extra
**MENÙ TURISTICO**
L 25,000, 3 courses, cover and
service included, beverage
included
**COVER & SERVICE CHARGES**
Cover L 1,500, 10% service
added

Tito remains one of my Florentine favorites because it is so typically Tuscan, complete with yellowing walls lined with photos of dubious value, quick and friendly service, and reasonable prices for food of uncompromisingly good quality. It is also out of the tourist mainstream, thus attracting a very local crowd.

At lunchtime you will need a shoehorn to get in because it is so packed with regulars, who consider this their neighborhood command post. Cheap Eaters will like the all-inclusive *menù turistico*, but I recommend loosening the money belt a notch or two and ordering from the *piatti del giorno* (daily specials). Carbohydrate fans will have a field day with the long list of authentic pastas and rice dishes. The *ribollita* (reboiled vegetable and bean soup), ravioli with spinach and Gorgonzola cheese, and the *pappardelle alle salsiccia e funghi* (broad noodles with sausage and mushrooms) are especially good. Carnivores can choose from a range of top-quality meats, and fish eaters will like the grilled salmon or baked sole. In the event that there is room for dessert, try the *dolce della casa* (special house dessert of the day) or an assortment of Tuscan cheeses and another glass of wine.

**ENGLISH**
Yes

## (63) I PILASTRI
### via dei Pilastri, 16r

Takeout doesn't have to be tacky, and it is certainly anything but at this bustling bar, *enoteca,* gourmet deli, lunch counter, and grocery store. Whatever you need in the way of packaged food or drink, chances are I Pilastri has it.

The hot food is ready at noon. By 1:00 P.M., the place is teeming, the selection dwindling, and the tables all occupied. But if you arrive early, you are bound to be lost in the endless choices before you: lasagna with mushrooms or asparagus, zucchini torte, fat sausages with braised fennel, roast chicken, curried rice, fish fixed numerous ways, salads and veggies galore, and a myriad of meats and cheese to be stacked on fresh rolls. It will be impossible to leave hungry.

**AREA**
piazza S. Ambrogio
**TELEPHONE**
24-52-00
**OPEN**
Mon–Sat; Wed half-day only
**CLOSED**
Sun, Aug
**HOURS**
7:30 A.M.–7:30 P.M., Wed
7:30 A.M.–2 P.M., continuous service
**RESERVATIONS**
Not accepted
**CREDIT CARDS**
None
**À LA CARTE**
From L 3,500
**MENÙ TURISTICO**
None
**COVER & SERVICE CHARGES**
None
**ENGLISH**
Limited

## (64) MAXIMILIAN
### via Alfani, 10r

"How do you do it?" I asked Adelina Vicini, the energetic owner and one-woman virtuoso of Maximilian. She not only plans the menu, shops for the food, prepares and serves both lunch and dinner but does the clean-up six days a week. She told me she sleeps only four or five hours a night. That must be on a good night. I am exhausted just *thinking* about it all.

She has been in her little trattoria on this street away from the tourist masses for about five or six years. Because she must depend on repeat local business, she has found what works and cooks accordingly. Her food is not exotic or gourmet but the simple homecooking we all know and love . . . and wish we had more of. It is nice to start with an *insalata mista,* filled with assorted greens, carrots, and tomatoes and brought to the table with a cruet of olive oil and vinegar. Vegetarians will lap up any of her garlic-filled pastas and the grilled seasonal vegetables. Meat eaters are treated to fried brains, calves' liver with mashed potatoes, or succulent roast rabbit. If you don't see what you want on the menu, and she had the ingredients in the kitchen, she will be happy to fix it

**AREA**
piazza de Santissima Annunziata
**TELEPHONE**
24-78-080
**OPEN**
Tues–Sun
**CLOSED**
Mon, Aug (last 2 weeks)
**HOURS**
Lunch 1–3:30 P.M., dinner 7:30–10 P.M.
**RESERVATIONS**
Advised
**CREDIT CARDS**
AMEX, DC, MC, V
**À LA CARTE**
L 35,000, beverage extra
**MENÙ TURISTICO**
None
**COVER & SERVICE CHARGES**
Cover L 4,000, service not included
**ENGLISH**
Enough

for you. For dessert, even if you think you are full, you will find yourself scraping the bottom of the generous dish of profiteroles, smothered in thick chocolate.

As you can imagine, when the tables are full, service may be a little slow. Don't worry, order a bottle of good Chianti Classico, sit back, enjoy the experience, and give Adelina great credit for a job very well done.

## Food Shopping in Florence

Probably the Cheapest Eat you will have in Florence is the one you prepare yourself. It may be an ambitious three-course meal prepared in your apartment kitchen or a snack purchased from the market and eaten on the run or on a pretty piazza. Even if you just wander through an Italian outdoor market or cruise the aisles of a supermarket, you will get a good look at the everyday Italian way of life. In Florence, here are the places I like to shop for food.

### INDOOR/OUTDOOR MARKETS
#### Mercato della Cascine
*Cascine Park along the Arno River*
*Tues only, 7 A.M.–1 P.M.*

A weekly outdoor market that is a cross between an outdoor food market and a discount department store. Go early for the best selection. Watch your wallets and purses. Take your own shopping bags.

#### Mercato Centrale de San Lorenzo
*Piazza del Mercato Centrale*
*Indoor food market: Mon–Sat 7 A.M.–1 P.M.*
*Outside stalls: Tues–Sat 9 A.M.–6 P.M., winter; Tues–Sun 9 A.M.–9 P.M., summer*

A *must* for every visitor to Florence. Inside on two levels are stalls selling every sort of meat, fish, cheese, fruit, and vegetable imaginable. This is the best in Italy, and the largest covered market in Europe. Outside are hundreds of stalls with hawkers selling a variety of fake Gucci scarves and bags, T-shirts for everyone on your list, Florentine paper products, leather goods, and more. Not much bargaining in the prices, so pick the seller with the best attitude. No one has a monopoly on any items . . . there are dozens of sellers all selling the same things at the same prices. Very touristy, but fun and worth at least an hour or so.

### Mercato Sant' Ambrogio
*Piazza Ghiberti (near Santa Croce)*
*Mon–Sat 7 A.M.–1 P.M.*

A lively indoor/outdoor neighborhood market selling to the locals. All the same meats, fish, dairy products, fruits, and vegetables found at the Mercato Centrale, but at slightly better prices. The dry goods stalls outside have some good buys in cotton underwear and socks.

## SUPERMARKETS
### Esselunga
*Via Pisana, 130*
*Viale de Amicis, 89*
*Mon–Sat 9 A.M.–7 P.M.; closed Wed afternoons*
*No credit cards*

This American-style supermarket has free parking, but avoid it on Saturdays.

### Standa
*Via de' Panzani, 31 (near Santa Croce and most central)*
*Tel: 28-30-71*
*Tues–Sat 9 A.M.–7:30 P.M., Mon 2–7:30 P.M.; closed Sun*
*Credit cards: MC, V*

This is the K-Mart of Italy, with a food section in back. The other locations are: Via dei Mille, 140, and Via Pietraplana, 42–44.

## HEALTH FOOD STORE
### Sugar Blues Health Food Store
*Via XXVII Aprile, 46–48*
*Tel: 48-36-66*
*Via dei Serraglia, 57*
*Tel: 26-83-78*
*Mon, Tues, Thur 9 A.M.–1:30 P.M. and 4–7:30 P.M.;*
*closed Wed afternoon*
*No credit cards*

A good health food store selling vitamins, packaged foods, a small selection of deli items, cereals, juices, teas, honey, yogurt, and cosmetics. The produce leaves something to be desired.

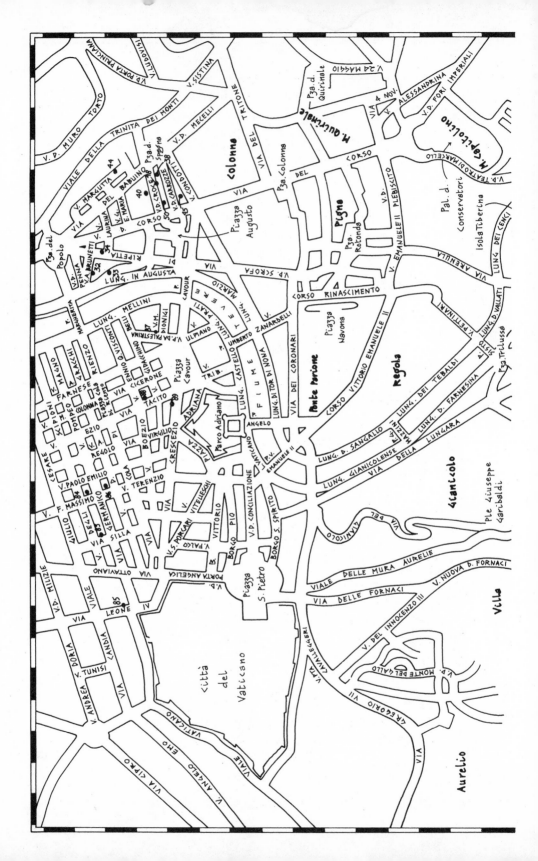

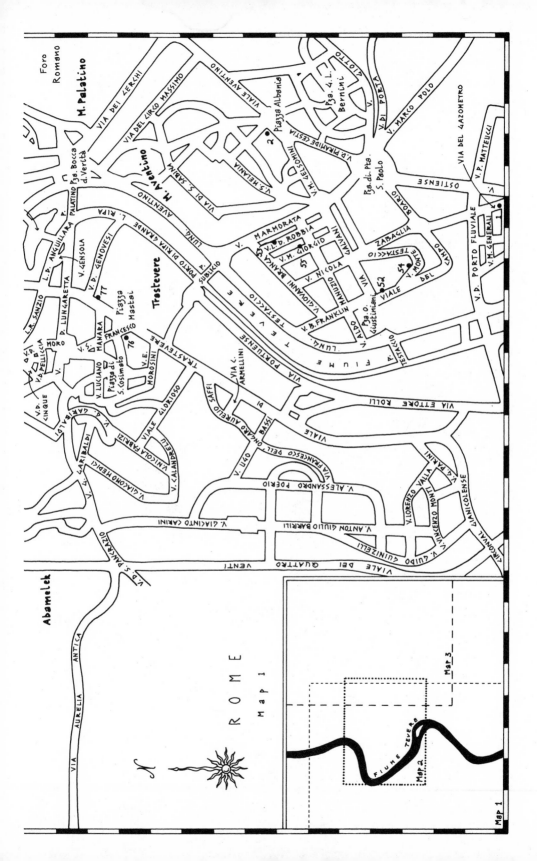

Map 1

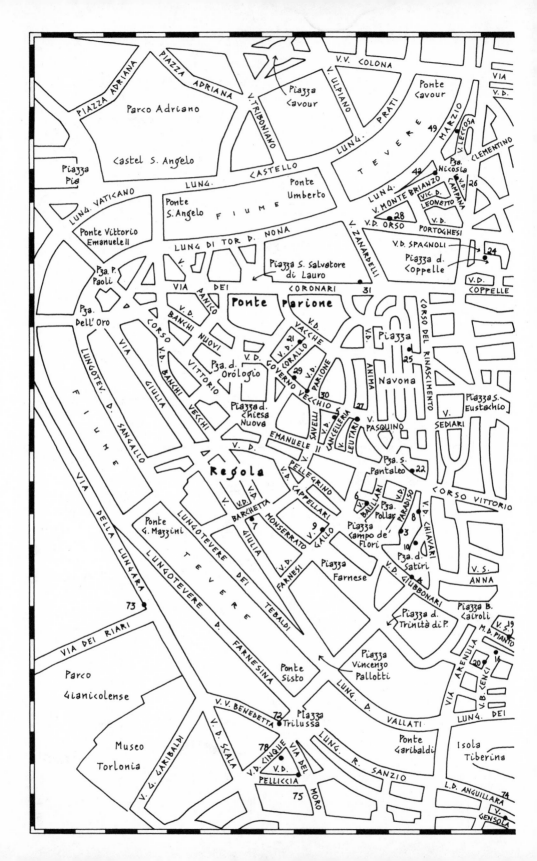

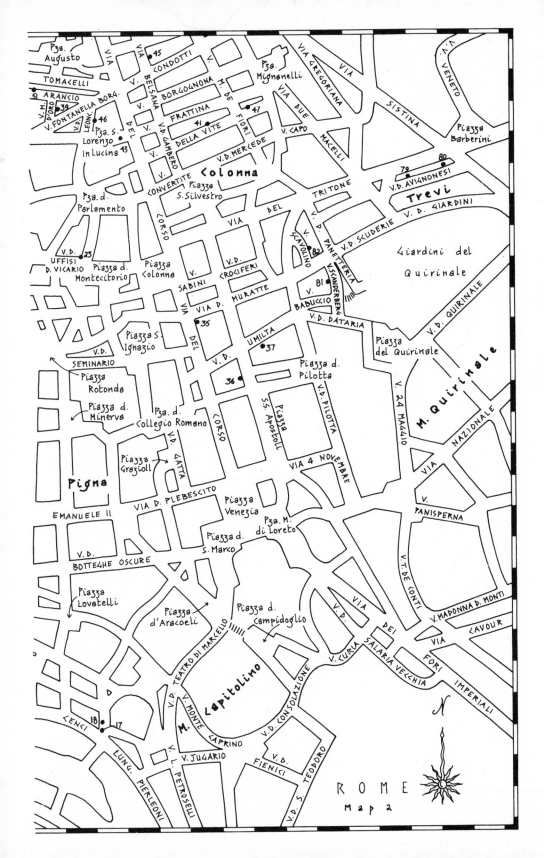

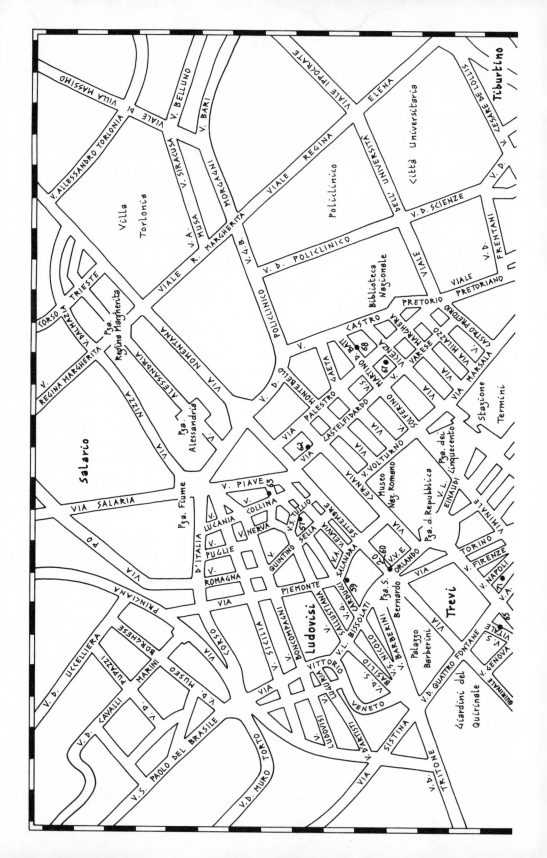

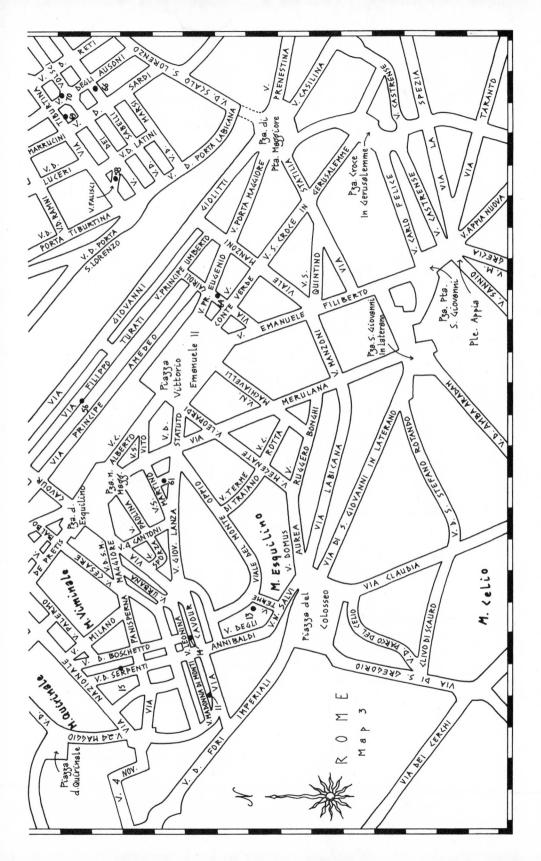

# Rome

**Every road does not lead to Rome, but every road in Rome leads to eternity.**
—*Arthur Symons,* Cities, *1903*

**When thou are in Rome, do as they do at Rome.**
—*Cervantes,* Don Quixote

In the eternal city of Rome, antiquity and history are taken for granted as part of normal life. A leisurely stroll or a bus ride can take you past some of Western civilization's greatest monuments, piazzas, and landmarks. This city, teeming with humanity and choked with traffic, happily lives amid the testimonies of her past.

Romans are famous for their passion for eating. While Rome cannot claim to be the gastronomic capital of Italy, it is the city where food is most pleasurably consumed. Romans were the originators of the first developed cuisine in the Western world. Today, Roman cuisine is rich in flavors and aromas, but there is nothing fancy about it. In fact, some may think it almost primitive because many of the famous dishes are based on innards, such as *coda all vaccinara* (oxtail stew with vegetables), *trippa all roman* (tripe cooked with meat sauce, mint, and *pecorino* cheese), and *cervella fritta* (fried calves brains). The Jewish community in Rome favors deep frying and has raised this cooking method to a delicate art form. Consider *carciofi alla giudia* (artichokes flattened and fried until brown and crisp) and zucchini blossoms stuffed with ricotta cheese and anchovies and quickly deep fried.

In Rome there are literally thousands of dining choices, from the elegant citadels of fine cuisine to the rapidly vanishing little family-owned and -run trattorias. As in every major world capital, fast food chains have invaded the city. The good news is that serious chefs are sticking with regional standbys and the basic *cucina* everyone wishes Mama still had the time and desire to prepare. Roman restaurants of all types are noted for serving the same specialties on the same days of the week. Tuesday and Friday, look for fresh fish. On Thursday, it is gnocchi, and on Saturday, tripe. For a traditional Sunday lunch with the extended family, plan on rich lasagna. Favored starters and pastas are *stracciatella* (chicken broth with egg and cheese stirred in just as it is served), *penne all'amatriciana* (pasta with tomatoes, onions, bacon, and hot pepper), *spaghetti alla carbonara* (pasta with bacon, onion, eggs, cheese, and wine), and mouthwatering displays of vegetable, meat, and seafood antipasti laid out with the precision of a fine jeweler. Popular entrées are *saltimbocca* (which means "hop into the mouth," and consists of thin slices of prosciutto and veal sautéed in butter and wine), *abbacchio* (lamb roasted to perfection over an open fire), and *baccalà* (dried salt cod, usually dipped in butter and fried in olive oil). Desserts are kept simple: a piece of fruit or a dish of fresh fruit. If something more is desired, there is the ever-present *dolci* darling of the decade, *tiramisù* (which means "pick me up"), a rich mix of coffee, cake, chocolate, and Mascarpone cheese.

## RESTAURANTS IN ROME

*Restaurants marked with an asterisk (*) are considered Big Splurges.

## Restaurants in Aventine

### (1) L'INSALATA RICCA III
### via del Gazometro, 62/64/66

For description, see L'Insalata Ricca I, campo de' Fiori, page 80.

AREA: Below Aventine
TELEPHONE: 57-51-76
OPEN: Mon, Tues, Thur–Sun
CLOSED: Wed
HOURS: Lunch 12:30–3 P.M., dinner 7:30–11:30 P.M.

### (2) L'INSALATA RICCA IV
### piazza Albania, 5

For description, see L'Insalata Ricca I, campo de' Fiori, page 80.

AREA: Aventine
TELEPHONE: 57-43-877
OPEN: Mon, Tues, Thur–Sun
CLOSED: Wed
HOURS: Lunch 12:30–3 P.M., dinner 7:30–11:30 P.M.

## Restaurants near Campo de' Fiori and Piazza Farnese

### (3) COSTANZA
**piazza del Paradiso, 63/65**

AREA
campo de' Fiori

TELEPHONE
68-61-717, 68-80-1002

OPEN
Mon–Sat

CLOSED
Sun, Aug

HOURS
Lunch 1–3 P.M., dinner
8–11:30 P.M.

RESERVATIONS
Essential

CREDIT CARDS
AMEX, DC, MC, V

À LA CARTE
L 50,000, beverage extra

MENÙ TURISTICO
None

COVER & SERVICE CHARGES
Cover L 4,000, service not
included

ENGLISH
Yes

A rather anonymous exterior masks the warmth of Costanza, a multiroom *hostaria* that sits on part of the ruins of the Theater de Pompeo, sections of which are displayed inside behind glass fronts. The attractive interior is a mix of stuccoed walls, low ceilings, and beams long with the expected round-up of wine bottles, paintings, candles at night, and other bric-a-brac. This dark, cozy atmosphere makes it the perfect place for a romantic meal with a special person.

The wide-ranging menu, which holds few disappointments, is admittedly for diners with more flexible budgets. On the pasta front, the *pasta e fagioli Costanza,* a carbohydrate festival of white beans and pasta in a broth with onions, bacon, and tomato sprinkled with grated cheese, is delicious. So are any of the risottos and the *tagliolini* with salmon and radicchio. From here, you safely pass to a number of main course dishes, ranging from steak tartare, grilled or roasted veal and beef to fresh fish and vegetables. The ever-present *dolci, tiramisù,* is featured and is especially rich, as are most of the other homemade desserts. I love the *torta di mirtilli* (blueberry tart) or, for a lighter choice, their own honey and almond cookies served with a glass of sweet wine for dipping.

### (4) DAR FILETTARO A SANTA BARBARA
**largo dei Librari, 88**

AREA
campo de' Fiori

TELEPHONE
68-64-018

OPEN
Mon–Sat dinner only

CLOSED
Sun, Aug, Dec 24–Jan 3

HOURS
5:30–10:30 P.M.

You need only remember one thing about this hidden Cheap Eat: *filleto di baccalà,* or deep-fried cod fish, their specialty.

All the fast-food fish fanciers in this section of Rome flock here. Their version is batter dipped and quickly deep fried, leaving the inside moist and the outside crisp.

Add a glass of wine and maybe a salad and you should be filled and ready for the next round of sightseeing.

RESERVATIONS
Not accepted
CREDIT CARDS
None
À LA CARTE
L 10,000, beverage extra
MENÙ TURISTICO
None
COVER & SERVICE CHARGES
No cover, service included
ENGLISH
Limited

## (5) GRAPPOLO D'ORO
### piazza della Cancelleria, 80/81

As with most popular Roman restaurants, the tourists eat early and the Italians late, so time your visit accordingly at this exceptionally popular location near campo de' Fiori. However, do not confuse this with two other restaurants in Rome bearing this same name.

Predictable trattoria decor, prices, and traditions prevail, down to the old-time white-jacketed headwaiter managing an overworked staff, who have only a nodding acquaintance with English and offer distracted service when the rush is on. However, the excellent food, the warm plates, the good-sized servings, and the eclectic crowd make up for the few shortcomings of the service. *Fettuccine con trote* (with trout) or risotto with truffles and mushrooms are good first courses. Veal kidneys with polenta, brains cooked in butter, or grilled liver may appeal to some. Less adventurous diners will like the scalloped veal in wine sauce, the *saltimbocca,* or the grilled lamb chops. The *insalata mista* is good, full of designer greens, radicchio, and tomatoes. For dessert, the *tartufo nero* (chocolate ice cream rolled in dark chocolate pieces) is my choice. Otherwise, there is the usual *tiramisù, torta del giorno* (daily cake or tart), or *panna cotta.*

AREA
campo de' Fiori
TELEPHONE
68-64-118, 68-97-080
OPEN
Mon–Sat
CLOSED
Sun, Aug (dates vary)
HOURS
Lunch noon–3 P.M., dinner 7–11 P.M.
RESERVATIONS
Strongly advised
CREDIT CARDS
AMEX, DC, MC, V
À LA CARTE
L 35,000, beverage extra
MENÙ TURISTICO
None
COVER & SERVICE CHARGES
Cover L 2,500, service included
ENGLISH
Limited

## (6) HOSTARIA FARNESE
### via dei Baullari, 109

At the Hostaria Farnese located between campo de' Fiori and piazza Farnese, you will enjoy homemade food served in a pleasant family atmosphere. The inside hasn't many froufrous . . . just black bentwood chairs, tables with green tablecloths, and a few outside tables during the summer months. Everyone gets into the act with the food and service: Mamma cooks and Papà and their daughter serve. The menu is one of utmost simplicity and goodness, featuring healthy minestrone, spinach

AREA
Between campo de' Fiori and piazza Farnese
TELEPHONE
68-80-1595
OPEN
Mon–Wed, Fri–Sun
CLOSED
Thur, Aug
HOURS
Lunch noon–3 P.M., dinner 7 P.M.–midnight

ravioli, roast lamb, grilled meats, veal scaloppine, pizza for lunch and dinner, and a few desserts. The portions will not overwhelm you, and neither will your bill.

RESERVATIONS
Advised
CREDIT CARDS
AMEX, DC, MC, V
À LA CARTE
L 35,000, beverage extra
MENÙ TURISTICO
None
COVER & SERVICE CHARGES
Cover L 2,500, service not included
ENGLISH
Yes

### (7) HOSTARIA GIULIO
**via della Barchetta, 19**

AREA
piazza Farnese and campo de' Fiori
TELEPHONE
68-80-6466
OPEN
Mon–Sat
CLOSED
Sun, Aug (dates vary)
HOURS
Lunch 12:30–3 P.M., dinner 7 P.M.–midnight
RESERVATIONS
Advised for terrace
CREDIT CARDS
AMEX, MC, V
À LA CARTE
L 45,000, beverage included
MENÙ TURISTICO
L 28,000, 2 courses, cover and service included, beverage extra
COVER & SERVICE CHARGES
Cover L 2,500, 15% service added
ENGLISH
Yes, also Spanish and Portuguese

Hostaria Giulio is in a wonderful old Roman building that dates back to the early 1400s. The present owners are into their fourth decade of serving and pleasing their guests. The small inside dining room has arched ceilings, a beautifully tiled floor, and stone walls lined with paintings by local artists. The fifteen tables are covered with light yellow linens and bouquets of fresh flowers. During the steaming summertime, be sure to reserve one of the sought-after tables on the streetside terrace.

The menu features a parade of seasonal dishes. Depending on the time of your visit, you will find good renditions of homemade ravioli filled with spinach and ricotta cheese, and of fettuccine with garlicky pesto or topped with truffles in a white sauce. Gnocchi is served every Thursday year round. Veal and fresh fish are always on, along with vegetables, assorted cheeses, and the usual desserts. When all is said and done, you will not have spent much more than L 40,000 per person, including a glass or two of the drinkable house wine.

### (8) L'INSALATA RICCA I
**largo dei Chiavari, 85**

AREA
campo de' Fiori
TELEPHONE
68-80-3656
OPEN
Mon, Tues, Thur–Sun
CLOSED
Wed
HOURS
Lunch 12:30–3 P.M., dinner 7:30–11:30 P.M.
RESERVATIONS
Strongly advised

L'Insalata Ricca is a small chain of popular, casual trattorias strategically located around Rome. You will find L'Insalata Ricca II near Piazza Navona, number III in the Aventine section, and the newest, number IV, a bit further afield, but also in the Aventine.

All are bustling with families and foreign residents and offer great value and variety and stretch your lire admirably. For both lunch and dinner, plan to arrive early, because within ten minutes of opening, there is a crowd standing outside waiting for a seat. Once inside, everyone sits at closely packed tables, delighting in the mammoth helpings of antipasti, pastas, and huge salads. you can always count on at least seven or eight regular pastas plus several pasta specials, along with beef, veal, and turkey, omelettes made to order, and ham and fried cheese. There are twenty salads, ranging from a basic green to corn, tuna, shrimp, and walnut or cheese and pears. Dense chocolate cake, fruit tarts, mousses, and *tartufo* round out the successful meal. House wine is cheap and good. Other pluses included an English menu and a nonsmoking area that is enforced.

**CREDIT CARDS**
AMEX
**À LA CARTE**
L 15,000–25,000, beverage extra
**MENÙ TURISTICO**
None
**COVER & SERVICE CHARGES**
Cover L 2,000, service not included
**ENGLISH**
Yes, and English menu
**MISCELLANEOUS**
Nonsmoking area

## (9) OSTARIA AR GALLETTO
### vicolo del Gallo, 1, piazza Farnese, 102

Ostaria ar Galletto is a perennial favorite because it is a family-owned place where every member has a part to play. Mamma, the *real* boss, runs the kitchen. Papà holds court in the dining room, seating and serving guests, who swap stories about their favorite soccer teams. One of the sons-in-law, a colonel in the Italian army, jokes that he ate here as a young man and loved the restaurant so much that he married the owner's youngest daughter. After one meal you will understand his enthusiasm. The inside is charming, with its wood-beamed ceiling festooned with hanging hams, hunting murals along the walls, and bright orange linen on the well-spaced tables. On warm days, reserve a table outside on the piazza Farnese, a beautiful Baroque square with fountains at either end, an ideal place to lose touch with everything but what is on your plate and who is across the table.

A full meal can creep into the Big Splurge category if you are not watchful, but with a little care and a liter of the house wine you should be fine. I recommend going easy on the appetizers, thus saving room for a bowl of Mamma's homemade ravioli, gnocchi, or fettuccine noodles tossed with zucchini. If you like fish, be sure to order the special *frito misto Italiano* when you reserve your table. Meat eaters lean toward the *saltimbocca alla Romana,* thin slices of veal seasoned with fresh sage, covered with ham, and sautéed in butter with a splash of white wine. The beef, slowly cooked in red wine with carrots and fresh mushrooms, is another favorite. The desserts are all homemade, but I have never had any room for more than the *fragole con gelato,* fresh strawberries spooned over vanilla ice cream.

**AREA**
piazza Farnese
**TELEPHONE**
68-61-714
**OPEN**
Mon–Sat
**CLOSED**
Sun, Dec 22–Jan 10
**HOURS**
Lunch 12:30–3 P.M., dinner 7:30–11:30 P.M.
**RESERVATIONS**
Advised, especially for outside table
**CREDIT CARDS**
Not accepted
**À LA CARTE**
L 30,000, beverage extra
**MENÙ TURISTICO**
None
**COVER & SERVICE CHARGES**
Cover L 3,000, 15% service added
**ENGLISH**
Yes

## (10) RISTORANTE DER PALLARO
### largo del Pallaro, 15

**AREA**
piazza Farnese and campo de' Fiori
**TELEPHONE**
68-80-1488
**OPEN**
Tues–Sun
**CLOSED**
Mon, Aug 10–25
**HOURS**
Lunch 1–3 P.M., dinner 8 P.M.–12:30 A.M.
**RESERVATIONS**
Advised
**CREDIT CARDS**
None
**À LA CARTE**
None
**MENÙ TURISTICO**
L 30,000, 4 courses, cover and service included, beverage included
**COVER & SERVICE CHARGES**
Both included
**ENGLISH**
Enough

Ristorante der Pallaro will not thrill you with a glitzy location or a snappy interior design, but it displays the loving attention of a chef-owner husband-and-wife team who really care about what is put on your plate—and after all, that is still the bottom line when it comes to eating out. The cast of characters in the three-room, knotty pine *ristorante* usually includes a lively mix of families, spry senior citizens, a yuppie or two, and anyone else on the prowl for a satisfying Cheap Eat in Rome.

When you arrive, look a little to the right of the beaded curtains covering the entry and you will see Paola Fazi busily working in her tiny kitchen. Her husband, Mario, helps out front. They offer no à la carte menu . . . whatever Paola cooks is what you eat, and portions are so large that even a veteran coal miner after a ten-hour shift would have trouble finishing them. You will start with an antipasto, then be served the pasta of the day, which might be spaghetti with marinara sauce, ravioli, or *fettuccine carbonara*. Next comes the main course, perhaps roast beef, veal, fresh cod on Fridays, or meatballs, garnished with one or two vegetables. Finally there is a piece of homemade cake, all washed down with tangerine juice, mineral water, or wine. Coffee is not available.

## Restaurants near the Coliseum and Forum

## (11) ENOTECA CAVOUR 313
### via Cavour, 313

**AREA**
Coliseum/Forum
**TELEPHONE**
67-85-496
**OPEN**
Mon–Fri; Sat dinner only
**CLOSED**
Sun, Aug
**HOURS**
Lunch 12:30–2:30 P.M., dinner 7:30 P.M.–12:30 A.M.
**RESERVATIONS**
Advised for dinner
**CREDIT CARDS**
None
**À LA CARTE**
L 10,000–20,000, beverage extra

For a light lunch or dinner accompanied by a few glasses of fine wine, it will be hard to beat the Enoteca Cavour 313, one of the most complete wine bars in Rome. This appealing location features more than six hundred different wines and champagnes from every wine-growing region in Italy, as well as wines from France, California, and Australia. The casual atmosphere, with wooden tables and booths, draws everyone from workers in dusty shoes on their way home from the job site to socialites dressed to the nines. Angelo, one of the owners, speaks English and knows his wines. He will be happy to make suggestions or to discuss whatever wines he is featuring at the time. Lingering is encouraged, and you are free to order as much or as little as you want to eat. Don't expect pizza, pasta, or three-course meals. Instead you will be tempted by beautiful salads, smoked fish, cold meats, cheeses, pâtés, and rich desserts.

## (12) IL RE DEL TRAMEZZINO
### via Mecenate, 18A

There is no telephone number to call for reservations in this residential neighborhood bar within walking distance of the Coliseum and the Forum. Management does not stand on ceremony; they only care about providing good food and lots of it to hungry eaters in search of a big lunch at a decent price. When you go, check the menu written on a board by the bar or in the front window. You can sit at the bar that wraps around a colorful antipasti display, or in summer, nab one of the sidewalk tables. The typical menu at this lunch-only place should put you in good spirits, especially when it results in such dependable standbys as gnocchi, eggplant *alla parmigiana,* and pasta *all'amatriciana* (bacon, garlic, tomatoes, hot red peppers, and onion). In addition to the daily hot specials, they offer different salads, cold meat plates, sandwiches, and a homemade dessert to wrap up the meal. Because it is a Cheap Eat in a pricey area, it is a very popular destination. You must time your visit to beat the rush because they often run out of the best dishes early.

## (13) OSTARIA DA NERONE
### via delle Terme di Tito, 96

This classic restaurant is a smart choice for a leisurely lunch between sightseeing rounds near the Coliseum and the Forum. The emphasis is firmly on good old-fashioned value, and that is evidenced by the many regulars who have been eating here for decades. The interior is mighty basic: whitewashed walls with a picture or two, white linens on the tables, uniformed waiters who came with the building, hard chairs, and a pay telephone by the front door. In warm weather, tables are set up outside so you can dine with a view of the Coliseum.

Before ordering, be sure to take a good look at the beautiful antipasti display and the lovely desserts and plan the rest of your meal accordingly. For the first course, hope that the homemade ravioli stuffed with

**MENÙ TURISTICO**
None

**COVER & SERVICE CHARGES**
Cover L 1,000 for wine only, L 1,500 for food; service included

**ENGLISH**
Yes

**AREA**
Coliseum/Forum

**TELEPHONE**
None

**OPEN**
Mon–Sat bar and lunch only

**CLOSED**
Sun, Aug

**HOURS**
Bar 7:30 A.M.–8 P.M.; lunch 12:30–3 P.M.

**RESERVATIONS**
Not accepted

**CREDIT CARDS**
None

**À LA CARTE**
L 8,000–18,000, beverage extra

**MENÙ TURISTICO**
None

**COVER & SERVICE CHARGES**
None at the bar; cover L 1,500 at a table, service included

**ENGLISH**
Minimal

**AREA**
Coliseum/Forum

**TELEPHONE**
47-45-207

**OPEN**
Mon–Sat

**CLOSED**
Sun, Aug

**HOURS**
Lunch 12:30–3 P.M., dinner 7–11 P.M.

**RESERVATIONS**
Advised

**CREDIT CARDS**
MC, V

**À LA CARTE**
L 30,000, beverage extra

**MENÙ TURISTICO**
None

ricotta cheese and sage in a butter sauce is on the menu. On Thursday, you can depend on gnocchi, and every day you can order their specialty, *fettuccine alla Nerone*, a creamy dish with salami, ham, peas, mushrooms, and eggs. The fish is mostly frozen, so avoid it. For your main course, order roast lamb, the chicken with tomatoes and peppers in a wine sauce, or the roast rabbit. If you are in a more daring culinary mood, try the calves' brains sautéed with mushrooms and butter. The desserts are worth every calorie. To ease your pangs of guilt, remember, you can walk back to your hotel or spend the afternoon strolling around the Forum and the Coliseum.

### (14) PIZZERIA LEONIA
### via Leonina, 84

AREA
Monti, near the Coliseum
TELEPHONE
48-27-744
OPEN
Mon–Fri
CLOSED
Sat, Sun, Aug (dates vary)
HOURS
7 A.M.–8 P.M., continuous
service
RESERVATIONS
Not accepted
CREDIT CARDS
None
À LA CARTE
From L 1,500 per slice
MENÙ TURISTICO
None
COVER & SERVICE CHARGES
None
ENGLISH
Limited

One of the best slices of pizza you will have in Rome will be at this stand-up pizza bar within walking distance of the Coliseum and the Forum. It is a virtual mob-scene around lunchtime, when the wait for your number to be called seems endless and the crowd ahead of you multiplies, never looking as though it will move on. The big trays of piping hot pizzas are brought from the oven every ten to fifteen minutes, so early or late you will still be guaranteed a delicious choice. The pizzas are cut into pieces as big or as small as you want. I suggest trying two or three varieties, saving plenty of room for a healthy sampling of their apple pizza, replete with warm apple slices and raisins under a light dusting of cinnamon. There are twenty-three other choices that you can eat here or munch as you go.

### (15) TRATTORIA L'ALBANESE
### via dei Serpenti, 148

AREA
Coliseum/Forum
TELEPHONE
47-40-777
OPEN
Mon, Wed–Sun
CLOSED
Tues, July 25–Aug 25
HOURS
Lunch noon–3 P.M., dinner
7–11 P.M.
RESERVATIONS
Not necessary
CREDIT CARDS
AMEX, MC, V

There is nothing overly glamorous about the Trattoria l'Albanese, but it is a clean and hospitable family-run restaurant near the Coliseum. There is a garden dining area in back and a plain front room that fills quickly at lunch with committed followers, who indulge in the rich food that is much more familiar to a working farmer than to anyone in the health-conscious '90s.

Dieters need not apply for their pasta specials, especially the *bombolotti* (an egg-rich pasta ladened with sausage, mushrooms, and peas in a Parmesan sauce) or the cannelloni (fat pasta tubes stuffed full of ground meat, cheese, and vegetables and covered with a thick tomato sauce). The *menù turistico* is a Cheap Eat joy that includes several choices of soup or pasta, a meat main course, vegetables, and fresh fruit for dessert. Service and drinks are extra, and so is a slice of the decadent Dominican chocolate cake. To make this even more popular, it is open on Sundays and serves low-cost pizzas and *crostini* in the evening.

**À LA CARTE**
L 30,000, beverage extra
**MENÙ TURISTICO**
L 20,000, 2 courses, cover included, service not included, beverage extra
**COVER & SERVICE CHARGES**
Cover L 2,000, 12% service added
**ENGLISH**
Limited, but friendly

## Restaurants in the Jewish Quarter

### (16) AL POMPIERE
### via S. Maria del Calderari, 38 (off via Arenula)

The Jewish Quarter in Rome is a fascinating maze of tiny piazzas, cobblestone streets, small shops, restaurants, and ancient ruins. In the heart of this you will find Al Pompiere, a charming restaurant located on the second floor of the Cenci Bolognetti Palace, which dates from the 1600s. The three simple dining rooms have dark ceilings frescoes, rustic wooden tables and chairs, and not much else. The emphasis here is on real food for real people at realistic prices.

This is the place to sample Roman-Jewish cooking at its best. For the antipasti, *do not miss* the *carciofo alla guidia,* a flattened, fried artichoke that looks like a pressed flower. Another must, whenever they are in season, are the *fior di zucca ripieni,* zucchini blossoms stuffed with mozzarella and anchovies then deep fried. Other house specialties include daily homemade pastas, succulent roast baby lamb, *baccalà* (salt dried cod), and *fritto vegetale,* a plate of crisply fried vegetables. The desserts to order include ricotta cheesecake and the *gran misto del Pompiere,* a taste of everything. Cheap Eaters will be pleased to note the lunch menu can be ordered in sections (i.e., just a pasta, or only the main course), or if four courses are ordered, it will not top L 26,000.

**AREA**
Jewish Quarter
**TELEPHONE**
68-68-377
**OPEN**
Mon–Sat
**CLOSED**
Sun, July 20–Aug 31
**HOURS**
Lunch 12:30–3 P.M., dinner 7:30–12:30 P.M.
**RESERVATIONS**
Advised
**CREDIT CARDS**
None
**À LA CARTE**
L 40,000, beverage extra
**MENÙ TURISTICO**
Lunch only, L 26,000, 4 courses, cover and service included, beverage extra
**COVER & SERVICE CHARGES**
Cover L 3,500, service included
**ENGLISH**
Yes

### (17) DA GIGGETTO AL PORTICO D'OTTAVIA
### via del Portico d'Ottavia, 1/e

Any trip to Rome would be incomplete without sampling Roman-Jewish cuisine. Nowhere will it be more authentic than in this family-owned trattoria next to the ruins of the Theater of Marcellus. Out front there is a large seating area shaded by umbrellas. The inside consists of four rooms done in the usual rustic style with

**AREA**
Jewish Quarter
**TELEPHONE**
68-30-7937
**OPEN**
Mon, Wed–Sat; Sun lunch only

**CLOSED**
Tues, Aug
**HOURS**
Lunch 12:30–3 P.M., dinner
7:30–11 P.M.
**RESERVATIONS**
Advised
**CREDIT CARDS**
AMEX, DC, MC, V
**À LA CARTE**
L 40,000–45,000, beverage
extra
**MENÙ TURISTICO**
None
**COVER & SERVICE CHARGES**
Cover L 3,000, service included
**ENGLISH**
Yes, and English menu

terra-cotta floors, ropes of garlic hanging from the ceiling, and white linens covering light green tablecloths. The ambitious menu is thankfully translated into English.

For your appetizer course, you must try one of their specialties: crisp, tender fried artichokes, fried zucchini flowers filled with mozzarella cheese and anchovies, fried cod fish fillets, rice balls filled with mozzarella cheese and covered with a tomato sauce, or potato croquettes. If I order meat, I usually like to stay light with the pasta, selecting a simple spaghetti with butter and Parmesan cheese. When I skip the meat and fish dishes, I order something more substantial, say the *spaghetti carbonara* or the *spaghetti con vongole veraci* (with fresh clams). If you are having meat, the *osso buco* with mushrooms and peas is a filling choice, as is the roast lamb or veal. True to Roman tradition, many unusual cuts of meat are featured. If you're not careful, the beef tongue in parsley sauce or the fried brains with mushrooms, artichokes, and zucchini will make a convert out of you. The pace doesn't let up with dessert, which offers fresh fruit, ice cream, or a sinfully fattening delicacy from La Dolceroma next door, an American-Austrian bakery run by the owner's son (see below).

## (18) LA DOLCEROMA
### via del Portico d'Ottavia, 20/B

Stefano Ceccarelli's family has owned the restaurant next door for generations (see Da Giggetto al Portico d'Ottavia above). But Stefano wanted to do something on his own. Since he has always been interested in baking, it was natural for him to open La Dolceroma, now one of Rome's most popular and well-known bakeries, which sells American and Austrian delicacies.

In this tiny place you can see directly into the kitchen from the front room, which has a display case and a table with chairs. Stefano does all the baking himself, listing the ingredients so you will know exactly what you are eating. And what will you be eating? The list is endless: perhaps chocolate, orange, or blueberry muffins, or one of several types of cookies, including chocolate chip, peanut butter, and oatmeal raisin. He makes brownies, cheesecake, carrot cake, chestnut cake, pecan pie, and *Sachertort*. At Christmas time you will find *stollen* and *Linzertort*. If you are not in the mood for any of these, try his hand-dipped chocolates. Everything is sold by weight

**AREA**
Jewish Quarter
**TELEPHONE**
68-92-196
**OPEN**
Tues–Sat; Sun morning only
**CLOSED**
Mon, Aug
**HOURS**
7:30 A.M.–1:30 P.M., 4–8 P.M.;
Sun 10 A.M.–1 P.M.
**RESERVATIONS**
Not accepted
**CREDIT CARDS**
None
**À LA CARTE**
From L 2,000 per pastry
**MENÙ TURISTICO**
None
**COVER & SERVICE CHARGES**
None
**ENGLISH**
Yes

and packaged to go. If you are here from late spring until October, American coffee and cappuccino will be served.

## (19) L'ENOTECA DI ANACLETO BLEVE
### via S. Maria del Pianto, 9A/11

Rising prices for food and services have forced many small restaurants and trattorias out of business in Italy. Coming along in their place are *enoteche* (wine bars) that sell wine by the case, bottle, or glass. In addition, many of these places offer lunch and light snacks that are geared to complement the wines as well as your pocketbook.

Whenever I am in the Jewish Quarter in Rome, I head for this *enoteca,* where I can depend on having a nice lunch and a glass of good wine. On display are artistically arranged salads, assorted cheeses, and several hot daily specials. After eating, I take a minute or two to browse through their gourmet grocery section, which features jams, preserved fruits, olives, and olive oils.

**AREA**
Jewish Quarter

**TELEPHONE**
68-65-970

**OPEN**
Mon–Sat, bar and lunch only

**CLOSED**
Sun

**HOURS**
Bar 9 A.M.–8 P.M.; lunch 12:30–3 P.M.

**RESERVATIONS**
Advised for lunch

**CREDIT CARDS**
AMEX, MC, V

**À LA CARTE**
L 6,000–12,000, beverage extra

**MENÙ TURISTICO**
None

**COVER & SERVICE CHARGES**
No cover, service included

**ENGLISH**
Limited

## (20) SORA MARGHERITA
### piazza della Cinque Scole

For those who wear sunglasses at night and would not be caught dead without a cellular telephone, Sora Margherita will have no appeal. But for Cheap Eaters in Rome it is very appealing. The menu is handwritten on a piece of grid paper ripped out of a notebook. Wine is served in juice glasses, which are placed on paper overlays covering Formica tables. In this basement hideaway behind a green door with no sign, owner-chef Margherita Tomassini turns out some of the heartiest and simple Jewish cooking in the quarter. She wears slippers to work and stands on tradition, never changing her time-worn menu, which is served only for lunch.

She always fixes fettuccine with cheese, black pepper, and tomatoes or cream sauce, and her specialty—*agnolotti*—a type of meat ravioli. On Thursday she adds gnocchi with tomato sauce. Grilled fish is the Friday highlight, but before ordering, be sure you check the price: is it sold by the gram or the piece? Meatballs are a daily dish and so are the fried artichokes and the veal chops. However, Margherita doesn't bother with dessert.

**AREA**
Jewish Quarter

**TELEPHONE**
68-64-002

**OPEN**
Mon–Fri lunch only

**CLOSED**
Sat, Sun, Aug

**HOURS**
Noon–3 P.M.

**RESERVATIONS**
Not accepted

**CREDIT CARDS**
None

**À LA CARTE**
L 25,000, beverage extra

**MENÙ TURISTICO**
None

**COVER & SERVICE CHARGES**
No cover, service included

**ENGLISH**
None

# Restaurants near Piazza Navona and the Pantheon

## (21) DA FRANCESCO
### piazza del Fico, 29, at via della Fossa (corner of via del Corallo)

**AREA**
. piazza Navona
**TELEPHONE**
68-64-009
**OPEN**
Mon, Wed–Sun
**CLOSED**
Tues, Aug (2 weeks)
**HOURS**
Lunch 12:15–3 P.M., dinner 7 P.M.–1 A.M.
**RESERVATIONS**
Not accepted
**CREDIT CARDS**
None
**À LA CARTE**
L 20,000, beverage extra; pizza L 8,000–15,000
**MENÙ TURISTICO**
None
**COVER & SERVICE CHARGES**
Cover L 2,000, service included
**ENGLISH**
Limited

"What are they giving away?" my friend asked as we strolled by this local favorite. At lunchtime it boasted wall-to-wall people inside and almost as many milling outside waiting to get in. What they do is prepare good food at fair prices in a lively atmosphere—proving that the public will still support a good thing. The food packs a punch, starting with fettuccine covered in a mushroom cream sauce, *penne all'arrabbiata,* or *tonnarelli* with artichokes. Meatballs in a gutsy tomato sauce, pork stewed in white wine, or ham and beans will keep you going for hours. At night, everyone is back for the self-service antipasti table and the pizza, bursting with tomatoes, mozzarella cheese, and all the usual toppings. It is all very informal, with paper table covers and wine poured into drinking glasses by prompt, if inelegant, waiters.

## (22) FIAMMETTA
### piazza Fiammetta, 8/9/10

**AREA**
piazza Navona
**TELEPHONE**
68-75-777
**OPEN**
Mon, Tues, Thur–Sun
**CLOSED**
Wed, Aug
**HOURS**
Lunch 12:30–3 P.M., dinner 7–11:30 P.M.
**RESERVATIONS**
Advised, especially for dinner
**CREDIT CARDS**
AMEX, DC
**À LA CARTE**
L 35,000, beverage extra; pizza L 8,500–14,000
**MENÙ TURISTICO**
None
**COVER & SERVICE CHARGES**
Cover L 2,500, service included
**ENGLISH**
Limited

The pizza chef in his white undershirt has the ovens stoked and ready to go by 7 P.M., when the first dinner guests begin to stream in. By 9:30 P.M., there is not an empty seat at this all-purpose pick near piazza Navona. The rustic rooms have "old West–style" chandeliers with wine carafes as lamp shades. There is a wall mural of the Ponte Vecchio in Florence, a collection of hanging pots, and the mandatory table displaying antipasti and desserts.

The waiters speak varying degrees of English. My favorite server is Silvio, who has been delivering heaping plates to happy diners since 1977. He is full of fun and works hard, somehow making you forget about the lag between the first and second courses. When you order, watch the daily specials attached to the corner of the menu. Skip the boring salads and focus on one of the pizzas (evenings only) or a grilled meat or fish. For dessert, I would suggest the *vin santo Toscano* . . . a glass of sweet wine with *biscotti* to dip into it.

## (23) GIOLITTI
### via Uffici del Vicario, 40

When ice cream is mentioned in Rome, the hands-down favorite is Giolitti, an always-crowded Art Nouveau *gelateria* near the Pantheon where generations of the same family have been selling their *gelato* since 1900. In the early morning, fifteen flavors of ice cream are available, along with cappuccino and a counter full of waist-expanding pastries. On Tuesday through Saturday, light lunches of salads, omelettes, and a few hot dishes are served in an upstairs dining room. Standing at the bar you can order a quick sandwich or more pastries. By 2:30 in the afternoon, there is a three-deep crowd ordering cones or dishes from more than fifty-seven revolving varieties of pure *gelato*. First you pay for the size you want and then take your order to the counter. There is no real place to sit while eating your ice cream, but it is fun to join the throng standing around outside and indulge in the premier people-watching this place always affords.

**AREA**
Pantheon

**TELEPHONE**
69-91-243

**OPEN**
Tues–Sat; Sun *gelateria* only

**CLOSED**
Mon

**HOURS**
*Gelateria* 7 A.M.–2 A.M.; lunch noon–2 P.M.

**RESERVATIONS**
Not accepted

**CREDIT CARDS**
None

**À LA CARTE**
Ice cream L 2,500–11,000; lunch L 12,000–15,000, beverage extra

**MENÙ TURISTICO**
None

**COVER & SERVICE CHARGES**
None

**ENGLISH**
Yes

## (24) IL BACARO
### via degli Spagnoli, 27

I am always happy to stumble upon places like Il Bacaro. Hidden on a back street, just far enough from the maddening crowds to be real, it caters to a well-dressed, sophisticated clientele who know and appreciate good food. It is open only for dinner, with two reservation-only seatings. Diners can book for either the 8 P.M. or the 9:30 P.M. seatings in either the umbrella-shaded terrace or inside in the small, understated room, which has a bar in one corner and rather loud music playing over it all.

No matter what time of the year you are here, or where you sit, you can depend on an imaginative meal, well-executed, and politely served. Antipasto is not served. You can start with the house salad, which is a pretty array of thin slices of zucchini and fresh Parmesan cheese on a bed of fancy greens, garnished with finely chopped carrots and fennel, and dressed with a light vinaigrette. The pastas are all made here and presented in different combinations. I thought the *risotto radicchio e gorgonzola* (risotto with radicchio and Gorgonzola cheese) was a creamy delight. The *bombolotti con broccoli e salsicce* combines small macaroni and broccoli with fat, slightly

**AREA**
Pantheon/piazza Navona

**TELEPHONE**
68-64-110

**OPEN**
Mon–Sat dinner only

**CLOSED**
Sun, Aug, Christmas (2 weeks)

**HOURS**
Dinner seatings at 8 P.M. and 9:30 P.M.

**RESERVATIONS**
Required

**CREDIT CARDS**
AMEX, MC, V

**À LA CARTE**
L 48,000, beverage extra

**MENÙ TURISTICO**
None

**COVER & SERVICE CHARGES**
No cover, service included

**ENGLISH**
Limited

spicy sausages. Meat and fish dishes are prepared with simple respect and without sauces to mask the real flavor of the food. Try the *carpaccio alto di manzo,* tender beef slices cooked on one side and served with chicory and white truffle oil. Mmm, good. Also delicious is the *scaloppe alle mele,* veal escalopes with apples in a cream sauce, and the smoked goose with kiwi sauce. Fish is as innovatively conceived as the rest of the menu. An all-encompassing choice is the *misto di affumicati ai tre aromi,* mixed smoked fish with herbs and spices.

And don't forget dessert! The winner here is the warm pear tart, dusted with powdered sugar and drizzled with hot dark chocolate sauce. The house wine is realistically priced by the bottle, or you can order other vintages by the glass. After-dinner coffee is not served.

### (25) I TRI SCALINI
### piazza Navona, 28/32

For a *tartufo* to die for, I Tri Scalini is *the* place. It is big and barnlike, with a long bar, a dreary tearoom upstairs, and lots of tables on the piazza Navona. Dedicated Cheap Eaters will order their *tartufo* (chocolate ice cream and cherries covered with a bittersweet chocolate casing and swathed in whipped cream) standing at the bar. It will cost double to have it served at a table. If you do sit outside, tell whoever seats you that you are just having a *tartufo,* or you could be seated in the dining section where ordering just dessert would not be acceptable. As noted, full lunches and dinners are served, but they are basically high-priced tourist fare that I cannot recommend.

A word of warning: Don't be fooled by imitations and mistakenly go to I Tre Tartufi next door.

### (26) LA CAMPANA
### vicolo della Campana, 18

It is nice occasionally to have starched linen tablecloths with proper table settings and polite service by accomplished Italian waiters in rooms filled with up-market diners. You will find this, along with excellent value-for-money food, at La Campana, one of Rome's oldest restaurants.

The servings are big and the food robust, so I suggest following the lead of the regulars and ordering as you go along. Start with either the house red or white wine to

**AREA**
piazza Navona
**TELEPHONE**
68-79-148
**OPEN**
Mon, Tues, Thur–Sun
**CLOSED**
Wed, Dec and Jan (dates vary)
**HOURS**
8 A.M.–midnight
**RESERVATIONS**
Not necessary
**CREDIT CARDS**
None
**À LA CARTE**
*Tartufo* at bar L 5,000, at a table L 10,000
**MENÙ TURISTICO**
Not recommended
**COVER & SERVICE CHARGES**
None for *tartufo*
**ENGLISH**
Limited

**AREA**
piazza Navona
**TELEPHONE**
68-67-820, 68-75-273
**OPEN**
Tues–Sun
**CLOSED**
Mon, Aug (last 2 weeks)
**HOURS**
Lunch 12:45–3 P.M., dinner 7:30–11 P.M.

sip with the *antipasti misto,* which is big enough to share. Next, try the spicy *spaghetti puttanesca* or the fettuccine with butter and mushrooms if you plan on ordering a second meat or fish course. Otherwise, the *pappardella con salsa lepre* (wide noodles with hare sauce) or the Thursday special of gnocchi are heavy duty enough to require only a salad or vegetable accompaniment.

The important thing is to save enough room for dessert. La Campana also wants to make sure you will not miss this course, and most of their offerings are seductively displayed on tables by the entrance, resulting in oohs and aahs of anticipation. Their version of *tarte Tatin* has a spongy base covered with glazed apples. It is not too sweet and is laced with just enough cream to give it an interesting edge. If that does not speak to you, surely one of the cakes, tarts, puddings, abundant fruit creations, or a simple dish of *gelato* will.

**RESERVATIONS**
Advised

**CREDIT CARDS**
AMEX, DC, MC, V

**À LA CARTE**
L 30,000–40,000, beverage extra

**MENÙ TURISTICO**
None

**COVER & SERVICE CHARGES**
Cover L 3,000, service included

**ENGLISH**
Limited

## (27) L'INSALATA RICCA II
**piazza Pasquino, 72**

For description, see L'Insalata Ricca I, campo de' Fiori, page 80.

AREA: piazza Navona
TELEPHONE: 68-30-7881
OPEN: Mon, Tues, Thur–Sun
CLOSED: Wed
HOURS: Lunch 12:30–3 P.M., dinner 7:30–11:30 P.M.

## (28) ORSO '80
**via dell' Orso, 33**

It remains true every year—all I want for Christmas besides a fiery red Jeep is another great meal at this wonderful trattoria in the heart of Old Rome. The restaurant has been owned for almost two decades by brothers Alfredo and Memmo and their longtime friend Antonio, the talented chef. Here you will eat truly memorable food, served with gusto and guaranteed to ignite even the most jaded palates. Because the prices tend to be higher than most, reserve this dining experience for a Big Splurge.

The restaurant is justly known for its fabulous antipasti tables, and I agree—it is one of the best I sampled in Italy. You name it and it is here, from seasonal vegetables prepared six different ways to dozens of bowls of fish and shellfish. If you are not careful, you could make this your entire meal. But save room, please, for

**AREA**
piazza Navona

**TELEPHONE**
68-64-904, 68-61-710

**OPEN**
Tues–Sun

**CLOSED**
Mon, Aug

**HOURS**
Lunch 12:30–3:30 P.M., dinner 7–11 P.M.

**RESERVATIONS**
Necessary, especially for dinner

**CREDIT CARDS**
AMEX, DC, MC, V

**À LA CARTE**
L 55,000–60,000, beverage extra

one of the homemade pastas, such as the *papparadelle al salmone,* wide buttery noodles smothered in a creamy salmon sauce, or the spaghetti with fresh clams. Grilled meats are another specialty, as is the impressive lineup of fresh fish. In the evenings, the wood-fired pizza oven is roaring, turning out a limited but delicious selection of crisp-crusted pizzas. After a meal such as this one, dessert hardly seems possible, but I do recommend a bowl of the sweet strawberries as the perfect finish.

### (29) PALLADINI
**via del Governo Vecchio, 29**

**MENÙ TURISTICO**
None
**COVER & SERVICE CHARGES**
Cover L 4,000, service included
**ENGLISH**
Yes

There is no sign outside, no seating inside, positively no charm, and definitely no English spoken in this spartan deli, a great place for anyone whose lire are in danger of running out . . . or for those who appreciate a really great sandwich. Only sandwiches are available, made on freshly baked chunks of pizza *bianca* (pizza bread) that are brushed with olive oil and stuffed with fillings of your choice by two old men wearing undershirts and faded Levis. Surprisingly enough, these are sensational sandwiches, especially the *bresaola e rughetta,* smoked meat and arugula sprinkled with Parmesan cheese and lemon juice. You can either join the lunch bunch and eat standing by the cases of soft drinks and beer that line the room or take your creation with you and eat it as you go.

**AREA**
piazza Navona
**TELEPHONE**
68-61-237
**OPEN**
Mon–Fri, Sat lunch only
**CLOSED**
Sun, Aug
**HOURS**
7 A.M.–2 P.M. and 5–8 P.M.;
sandwiches noon–2 P.M.
**RESERVATIONS**
Not accepted
**CREDIT CARDS**
None
**À LA CARTE**
Sandwiches from L 3,500
**MENÙ TURISTICO**
None
**COVER & SERVICE CHARGES**
None
**ENGLISH**
None

### (30) PIZZERIA DA BAFFETTO
**via Governo Vecchio, 114**

**AREA**
piazza Navona
**TELEPHONE**
68-61-617
**OPEN**
Mon–Sat
**CLOSED**
Sun
**HOURS**
Lunch noon–3 P.M., dinner
7:30 P.M.–1 A.M.
**RESERVATIONS**
Not accepted
**CREDIT CARDS**
None
**À LA CARTE**
Pizza L 10,000–12,000

In Rome, Pizzeria da Baffetto is synonymous with good pizza, and the line that forms at the front door of this matchbook-sized spot attests to this. Expect to share your table in this tiny room, which is dominated by a pizza oven, a menu board on one wall, and a small cash desk. The seats are hard, and long stays are discouraged.

The only things on the menu besides the sizzling pizzas are *bruschette,* the traditional preparation of grilled bread covered with garlic, basil, and ripe red tomatoes; *crostini,* toasted bread with mozzarella cheese and a variety of simple toppings; a few pastas; and some entirely forgettable meat dishes. Here, you order pizza . . . period.

### (31) TRI ARCHI
**via dei Coronari, 233**

Tri Archi is the sort of folksy place people go to when no one feels in the mood to cook. The prices are firmly in the Cheap Eat category, making this an address to remember if you want a glimpse of average Romans and the food they thrive on. The clientele, which ranges from families with noisy children to gray-haired couples who have staked out regular tables, makes for some interesting people-watching.

The inside is neat and utilitarian, with orange tablecloths, a few green plants, and a mural along one wall. The one waiter is a study in efficiency and grace under pressure.

The food is simple, standard fare: minestrone soup, pastas with the familiar *ragù,* daily specials, above-average salads, and desserts in the never mind column. The house wine is perfectly adequate.

## Restaurants near Piazza del Popolo

### (32) AL 59 RISTORANTE DA GIUSEPPE
**via Angelo Brunetti, 59**

The food at Al 59 Ristorante da Guiseppe is a triumph of Bolognese cooking and a good reason to make a pilgrimage across Rome. If you can stretch your budget only once or twice for a special meal in Rome, this is a worthy choice. The clean and classic interior is elegant and so is the superb food, passionately prepared by master chef and owner Giuseppe, who is, naturally, from Bologna. Everything from start to finish is made inhouse. If you walk by before lunch, you will see several gray-haired men sitting around a large table hand rolling the tortellini, which is the trademark pasta of Bologna. The meal could begin with antipasto or soup, but I always start with the tortellini with pumpkin or the heaven-sent spinach ravioli filled with ricotta cheese and lightly sauced with fresh tomatoes. Next consider the *bolliti misti,* which is served from a special cart rolled to your table. With a side of vegetables or a mixed salad,

**MENÙ TURISTICO**
None
**COVER & SERVICE CHARGES**
Cover L 1,500, service included
**ENGLISH**
English menu

**AREA**
piazza Navona
**TELEPHONE**
68-65-890
**OPEN**
Mon–Sat
**CLOSED**
Sun, Aug
**HOURS**
Lunch 12–3 P.M., dinner 7–11 P.M.
**RESERVATIONS**
Advised for dinner
**CREDIT CARDS**
AMEX, DC, MC, V
**À LA CARTE**
L 25,000–30,000, beverage extra
**MENÙ TURISTICO**
L 20,000, 3 courses, cover and service included, beverage extra
**COVER & SERVICE CHARGES**
Cover L 2,500, service included
**ENGLISH**
No

**AREA**
piazza del Popolo
**TELEPHONE**
32-19-019
**OPEN**
Mon–Sat
**CLOSED**
Sun, Aug
**HOURS**
lunch 1–3 P.M., dinner 8–11 P.M.
**RESERVATIONS**
Essential
**CREDIT CARDS**
AMEX
**À LA CARTE**
L 50,000–60,000, beverage extra
**MENÙ TURISTICO**
None

you will have a very filling meal. The sheer culinary bliss continues with the desserts, whether it be the plump baked apple or the *crostata* filled with jam. Because this is so popular with the locals, reservations are absolutely essential, especially for dinner, which is still humming at 10:30 P.M.

### (33) ANTICO BOTTARO
### passeggiata di Ripetta, 15

There is no sign outside . . . just a polished brass plaque to the right of the door discreetly displaying the name of the most upscale vegetarian restaurant in Rome. Owner Claudio Vannini knows what he is doing with his two vegetarian restaurants (see I Margutta, page 100). At Antico Bottaro, the mood is elegant and sophisticated. The mirrored walls, grand piano, graceful archways, and columns combine with soft pink linen, heavy silver and crystal, beautiful plants, and masses of fresh flowers to create a luxurious and romantic setting where well-trained waiters pamper the stylishly dressed, loyal clientele.

The food keeps pace with the surroundings and is, in a word, wonderful. Using only the freshest ingredients, completely free of additives, the imaginative chef creates a daily changing array of vegetarian dishes that even the most militant carnivore will appreciate and enjoy. You might start with the *charlotte de pomodoro con crostini all'aglio* (a flaky pastry with tomato and garlic) or the *pâté maison* made with pistachios and truffles. The ravioli seasoned with cumin and bathed in a light cream sauce is a match made in food heaven. So is the light potato soufflé with a dusting of almonds. For a lavish finish, sample the chocolate *torta* or the *degustazione dolci,* an assortment of their most popular desserts. Naturally, all of this does not fall into the budget category, but it will be worth ever extra lire you spend.

### (34) LA BUCA DI RIPETTA
### via di Ripetta, 36

An interesting neighborhood crowd reflecting the upmarket neighborhood two blocks down from the piazza del Popolo gathers daily for lunch and dinner at this popular whitewashed trattoria. The one-room restaurant with banquette seating around the sides is always crowded, a sure sign that the food is good and the prices affordable. It has been run by the same family for almost

---

**COVER & SERVICE CHARGES**
Cover L 4,000, service included
**ENGLISH**
Limited

**AREA**
piazza del Popolo
**TELEPHONE**
32-40-200
**OPEN**
Tues–Sun
**CLOSED**
Mon, Aug
**HOURS**
Lunch 1–3 P.M., dinner 8 P.M.–midnight
**RESERVATIONS**
Strongly advised
**CREDIT CARDS**
AMEX, DC, MC, V
**À LA CARTE**
L 55,000, beverage extra
**MENÙ TURISTICO**
None
**COVER & SERVICE CHARGES**
No cover, service included
**ENGLISH**
Yes
**MISCELLANEOUS**
Piano music on Sat and Sun from 9 P.M.

**AREA**
piazza del Popolo
**TELEPHONE**
68-95-78
**OPEN**
Tues–Sat, Sun lunch only
**CLOSED**
Mon, Aug (last 2 weeks)

forty years and has the kind of warm atmosphere and comfortable service that puts you in a happy mood immediately. Service by three waiters and the owner is swift and efficient enough to somehow turn the tables every hour or so without making guests feel rushed.

A carafe of the house red or white wine will complement any of the daily pastas, perhaps *pesto alla genovese* or buttery linguine bathed in a lemon sauce. Don't overlook the roast lamb served with clouds of puréed potatoes or any of the veal dishes. You can, however, overlook the desserts, which tend to be heavy and overpriced.

**HOURS**
Lunch 12:15–3:00 P.M., dinner 7:30–11 P.M.
**RESERVATIONS**
Essential
**CREDIT CARDS**
AMEX
**À LA CARTE**
L 30,000–35,000, beverage extra
**MENÙ TURISTICO**
None
**COVER & SERVICE CHARGES**
Cover L 2,500, service included
**ENGLISH**
Yes

## Restaurants near Piazza Venezia

### (35) ALEMAGNA
**via del Corso, 181**

Alemagna has been around forever. In fact, it served as the last bastion for intellectuals opposing the rule of Mussolini. Today it is an all-purpose *caffè* strategically positioned on the busy via del Corso halfway between piazza del Popolo and piazza Venezia. No matter what you are in the mood for at any time of the day, chances are you will find it at Alemagna, a self-service restaurant, tearoom, stand-up coffee bar, bakery, sandwich counter, and candy and ice cream dispensary.

If you are rushed, you can grab a toasted sandwich or a slice of pizza to go, or eat your snack standing at one of the sandwich tables in the center of the big room. For a sit-down lunch, the self-service *tavola calda* cafeteria line with seating at the linen-covered tables is another alternative, albeit a little more expensive. For an afternoon tea break, or an ice cream sundae that looks like Vesuvius erupting, sit at one of the outside tables and watch the passing parade. It is guaranteed to amuse.

**AREA**
piazza Venezia
**TELEPHONE**
67-89-135
**OPEN**
Mon–Sat
**CLOSED**
Sun
**HOURS**
Bar 7:30 A.M.–10 P.M., lunch noon–3 P.M., dinner 6–9 P.M.
**RESERVATIONS**
Not necessary
**CREDIT CARDS**
MC, V
**À LA CARTE**
L 12,000–18,000, sandwiches for L 3,000
**MENÙ TURISTICO**
None
**COVER & SERVICE CHARGES**
Tearoom only, L 1,500 cover, service included
**ENGLISH**
Limited

### (36) BIRRERIA PERONI
**via San Marcello, 19**

There is no spa cuisine at Birreria Peroni, only hearty, stick-to-your-ribs plates of pasta, beans, beef, pork, and veal that appeal to strong-hearted souls who have put in a hard day's work. With the unbeatable combination of enormous portions and reliable prices, all washed down with tall mugs of beer (no wine or coffee is served), it is no wonder that this restaurant has such a following.

**AREA**
piazza Venezia
**TELEPHONE**
67-95-310
**OPEN**
Mon–Fri, Sat dinner only
**CLOSED**
Sun, Aug
**HOURS**
Lunch 12:30–2:45 P.M., dinner 6:30–11:15 P.M.

**RESERVATIONS**
Not accepted
**CREDIT CARDS**
None
**À LA CARTE**
L 8,000–16,000, beverage extra
**MENÙ TURISTICO**
None
**COVER & SERVICE CHARGES**
No cover, 17% service added
**ENGLISH**
Limited

Unless you arrive early, or go late and run the risk of your favorite dish being sold out, you can expect to stand and wait for a table during the crowded lunch hour. Service is hectic at best, with waiters shouting orders to a harried cashier who somehow keeps it all straight and rings up everyone's order. Things calm down somewhat at night, but you can still count on sitting mighty close to your neighbor or sharing a table in one of Rome's oldest and most atmospheric restaurants.

### (37) L'ARCHETTO
### via dell' Archetto, 26

**AREA**
piazza Venezia
**TELEPHONE**
67-89-064
**OPEN**
Tues–Sun
**CLOSED**
Mon, Aug (dates vary)
**HOURS**
Lunch 12:30–3 P.M., dinner 7 P.M.–1 A.M.
**RESERVATIONS**
Advised for dinner
**CREDIT CARDS**
AMEX, DC, MC, V
**À LA CARTE**
L 20,000–28,000, beverage extra
**MENÙ TURISTICO**
None
**COVER & SERVICE CHARGES**
Cover L 2,500, service included
**ENGLISH**
Yes, and English menu

An impressive selection of pastas served in copious portions, along with a full complement of pizzas, *crostini, bruschettas,* and meat dishes make l'Archetto one of the restaurants most frequented by Cheap Eaters in this part of Rome.

By all means, try not to be seated upstairs, which is a small area jumbled with posters, fringed lamp shades, garlic braids, and dried peppers hanging from the rafters along with a display of aging postcards sent by customers. There is just too much going on here, with hustling waiters zipping around as if they are in training for the next Olympics and diners wandering by en route to better seating downstairs (the best tables are in the second room of the basement).

The *only* things to consider ordering are the pasta dishes, pizzas, *bruschetta,* or *crostini.* Pasta aficionados will have a delicious meal with any of the sixty-seven varieties. There is everything from a simple garlic, olive oil, and parsley rendition to fresh seafood (Tuesday and Friday only) and the *Chanel,* topped with tomato, garlic, lobster, brandy, cream, and pepper. Pizza eaters have twenty-five choices. For the antipasto course, order a simple *bruschetta* (toasted Italian bread covered with olive oil, garlic, and a variety of other toppings). *Primo* dessert temptations include homemade cakes, *tortas, gelato, tiramisù,* or *panna cotta.*

# Restaurants near Piazza di Spagna (Spanish Steps) and Via Condotti

## (38) AL 34
### via Mario de'Fiori, 34

Popular, crowded, and romantic, Al 34 was recently voted Best Value Trattoria in its price category by American Express cardholders in Rome. Reservations are essential and recommended for 9 or 9:30 P.M. If you eat much earlier, you will be dining with other tourists, and any later could put you standing in the aisles waiting for your table to clear. The cozy, wood-beamed interior is lit at night with ceramic table lights. Both dried and fresh flowers add a nice touch. The menu is typically Roman. Waiters in bow ties and black vests serve big bowls of soup, the best spinach salad in the area, wonderful pastas with imaginative toppings, well-executed meat dishes, and fresh seasonal vegetables. For dessert, the chocolate torte can be safely avoided and so can the banana split. Not so the *tiramisù*.

**AREA**
Spanish Steps

**TELEPHONE**
67-95-091

**OPEN**
Tues–Sun

**CLOSED**
Mon, Aug (3 weeks)

**HOURS**
Lunch 12:30–3 P.M., dinner 7:30–11 P.M.

**RESERVATIONS**
Essential

**CREDIT CARDS**
MC, V

**À LA CARTE**
L 45,000–55,000, beverage extra

**MENÙ TURISTICO**
None

**COVER & SERVICE CHARGES**
Cover L 3,500, service included

**ENGLISH**
Some, and English menu

## (39) ARANCIO D'ORO
### via Monte d'Oro, 17

Located near the daily antiques market on the piazza Borghese, this typical trattoria is a popular lunchtime rendezvous for the many businesspeople who have offices nearby. In the evening, the mood slows down, and it fills with residents and a stray tourist or two. Arancio d'Oro and its cousins, Settimio all'Arancio (see page 104) and Piccolo Arancio (see page 120), are owned by the Cialfi family and are equally well-known for their friendly hospitality and good food at realistic prices. The only time I can see that they fall a little short is on major holidays (i.e., Christmas or New Year's Day), when other restaurants are closed but they choose to stay open. The help and the kitchen staff operates on a limited basis during these holiday times, and it is reflected in the food and service, which can be mediocre. At all other times, the cooking tempts you with pastas in creamy sauces, sizzling platters of grilled meats, and a lemon mousse dessert you wish was double in size. Pizzas are served in the evenings only.

**AREA**
via Condotti

**TELEPHONE**
68-65-026

**OPEN**
Tues–Sun

**CLOSED**
Mon, Aug

**HOURS**
Lunch 12:30–3:30 P.M., dinner 7:30–11 P.M.

**RESERVATIONS**
Advised

**CREDIT CARDS**
AMEX, DC, MC, V

**À LA CARTE**
L 30,000, beverage extra

**MENÙ TURISTICO**
None

**COVER & SERVICE CHARGES**
Cover L 2,500, service included

**ENGLISH**
Yes, and English menu

## (40) BELTRAMME DA CESARETTO FIASCHETTERIA
### via della Croce, 39

**AREA**
Spanish Steps

**TELEPHONE**
None

**OPEN**
Mon–Sat

**CLOSED**
Sun, Aug

**HOURS**
Lunch noon–3 P.M., dinner
7:30–10:30 P.M.

**RESERVATIONS**
Not accepted

**CREDIT CARDS**
None

**À LA CARTE**
L 35,000, beverage extra

**MENÙ TURISTICO**
None

**COVER & SERVICE CHARGES**
Cover L 3,200, service included

**ENGLISH**
Yes

I cannot claim to have discovered this uncut Cheap Eat gem because it has been a household name for over a century. It is now a declared national monument, and when you go, you will quickly see that not much has changed since the opening in 1879. There are still just seven tables with forty place settings. In the 1960s, it was the hangout of important painters, actors, and poets, as well as for the scriptwriters for *La Dolce Vita,* which was conceived over long lunches at the back tables. The restaurant is located on an interesting shopping street that has everything from fishmongers, flower stalls, and fancy bakeries to luxurious lingerie shops and trendy leather boutiques. It doesn't stand out as a flashy spot; in fact, the only name you will see at this address is the word *Fiaschetteria* positioned at the top of the building. The present mix of diners figures into the restaurant's continuing success. At lunchtime regulars sit at shared tables with napkins around their necks, downing their food and wine with earnestness. At night, it is mostly couples who live nearby and a few smart visitors who have been tipped off to some of the only affordable food in this expensive enclave of Rome.

No one has ever claimed that this is a health-food sanctuary for the calorie-conscious. There are no food puritans sitting at other tables rolling their eyes in horror as you delve into an outrageously rich fettuccine with veal sauce, rabbit in white wine, or a filling pork chop. The basic menu stays about the same, but watch for the daily handwritten specials, which reflect the best foods of the season.

## (41) CENTRO MACROBIOTO ITALIANO
### via della Vite, 14 (third floor)

**AREA**
Spanish Steps

**TELEPHONE**
67-92-509

**OPEN**
Mon–Fri

**CLOSED**
Sat, Sun, Aug

**HOURS**
10 A.M.–7:30 P.M.; hot lunch
12:30–2:30 P.M. (or until food
is gone)

**RESERVATIONS**
Not accepted

Serious vegetarians in Rome all know about the Centro Macrobioto Italiano, the first macrobiotic center in Italy, which is reached by three long flights of steep stairs or via a white-knuckle trip in a creaking elevator. You can either eat at one of the red marble-topped metal tables or take your food with you.

From appetizers to desserts, the food is made with organic products and uses no butter, and the daily changing menu offers something for every type of vegetarian. You can have macrobiotic grain casseroles, steamed veggie plates, a variety of salads and interesting breads, yogurt shakes, natural ice creams, and fresh fruit and vegetable juices and organic beer.

Because the center is a private organization, membership is required. Visitors are allowed to eat here by paying a L 2,000 surcharge and showing their passport. To buy something from the adjoining shop, a L 30,000 fee is levied. If you show your copy of *Cheap Eats in Italy,* the fee will be cut in half. If you are staying in Rome for any length of time, you may be interested in joining one of their monthly cooking, exercise, or yoga classes.

### (42) FRATERNA DOMUS
**via dell' Cancello, 9 (at via di Monte Brianzo, 62; close to piazza Nicosia)**

For an inspiring Cheap Eat in Rome, consider communal dining, family-style, at Fraterna Domus, a Holy Hotel run by nuns. In addition to providing accommodations (see *Cheap Sleeps in Italy*), the nuns serve lunch and dinner to both guests and nonguests every day but Thursday. Reservations are required, since each meal has only a single seating, and you must bring cash, as credit is not part of the deal. The smells coming from the spotless kitchen tell you the simply prepared food is going to be wonderful, and you can trust me that it is. There is only one set-price menu, so make sure you ask what they are serving if you have dietary restrictions. The menu includes a pasta or soup, the main course, a garnish, salad, and dessert or fruit. Wine is extra. They also offer special student prices.

### (43) GRAN CAFFÈ EUROPEO ROMA
**piazza San Lorenzo in Lucina, 33**

Rain or shine, every morning I was in Rome to work on *Cheap Eats* and *Cheap Sleeps,* I went out early for my usual three-mile walk. I would try to go in different directions, spotting places that caught my interest to check on later in the day. After I found this *caffè* on the piazza San Lorenzo, I looked no further for my morning cappuccino and pastry, which were guaranteed to provide enough caffeine and sugar to jump-start my day. The doors open at 7 A.M., and until closing at 1 A.M. the staff is still filling orders for hot and cold drinks, ice cream, and their famous Sicilian pastries. The service is sharp, almost ruthless at busy times, but I guarantee you there is not a bad pastry in sight. I can still taste their *connoli al cioccolato,* and chocolate cream–filled horn. If

**CREDIT CARDS**
None
**À LA CARTE**
L 10,000–15,000, beverage extra
**MENÙ TURISTICO**
None
**COVER & SERVICE CHARGES**
No cover, service included; L 2,000 surcharge for non-members
**ENGLISH**
Yes

**AREA**
Spanish Steps
**TELEPHONE**
06-688-02727
**OPEN**
Mon–Wed, Fri–Sun
**CLOSED**
Thur, some holidays
**HOURS**
Lunch 1 P.M., dinner 7:30 P.M.
**RESERVATIONS**
Required
**CREDIT CARDS**
None
**À LA CARTE**
None
**MENÙ TURISTICO**
L 20,000, 3 courses, cover and service included, beverage extra
**COVER & SERVICE CHARGES**
Both included
**ENGLISH**
Yes

**AREA**
via Condotti
**TELEPHONE**
68-76-3000
**OPEN**
Mon, Tues, Thur–Sun
**CLOSED**
Wed, Aug
**HOURS**
7 A.M.–1 A.M., continuous service
**RESERVATIONS**
Not necessary
**CREDIT CARDS**
AMEX, DC, MC, V
**À LA CARTE**
Pastries from L 3,000
**MENÙ TURISTICO**
None

**COVER & SERVICE CHARGES**
Cover L 2,000 at a table, service
included
**ENGLISH**
Limited

you stand at the bar, you will have your order in minutes and the bill will be almost half of what it would be if you occupied a table on the square.

**NOTE:** Hot lunches and dinners are served, but they are not the reason to eat here . . . the pastries are.

## (44) I MARGUTTA
### via Margutta, 119

**AREA**
Spanish Steps
**TELEPHONE**
67-86-003
**OPEN**
Mon–Sat
**CLOSED**
Sun, Aug
**HOURS**
Lunch 12:30–3 P.M., dinner
8–11 P.M.
**RESERVATIONS**
Necessary for dinner, advised
for lunch
**CREDIT CARDS**
AMEX, DC, MC, V
**À LA CARTE**
L 35,000–40,000, beverage
extra
**MENÙ TURISTICO**
None
**COVER & SERVICE CHARGES**
Cover L 4,000, service included
**ENGLISH**
Yes

You will not find drab people munching brown rice cakes and thumbing through yoga manuals at I Margutta, an upscale vegetarian restaurant owned by Claudio Vannini, who also runs Antico Bottaro (see page 94). At I Margutta, you can depend on delicious vegetarian food served in a relaxed, open, California-style atmosphere with well-spaced mahogany tables, comfortable cushioned chairs, attractive plants, and helpful waiters.

The chef deserves awards for creating inventive dishes for every course. The menu changes with the seasons, but some tried-and-true dishes always remain. For instance, the wild rice salad garnished with asparagus and fresh Parmesan cheese and the tomato cream *crostini* are two appetizers guests adore. All the pastas are made here. I always look forward to the *tagliolini ai fiori di zucca* for my second course. Seasonal favorites include risottos, grilled or quick-fried seasonal vegetables, and the soy hamburger made with mushrooms, spinach, potatoes, and tomatoes. The salads are varied and enormous, and if you are not starving, they could be meals in themselves when accompanied with whole-grain bread and a fancy dessert. Desserts are worth serious cheating on your diet, especially the *degustazione dolci,* which includes a taste of all the desserts they offer that day.

## (45) I NUMERI
### via Belsana, 30

**AREA**
via Condotti
**TELEPHONE**
67-94-969
**OPEN**
Mon–Sat; Sun dinner only
**CLOSED**
Aug (dates vary)
**HOURS**
Lunch 12:30–3 P.M., dinner
7:30–11:30 P.M.
**RESERVATIONS**
Not accepted

Paper cups, napkins, and tablecloths along with a real popcorn wagon keynote this large informal choice close to upper-crust shopping near via Condotti. The Italian-style fast food is surprisingly good and always fresh, thanks to the huge turnover for lunch.

Everyone orders the pastas, and believe me, they are really good. I like the fusilli tossed with barely cooked zucchini and the *tonarrelli al limone,* square noodles in a lemon-cream sauce. Other favorite orders are any of the daily specials and the sweet or savory crêpes, which range from the house special, with Mascarpone cream cheese and chocolate, to the Honeymoon, filled with honey and nuts.

**CREDIT CARDS**
AMEX, DC, MC, V
**À LA CARTE**
L 15,000–20,000, beverage extra
**MENÙ TURISTICO**
None
**COVER & SERVICE CHARGES**
Cover for lunch L 2,000, dinner L 3,000, service included
**ENGLISH**
No, but English menu

## (46) LA FONTANELLA
### largo della Fontanella Borghese, 86

La Fontanella is a beautiful choice, whether you sit inside in the main room with a shimmering gold mosaic–tiled mural or outside on the tree- and umbrella-shaded terrace. A formal and dignified tone is maintained by the cast of polite waiters wearing maroon vests and black bow ties, unobtrusively serving the attractively clad clientele. Heavy white damask table coverings, gleaming silver, and pretty china further enhance the appeal, as do the lighted hurricane candles and fresh flowers.

Dinner begins with a flute of champagne and a plate of nibbles to enjoy while you are reading the menu. Be sure to ask about the daily specials, and keep in mind as you decide on your courses that the food is rich and the portions generous. For a light antipasto, consider the fried artichoke, served slightly warm and crisply tender—not woody and greasy like the "pinecones," as I like to call them, that you often get. Another nice beginning is one of their salads, all of which are a little different. The *insalata Fontanella* has arugula, cheese, mushrooms, and prosciutto tossed in a light mustard vinaigrette. Serious mushroom lovers will like the raw mushrooms mixed with fresh slices of Parmesan cheese. There is also a baby leaf spinach salad and one made with hearts of palm.

Pastas are aimed at recreating the days when we did not feverishly count calories and fat grams. I think the spinach and ricotta ravioli is divine, as are the crêpes filled with black truffles. So is the spaghetti with seafood and the gamey *paparadelle al sugo di lepre,* wide noodles in a robust hare sauce. Perfectly roasted and grilled meats and fresh fish follow. The fish is expensive, but it is fresh and delicious, usually plainly grilled and served smelling fragrantly of olive oil and lemon.

If it is available, by all means try the fresh fruit tart for dessert, a lovely mixture of fresh raspberries,

**AREA**
via Condotti
**TELEPHONE**
68-71-092, 68-71-582
**OPEN**
Tues–Sun
**CLOSED**
Mon, Aug
**HOURS**
Lunch 12:30–3 P.M., dinner 7 P.M.–midnight
**RESERVATIONS**
Advised
**CREDIT CARDS**
AMEX, DC, MC, V
**À LA CARTE**
L 60,000, beverage extra
**MENÙ TURISTICO**
None
**COVER & SERVICE CHARGES**
Cover L 4,000, service included
**ENGLISH**
Yes

boysenberries, and cranberries with a layer of cream placed on a crisp cookie crust. The house wine is good and served by the bottle. You pay only for as much as you drink. While the final bill will be above the Cheap Eat category, this will be a special meal you will remember.

**NOTE:** If you go for lunch, be sure to take a few minutes to wander through the small antiques market held in the square.

## (47) MARIO
### via della Vite, 55

**AREA**
via Condotti and the Spanish Steps

**TELEPHONE**
67-83-818

**OPEN**
Mon–Sat

**CLOSED**
Sun, Aug

**HOURS**
Lunch 12:30–3 P.M., dinner 7–11 P.M.

**RESERVATIONS**
Strongly advised

**CREDIT CARDS**
AMEX, DC, MC, V

**À LA CARTE**
L 50,000, beverage extra

**MENÙ TURISTICO**
None

**COVER & SERVICE CHARGES**
No cover, service included

**ENGLISH**
Yes, and English menu

No one ever comes to pick and nibble at Mario's, a typical Tuscan-style trattoria with whitewashed walls, raffia-covered chairs, bottles of Chianti on the tables, and service that ranges from friendly and attentive to rather slow. For thirty-seven years it has been run by the Mariani family, and it's a popular eating destination for both Romans and visitors. It is fine for lunch but best for dinner, when there is a crowded, happy atmosphere. Because of the crunch during prime time, always arrive with a reservation.

This is definitely the place to sample classic Tuscan fare, including *ribollita,* a heavy bread-thickened soup, and the famous *bistecca alla fiorentina,* a big steak rubbed with olive oil and herbs and grilled until just pink. Other dishes to consider are the braised beef with polenta and, when they are in season, the wild boar and pheasant. For dessert, I recommend zeroing in on the *tiramisù,* a liqueur-soaked layering of cake, Marsala wine, espresso coffee, and creamy Mascarpone cheese.

## (48) PASTICCERIA D'ANGELO
### via della Croce, 29/30

**AREA**
via Condotti and the Spanish Steps

**TELEPHONE**
67-82-556, 67-83-924

**OPEN**
Mon, Wed–Sun bar and lunch only

**CLOSED**
Tues, Aug

**HOURS**
Bar 7 A.M.–8 P.M.; lunch 12:30–3 P.M.

**RESERVATIONS**
Not necessary

**CREDIT CARDS**
AMEX, DC, MC, V

For power snacking or lunching, the Pasticceria d'Angelo in the heart of Rome's premier shopping district is a *must.* It is open from 7 A.M. until 8 P.M., with continuous service from the bar and pastry counter and lunch service from 12:30 P.M. until 3 P.M. It's a good place to start the day with a quick cappuccino and a warm roll or other tantalizing delight. Later on, between shopping sprints, you can order lunch from the cafeteria line, where the daily offerings included assorted antipasti, salads, soups, pastas, and meats.

The nice thing about eating here is that you can have just a bowl of soup or indulge in a four-course blowout if you are stoking up for heavy-duty afternoon shopping. Freshly made sandwiches are also available, but these must be eaten standing at one of the bar tables in front. If you are on the run, ask to have your order wrapped to go: *da portare via*.

## (49) PIZZERIA AL LEONCINO
### via del Leoncino, 28

Look for pizza, pizza, and more pizza at Al Leoncino. The service is fast, the pizzas inexpensive, the ambience as informal as it gets, and the place popular. What more can any Cheap Eater ask?

The hardworking pizza chefs cook crisp-crust creations in the wood-fired oven in full view of the diners. Romans know their pizza, so when it is good and cheap, expect to wait, especially here, as few other pizzerias in the area are open for lunch. Wine sells for L 4,000 a half liter, and the meal-sized pizzas from L 8,000 to L 12,000. You will leave happily satisfied with this Roman Cheap Eat.

## (50) RE DEGLI AMICI
### via della Croce, 33B

The five-room restaurant is a Roman institution—it has red-and-white tablecloths, murals on the ceilings, local artists' works lining the walls, and brash waiters racing about madly. People continue to come here for the classic trattoria cooking which offers multiple-choice self-service antipasti, a full complement of pastas, succulent grilled meats, and wood-fired pizzas to hungry audiences. Re Degli Amici also upholds the long-standing Roman tradition of serving a particular dish on certain days of the week. On Tuesday and Friday fresh fish are the specials. On Thursday, you can count on gnocchi; Saturday is tripe. Pizzas are available every evening, and lasagna is baked daily. A big bonus for many Cheap Eaters is that you can order just a first or second plate, along with maybe a salad to start or a dessert to finish, and not suffer from a grumpy waiter who expects you to order the works.

**À LA CARTE**
L 10,000–18,000, beverage extra; sandwiches from L 3,500
**MENÙ TURISTICO**
None
**COVER & SERVICE CHARGES**
None
**ENGLISH**
Limited

**AREA**
via Condotti, Spanish Steps
**TELEPHONE**
68-76-306
**OPEN**
Mon, Tues, Thur–Sun
**CLOSED**
Wed, Aug
**HOURS**
Lunch 1–2:30 P.M., dinner 7 P.M.–midnight
**RESERVATIONS**
Not necessary
**CREDIT CARDS**
None
**À LA CARTE**
Pizzas from L 8,000–12,000
**MENÙ TURISTICO**
None
**COVER & SERVICE CHARGES**
None
**ENGLISH**
No, but English menu

**AREA**
Spanish Steps, via Condotti
**TELEPHONE**
67-95-380, 67-82-555
**OPEN**
Tues–Sun
**CLOSED**
Mon, July (first 2 weeks)
**HOURS**
Lunch 12:30–3 P.M., dinner 7:30–10 P.M.
**RESERVATIONS**
Advised for dinner
**CREDIT CARDS**
AMEX, DC, MC, V
**À LA CARTE**
L 50,000, beverage extra; pizza L 15,000
**MENÙ TURISTICO**
None
**COVER & SERVICE CHARGES**
Cover L 3,000, service included
**ENGLISH**
Yes

### (51) SETTIMIO ALL'ARANCIO
**via dell'Arancio, 50**

**AREA**
via Condotti
**TELEPHONE**
68-76-119
**OPEN**
Mon–Sat
**CLOSED**
Sun, Aug
**HOURS**
Lunch 12:30–3 P.M., dinner
6–11:30 P.M.
**RESERVATIONS**
Advised
**CREDIT CARDS**
AMEX, DC, MC, V
**À LA CARTE**
L 30,000, beverage extra
**MENÙ TURISTICO**
None
**COVER & SERVICE CHARGES**
Cover L 2,000, service included
**ENGLISH**
Some, and English menu

Settimio all'Arancio is part of a trio of trattorias run by the Cialfi family. The other two are Arancio d'Oro (see page 97) and Piccolo Arancio (see page 120). The mood here is exactly right for a neighborhood eating place, with wholesome, well-prepared food served in two small whitewashed dining rooms with pink and white table linens and a few fresh flowers.

Go for the fried zucchini or artichokes for your appetizers, the *fusilli alla melanzana* for your pasta dish, and on Fridays always order the grilled fish. Dreamy desserts include the lemon mousse or *tiramisù*. The menus at all three places are virtually the same.

## Restaurants in Testaccio

### (52) AL VECCHIO MATTATOIO
**piazza O. Giustiniani, 2**

**AREA**
Testaccio
**TELEPHONE**
57-41-382
**OPEN**
Wed–Sun; Mon lunch only
**CLOSED**
Tues, Aug
**HOURS**
Lunch 12:30–3 P.M., dinner
7:30–11 P.M.
**RESERVATIONS**
Advised
**CREDIT CARDS**
None
**À LA CARTE**
L 30,000, beverage extra
**MENÙ TURISTICO**
None
**COVER & SERVICE CHARGES**
Cover L 2,000, 12% service
added
**ENGLISH**
None

The Testaccio part of Rome is not known for its designer boutiques, dainty tearooms, or matrons who lunch. This was once the slaughterhouse area of Rome, and many butcher shops are still in full swing. As you can imagine, food was, and still is, geared for burly workers who do not worry about cholesterol or their waistline. The area is now high on the trendy index, and it is well worth a meal foray, especially for those eager to add another cuisine experience to their roster.

I think the best time to eat at Al Vecchio Mattatoio is for Sunday lunch, when the pine-paneled dining room is bursting with extended families all enjoying themselves to the fullest. Heaping plates of tripe, *pajata* (veal intestines), liver oxtail stew . . . name a body part and it is probably on the menu. For the conservatives among you, there is roast pork or veal, a lamb dish, and often beef. But, quite frankly, if you are going to venture into this corner of Rome, plan to order what the area is known for and what the chefs do best, otherwise it really is not worth the safari. Of course, there are plenty of antipasti, salads, vegetables, and desserts to round out the meal. Strong wines go well with this type of food, so if you go for lunch, you probably do not want to plan too active an afternoon.

## (53) BUCATINO
### via Luca della Robbia, 84/86

Bucatino is a popular tavern in the Testaccio section of Rome. There are three main rooms: two upstairs and a large one downstairs. I like to sit in the big room upstairs because it is more central to all the interesting action and not as claustrophobic and stuffy as the one downstairs. Avoid at all costs the little closet-sized anteroom to your left as you walk in the door.

For the most inexpensive meal in the evening, have a pizza or pasta with a salad and maybe a dessert. On Fridays, the *pasta e ceci*—pasta with garbanzo beans in an onion, garlic, and tomato sauce—is a wonderful choice. So is the *bucatini all'amatriciana,* spaghetti covered in a thick tomato and bacon sauce. Main-course standbys are the *trippa alla romana, coda alla vaccinara* (oxtail stew), the roast veal with potatoes, or any fresh fish. Those eager to engage in off-beat dining should be satisfied for a *long* time with the *coratella alla Veneta*: lamb's heart, lung, liver, and spleen cooked in olive oil and seasoned with lots of pepper and onion. You will need a strong, red wine to get you through this one.

**AREA**
Testaccio

**TELEPHONE**
57-46-886

**OPEN**
Tues–Sun

**CLOSED**
Mon, Aug

**HOURS**
Lunch noon–3 P.M., dinner 7–11 P.M.

**RESERVATIONS**
Advised

**CREDIT CARDS**
MC, V

**À LA CARTE**
L 32,000, beverage extra; pizza from L 7,000–10,000

**MENÙ TURISTICO**
None

**COVER & SERVICE CHARGES**
Cover L 2,800, service included

**ENGLISH**
Yes

## (54) CHECCHINO DAL 1887
### via Monte Testaccio, 30

I urge you: Please do not let the location, or the many unusual specialty dishes this restaurant is famous for, turn you off. Checchino dal 1887 is one of Rome's most elegant and sophisticated dining choices. When it opened in 1887, it was a place to drink wine. Today you can see the original wine license hanging on the wall next to a picture of the great-great-grandfather and -grandmother of the current-generation Mariani family, who are still firmly in command. In addition to its fine food, the restaurant is well known for its diversity of wines, with over four hundred varieties housed in a naturally temperature-controlled underground *cave* that dates back to 75 B.C. You can pay up to L 800,000 for a museum-quality wine, but there are also scores of wines available for L 12,000 to L 25,000, as well as monthly featured wines that are affordably priced.

The dining room is beautiful. The quality table settings are placed on original marble-topped tables

**AREA**
Testaccio

**TELEPHONE**
57-46-318, 57-43-816

**OPEN**
Tues–Sat; Oct–May, Sun lunch also

**CLOSED**
Mon, Aug, Christmas (1 week)

**HOURS**
Lunch 12:30–3 P.M., dinner 8–11 P.M.

**RESERVATIONS**
Advised

**CREDIT CARDS**
AMEX, DC, MC, V

**À LA CARTE**
L 40,000–50,000, beverage extra

**MENÙ TURISTICO**
None

**COVER & SERVICE CHARGES**
Cover L 4,000, 15% service
added
**ENGLISH**
Yes, and English menu

accented by fresh yellow roses, the favorite flower of the owner's mother, who can usually be found sitting behind the cash register at the entrance.

The menu is not only translated into English but each dish is explained so that you will know exactly what you are eating. You will soon realize that this is *very* important. The Testaccio location means an emphasis on meats of all kinds, especially entrails, which most Americans would never consider trying. I can promise you that even though you think you would never *taste,* let alone *like,* veal kidneys, lamb's brains, oxtail stew, or pig's trotters . . . here they are raised to a gourmet level and are indeed delicious. I admit, I was wary. But after one meal, I was impressed and eager to return. To begin, there is head cheese, macaroni with calf's intestines, rendered pig's cheeks with ewe's milk cheese, or veal foot, boiled, boned, and served in salad with carrots, beans, celery, and dressing. Any one of these is wonderful, I promise you. To follow, you will find oxtail stew, tripe, veal intestines stewed or grilled, and the jackpot entrée: *arrosto misto,* which offers a sampling of roasted sweetbreads, calf's small intestines, and marrow. Tamer tastes need not stay away as there are many other choices, including their specialty lamb dish: *abbacchio alla cacciatora,* bite-sized pieces of lamb sautéed in white wine, white vinegar, rosemary, and red pepper. If you order this, you get a bonus: a pretty ceramic plate from the restaurant to take home as a souvenir.

To finish your meal, you can order from a long list of interesting cheeses, or homemade sweets, each served with a glass of an appropriate wine. From beginning to end, the service is impeccable, the food delicious, and the time memorable. Please do yourself a favor and try it as a special Big Splurge.

### (55) DA FELICE
### via Mastro Giorgio, 29

**AREA**
Testaccio
**TELEPHONE**
57-46-800
**OPEN**
Mon–Sat
**CLOSED**
Sun, Aug
**HOURS**
Lunch 12:30–2:30 P.M., dinner
7:30–10 P.M.

What a place! What a find! Don't look for a sign outside, a printed menu anywhere, English to be spoken, coffee to be served, credit cards to be accepted, or much charm, other than the mega-dose of local color provided by the other patrons. You will dine in a simple room amid rough-cast laborers, rotund men mopping their plates with chunks of bread, and perhaps a teased, bleached blond in spike heels who keeps the mix interesting. The two hardworking waiters—one an original fixture in modern-day tennis shoes and the other with a ponytail and leather vest tossed on over a T-shirt— somehow keep the orders straight and the diners satisfied. The daily menu depends on the mood of the chef and what the market has to offer. There is nothing dainty about the recipes or the servings. It is all he-man fare guaranteed to put hair on anyone's chest. When you are through, you will have been wined and dined for around L 20,000.

**RESERVATIONS**
Not accepted
**CREDIT CARDS**
None
**À LA CARTE**
L 18,000, beverage extra
**MENÙ TURISTICO**
None
**COVER & SERVICE CHARGES**
Cover L 2,000, service included
**ENGLISH**
None

## Restaurants near the Train Station, San Lorenzo, and Santa Maria Maggiore

### (56) AL FAGIANETTO
### via Filippo Turati, 21

Restaurants near train stations tend to be overpriced tourist traps with uninspired chefs and bored waiters. Al Fagianetto is definitely not in this category, and it gets my vote for serving some of the best, well-priced, and satisfying fare in this difficult area.

The comfortable dining room is hospitable and justifiably busy, especially at lunch. For both the first and second courses there are more than twenty options to select from. I like to start with the *tonnarelli alla ciociara* (pasta with mushrooms, ham, and tomatoes) or the *risotto con funghi porcini.* Popular main courses include the house specialty: *fiagiano alla casareccia,* pheasant cooked with olives and mushrooms. They also do roast lamb and veal Marsala nicely.

For a light, easy-on-the-wallet meal, try one of the pizzas (served only for dinner) and a salad. With the exception of the ice cream, all the desserts are made here, so go ahead and have one of their cream-filled cakes or a seasonal fruit tart.

**AREA**
Train station
**TELEPHONE**
44-67-306
**OPEN**
Mon–Wed, Fri–Sun
**CLOSED**
Thur, Aug
**HOURS**
Lunch 12:30–3:30 P.M., dinner 7–11 P.M.
**RESERVATIONS**
Advised for 4 or more
**CREDIT CARDS**
AMEX, DC, MC, V
**À LA CARTE**
L 28,000, beverage extra
**MENÙ TURISTICO**
L 21,000, 3 courses, cover and service included, beverage included
**COVER & SERVICE CHARGES**
Cover L 2,000, service included
**ENGLISH**
Limited, but English menu

### (57) BOTTIGLIERA REALI
### via Servio Tullio, 8

Mario Paziani runs his lilliputian restaurant as if he believes you will be coming back, and believe me you will, just as all his other patrons do on a regular basis. In fact, many come back perfectly willing to stand patiently in line at 2 P.M. The atmosphere inside is

**AREA**
Train station
**TELEPHONE**
48-72-027
**OPEN**
Mon–Fri, Sat lunch only
**CLOSED**
Sun, Aug (1 week)

**HOURS**
Lunch noon–3 P.M., dinner
7–9 P.M.
**RESERVATIONS**
Not accepted
**CREDIT CARDS**
None
**À LA CARTE**
L 18,000–28,000, beverage
extra
**MENÙ TURISTICO**
None
**COVER & SERVICE CHARGES**
Cover L 1,200, service included
**ENGLISH**
Limited

chummy, with six tables on one side and six along the other. Paper table covers and napkins, coats hung by the door, and a portable heater rolled down the center aisle sum up the interior. Daily pastas, hearty soups, fresh fish, and a good selection of meaty main courses headline a menu that brings back the tastes and smells of Mom's kitchen. The food is not delicate or approaching gourmet, but there is plenty of it and the prices must drive the competition crazy.

### (58) DA FRANCO AR VICOLETTO
### via dei Falisci, 1A

**AREA**
Train station and San Lorenzo
**TELEPHONE**
49-57-675
**OPEN**
Tues–Sun
**CLOSED**
Mon, Aug 15–30
**HOURS**
Lunch 12:30–3:30 P.M., dinner
7:30–11:30 P.M.
**RESERVATIONS**
Advised for 6 or more
**CREDIT CARDS**
None
**À LA CARTE**
L 35,000–40,000, beverage
extra
**MENÙ TURISTICO**
None
**COVER & SERVICE CHARGES**
No cover, service included
**ENGLISH**
Limited

Restaurant groupies would be happy to wait in the street for a table here if they could only *find* the place. Da Franco ar Vicoletto is accessible *only* to the determined first-time guest who is armed with a compass and a detailed street map. Since there is no sign or name over the door, follow these directions once you get to the neighborhood: if you enter from largo Falisci, look for the second door on your left, with the number 6930 to the left of the glass doors with black metal frames. If you come by way of via Latini, turn right at the first corner and the restaurant entrance will be on the right side after Barberie Michele, a barber shop. If you arrive around noon, take a few minutes to check the local outdoor market at the corner of via dei Falisci and via dei Latini.

Is the hunt worth the effort? You bet it is, *if* you love fresh fish. Yes, they have a steak and a veal offering, but they are unremarkable. Here, stay with fish for every course from appetizer to main. Start by helping yourself to the fish antipasti. My vote for pasta goes to the fettuccine with shrimp and artichokes or to the spaghetti with fresh clams. For the second course, order the mixed grilled seafood platter or whatever is touted on the daily special list. Most of the fish is priced per 100 grams, so watch out or your bill will climb. Desserts are mundane: no need to plan on saving room.

### (59) DA GIOVANNI
### via Antonia Salandra, 1

**AREA**
Train station
**TELEPHONE**
48-59-50

The section around the train station can be a dicey, no-man's-land when it comes to dining. Many of the restaurants are either on unsafe streets, serve unsavory food, or both. Not so at Da Giovanni, founded over forty years ago by the Vittucci family, who still run it today. Seating is downstairs in two knotty-pine rooms, lined with coat hooks; the entrance is graced with hanging meats, and fresh flowers accent the dessert and appetizer table. Sunny yellow damask linens complete the picture.

The chef really struts his stuff when it comes to the pastas. One of his best is the *fettuccine alla giovanni,* a combination of butter, cheese, mushrooms, tomatoes, and peas that will go directly to your arteries, but what a delicious journey. The main course plates range from *abbacchio alla cacciatora con funghi* (lamb gently stewed in a tomato-mushroom sauce) to grilled veal chops, fresh fish, and fried brains in butter. For a finale, the top choices are a heady version of *tiramisù* or whole baked pears (in season). A very light alternative is the *frutta secca,* a serving of dried fruit and nuts that pairs well with an after-dinner espresso.

**OPEN**
Mon–Sat

**CLOSED**
Sun, Aug

**HOURS**
Lunch noon–3 P.M., dinner 7–10 P.M.

**RESERVATIONS**
Not necessary

**CREDIT CARDS**
MC, V

**À LA CARTE**
L 25,000, beverage extra

**MENÙ TURISTICO**
L 25,000, 3 courses, cover and service included, beverage included

**COVER & SERVICE CHARGES**
Cover L 2,000, 10% service added

**ENGLISH**
Yes

## (60) DAGNINO
### Galleria Esedra, via Vittorio Emanuele Orlando, 75

I was looking for a cafeteria/pastry shop near the railroad station. I can just see it, I thought pessimistically, as I looked for the Galleria Esedra arcade near piazza della Repubblica. Most restaurants in this area are simply terrible, overpriced greasy spoons with no thought of changing. What a surprise was in store when I reached Dagnino, which bills itself as a bar, *pasticceria, gelateria,* and a cafeteria specializing in Sicilian pastries and ice cream.

Time stopped somewhere in the fifties in this two-level monument to mirrors, marble, fat grams, and sweets. You can stop in during the early morning cappuccino and *cornetto* rush; hit the cafeteria line around noon before the hot choices get too picked over; or go later on in the day for a snack. I like to go in the late afternoon, look over the magnificent pastries displayed along one wall, pick several, and retire to a quiet table with a pot of tea. I always think I will take a few home with me, but I usually end up devouring them all right on the spot. If you have children in tow, the ice creams are wonderful, and the *granita di limone* (lemonade) is the best I have tasted.

**AREA**
Train station

**TELEPHONE**
48-16-660

**OPEN**
Daily June–Sept; Mon–Fri, Sun Oct–May

**CLOSED**
Sat from Oct–May

**HOURS**
7 A.M.–10 P.M., hot food noon–8 P.M., continuous service

**RESERVATIONS**
Not accepted

**CREDIT CARDS**
AMEX, MC, V

**À LA CARTE**
Pastries L 3,000–6,000, ice cream L 5,000–8,000, hot food L 6,000–10,000

**MENÙ TURISTICO**
None

**COVER & SERVICE CHARGES**
None

**ENGLISH**
Limited

### (61) DA SOR GIOVANNI
### via San Martino ai Monti, 40 (corner via Domenichino)

**AREA**
Train station/Santa Maria Maggiore Church

**TELEPHONE**
48-72-695

**OPEN**
Mon–Sat

**CLOSED**
Sun, Aug

**HOURS**
Lunch noon–3 P.M., dinner 7–10:30 P.M.

**RESERVATIONS**
Advised

**CREDIT CARDS**
None

**À LA CARTE**
L 28,000, beverage extra

**MENÙ TURISTICO**
None

**COVER & SERVICE CHARGES**
Cover L 2,000, service included

**ENGLISH**
Very limited

No one speaks English and the menu certainly is not translated, probably because no tourist has ever been able to find the place. Now you can, if you go to the corner of via Domenichino and via San Martino ai Monti, 40, in the neighborhood around Santa Maria Maggiore Church. Naturally there is no sign outside, only a red telephone plaque over the curtained door at the entrance. Why bother? Because this is one place that is purely local, and even more important, the food is worth the hunt.

Do not expect the red carpet treatment, especially at lunch when exercise and workout dropouts fill the smoky room with their jolly laughter and social banter. To get really Roman, order the house pasta favorite, *tonnarelli alla Monticiana* (egg pasta tossed with peas and mushrooms). Follow with the tripe, *osso buco,* or maybe the *Parmigiana di melanzane* (baked eggplant and Parmesan cheese) if it is one of the specials. A carafe of the *vini della casa* and the basket of country bread keeps the meal going until dessert, when you can have a house custard of *tiramisù.*

### (62) DA VINCENZO
### via Castlefidardo, 4/6

**AREA**
Train station

**TELEPHONE**
48-45-96

**OPEN**
Mon–Sat

**CLOSED**
Sun, Aug

**HOURS**
Lunch 12:30–3 P.M., dinner 7:00 P.M.–11 P.M.

**RESERVATIONS**
Advised

**CREDIT CARDS**
AMEX, DC, MC, V

**À LA CARTE**
L 45,000, beverage extra

**MENÙ TURISTICO**
None

**COVER & SERVICE CHARGES**
Cover L 2,000, service included

**ENGLISH**
Yes, and English menu

The menu is translated into English, and probably German, French, and Japanese, too, but the clientele is usually local. The setting is simple, the service friendly yet professional, the plates warmed when they should be, and the food delicious. From appetizers to dessert, there are fifty-six possibilities. Still, if you do not see what you want, just ask and chances are it can be prepared for you. Fresh fish is the kitchen's strong suit, and it is cooked and served with pride. My dinner guests all agreed that it was one of the best fish meals they had had in Rome.

If you are going all the way with fish, the sautéed clams or mussels and the smoked swordfish are nice starters. Spaghetti with clams and prawns or the rice with seafood are well-executed first courses. Besides fish, the *penne all'arrabiatta* (a hot combination of peppers, tomatoes, and garlic) is a reliable first course. The baked sea bass or flounder are served with potatoes and can be topped with a zesty tomato sauce. *Saltimbocca alla Romana* (veal and ham cooked in a wine sauce), grilled pork chops, or a roast chicken will keep the carnivores in your party pleased. Fresh fruit tarts, *gelatos,* and lemon-flavored *sorbetto* splashed with vodka will not lead you too far astray from your dieting resolutions. A shot of Sambucca, served if you order a full meal, will add to your desire to dine again at this wonderful Roman restaurant.

## (63) FIASCHETTERIA MARINI
### via Rafaele Cadorna, 9

Eating at an *enoteca,* or wine bar, is currently one of the "in" things to do in Rome, not only because the wine is good and the food choices lighter but because of the lower cost.

From Monday through Friday, the Fiaschetteria Marini serves lunches only to a packed house. Dinner is available by reservation for groups of ten or more. Please plan to go early, or be prepared to stand with the regulars gossiping at the bar while waiting for a table. The setting is casual, with paper covers on tiny marble-topped tables, which are set both inside amid crates of wine bottles and outside on the sidewalk when weather permits. The daily changing choices are limited, but all are absolutely delicious, especially the *pasta e fagioli* or any of the special German dishes that appear when the owner's mother, who is Austrian, gets busy in the kitchen.

**AREA**
Train station
**TELEPHONE**
47-45-534
**OPEN**
Mon–Fri lunch only
**CLOSED**
Sat, Sun, Aug
**HOURS**
Lunch 12:15–2:45 P.M.
**RESERVATIONS**
Not accepted
**CREDIT CARDS**
None
**À LA CARTE**
L 10,000–15,000, beverage extra
**MENÙ TURISTICO**
None
**COVER & SERVICE CHARGES**
Cover L 1,500, service included
**ENGLISH**
Enough
**MISCELLANEOUS**
Dinner for 10 or more by reservation only

## (64) GIOVANNI FASSI, PALAZZO DEL FREDDO
### via Principe Eugenio, 65/67 A

It is said that modern-day Romans hold the nation's *gelato* consumption record at more than five gallons per person per year. Judging from the amount I saw consumed at this century-old *gelateria* near the train station, I think that is an extremely low estimate. Giovanni Fassi began in 1816 as a little shop in piazza Navona, and in 1880 it moved to its present location. It has been run by the same family since the beginning and is considered to be the *gelato* Mecca by most connoisseurs in Rome.

The ice cream is displayed in glass cases with signs in English. Decide what size *cono* (cone) or *coppa* (cup) you want, pay the cashier, and give your receipt to a server. You can take your treat to one of the tables scattered around the cavernous room or eat it on the run. Prices

**AREA**
Train station
**TELEPHONE**
44-64-740
**OPEN**
Tues–Sun
**CLOSED**
Mon
**HOURS**
Winter noon–11 P.M.; summer noon–midnight, continuous service
**RESERVATIONS**
Not accepted
**CREDIT CARDS**
None
**À LA CARTE**
*Gelato* from L 2,000

start around L 2,000 and climb according to how elabo-rate and involved your order gets.

### (65) GRAN CAFFÈ LA STREGA
### piazza del Viminale, 27/31

Huge, brightly lit, and packed with animated Ital-ians—that is the Gran Caffè la Strega, a combination cafeteria, restaurant, and pizzeria catering to Ministry of the Interior workers and tourists at lunch and an eclectic crowd in the evening.

Smart lunch munchers skip the ready-made sand-wiches and head straight for the self-service cafeteria counter. They also bypass the diet-destroying display of desserts and concentrate on one of the twenty daily salads and ten or twelve hot specials. Seating is either in a room with the pizza ovens or on a large outdoor lighted terrace shielded from traffic and street noise by a ring of bushes and trees.

If you want to avoid the sometimes frustratingly long cafeteria line, you can opt for pizza, which is served separately for both lunch and dinner. The twenty-three wood-fired varieties run the gamut of a simple topping of tomato and cheese to "the works" with a fried egg on top.

In the evening, waiters serving only pizzas and salads replace the cafeteria line.

### (66) HOSTARIA DE PAOLO E LILIANA
### via dei Sabeli, 6/8

You won't find the name of this restaurant anywhere on the building. Instead, look for the red doors at 6–8 via dei Sabeli and follow your nose for one of the Cheap-est Eats in Rome.

Paper tablecloths, wine in juice glasses, worn tile floors, a slow-moving fan, a bouquet of flowers in a wine pitcher, a pay telephone, a coatrack in the corner . . . it's obvious that no restaurant designer has ever been con-sulted here. In fact, the status quo has been maintained for years in this little San Lorenzo spot, where the robust cook in her teased beehive hairdo and sensible slippers serves steaming bowls of pasta to a cast of blue-collar locals, who fill every seat by 1:00 P.M.

The handwritten, but legible, menu changes every day, and you can always count on he-man portions of pasta, meaty second courses, and basic seasonal vegetables. Desserts do not exist, except for fresh fruit.

### (67) I LEONI D'ABRUZZO
**via Vicenza, 44**

For serious cooking with good value for money, you will be unable to beat this Cheap Eat find near the train station. I like it not only for the exceptional food but for the personalized service from the owner, who greets guests, takes orders, helps out serving, and then bids everyone farewell. The location doesn't dazzle: it is in a newly redone basement room with bright lighting and white walls. Early in the evening it is full of nearby hotel guests—later the locals arrive.

There is a very basic *menù turistico* and a long à la carte menu translated into several languages. Forget them both. Instead do what the contented regulars do and order from the Italian *menu del giorno* (Italian daily menu). The choices for each course are not many, but they are seasonally fresh and delicious. Polish off the meal with a slice of the almond cake and a glass of the house *digestif,* which is brought to your table for you to pour. It is a dandy way to end a satisfying meal.

### (68) LA REATINA
**via S. Martino della Battaglia, 17**

Sunday night is never an easy night for dining out in Rome. That is not a problem here, where the promise of a Cheap Eat in Rome packs them into this typical *trattoria di quatiere* near the train station. For thirty years, six brothers and their wives and children have cooked for and served a weathered-looking neighborhood clientele. Neither the exterior nor the interior have any panache, but the bottom line, inexpensive food, is why you are here. They offer a *menù turistico* as well as one translated into four languages. Don't look at these unless you must. Ask instead for the handwritten Italian *menu del giorno,* which lists all the good stuff. The house pasta specialty is *farfalle impazzite,* a homemade bow-tie pasta tossed with cream and spinach that is a kissing cousin to fettuccine Alfredo. Fresh fish is not on the kitchen's shopping list, but meat and potatoes, veal creations, and season vegetables are. I have never been able to do dessert, but if you can, be sure it is made here.

**ENGLISH**
None

**AREA**
Train station
**TELEPHONE**
44-70-02-72
**OPEN**
Mon–Sat
**CLOSED**
Sun, Aug
**HOURS**
Lunch noon–3 P.M., dinner 6:30–11 P.M.
**RESERVATIONS**
Absolutely
**CREDIT CARDS**
MC, V
**À LA CARTE**
L 35,000, beverage extra
**MENÙ TURISTICO**
L 25,000, 3 courses, cover and service included, beverage extra
**COVER & SERVICE CHARGES**
Cover L 2,500, service included
**ENGLISH**
Yes, and English menu

**AREA**
Train station
**TELEPHONE**
49-03-14
**OPEN**
Mon–Fri, Sun
**CLOSED**
Sat, Aug 15–30, Christmas (10 days)
**HOURS**
Lunch noon–3 P.M., dinner 6:30–11 P.M.
**RESERVATIONS**
Not necessary
**CREDIT CARDS**
None
**À LA CARTE**
L 25,000, beverage extra
**MENÙ TURISTICO**
L 20,000, 3 courses, cover and service included, beverage included
**COVER & SERVICE CHARGES**
Cover L 2,500, service included
**ENGLISH**
Yes

## (69) PIZZERIA L'ECONOMICA
### via Tiburtina, 46

**AREA**
San Lorenzo
**TELEPHONE**
44-56-669
**OPEN**
Mon–Sat dinner only
**CLOSED**
Sun, Aug
**HOURS**
6:30–11:30 P.M.
**RESERVATIONS**
Not accepted
**CREDIT CARDS**
None
**À LA CARTE**
L 9,000–16,000, beverage extra
**MENÙ TURISTICO**
None
**COVER & SERVICE CHARGES**
No cover, 10% service added
**ENGLISH**
Yes

The name says it all. Pizzeria l'Economica is a bare-bones, family-run place with zero decor. Its wide-ranging claim to fame is that it serves the lowest cost, and its fans claim the best, pizzas in the San Lorenzo area of Rome, which is about a ten-minute bus ride east of the train station.

The giant wood-burning pizza fires are lit in the evening only from 6:30 to 11 P.M. If you don't want one of their super pizzas, the only other options are *crostini*, pieces of toast covered with any combination of ham, anchovies, sardines, mushrooms, tomatoes, and cheese, or an unbeatable antipasti selection. Desserts are definitely in the ho-hum category, so pass them up for another time, another place.

## (70) POMMIDORO
### piazza Sanniti, 44

**AREA**
Train station, San Lorenzo
**TELEPHONE**
44-52-692, 44-52-652
**OPEN**
Mon–Sat
**CLOSED**
Sun, Aug
**HOURS**
Lunch 12:30–3 P.M., dinner 7:30 P.M.–midnight
**RESERVATIONS**
Advised
**CREDIT CARDS**
AMEX, DC, MC, V
**À LA CARTE**
L 40,000–50,000, beverage extra
**MENÙ TURISTICO**
None
**COVER & SERVICE CHARGES**
Cover L 3,000, service included
**ENGLISH**
Enough

Anna and Aldo Bravi run a remarkable trattoria in the university district of San Lorenzo behind the train station. Opened by Aldo's grandmother as a wine shop, it was expanded into a restaurant by his father. Aldo has been on the payroll since he was seven, and now his sons and daughters and their spouses all work here. The wonderful food is the creation of his wife, Anna. The clientele is a wide sampling of locals—professors and students, workers in overalls, ladies draped in mink, businessmen making deals—all of whom are treated with the same degree of dignity and respect.

In the main room, with its arched brick ceilings, is a large open-fire oven and grill where seasonal game and other meats are cooked to perfection. Tables, set with yellow linens, are crowded into several rooms as well as outside on a raised terrace.

The value-packed menu is astonishing in its versatility, offering the kind of quality that brings diners back again and again. Order a liter of the house wine and a plate of the thinly sliced prosciutto with figs. Don't miss Anna's own fettuccini tossed with wild mushrooms or her *pappardelle* with wild boar sauce. If you appreciate wild game, nowhere in Rome is it prepared with more skill. Otherwise, the mutton stew is a smart alternative as are any of the grilled chops or fresh fish selections.

Desserts are all by Anna, and her repertoire is long and delicious. Just ask what she has made that day, and whatever you pick will be sweet and perfect.

## (71) TRATTORIA ABRUZZESE
### via Napoli, 3a/4

The generous cooking is more likely to please a hungry gourmand than a finicky gourmet at this two-room trattoria in the shadow of the opera. Red-coated waiters wearing black pants and bow ties serve a contented crew of diners who return again and again for straightforward food prepared with the best ingredients.

The best Cheap Eat is certainly the *menù turistico,* which includes everything from soup to service. The choices for each course are varied and include daily specials. The meat dishes are better than the fish, especially the soul-soothing *osso buco.* Typical Roman specialties of tripe or brains fried with artichokes offer different choices you can't get back home. If you stray from the set-price meal, you will pay more, but you will be able to indulge in the house pasta—*rigatoni bohème,* a cholesterol festival of cream cheese and sausage blanketed with Parmesan cheese.

For dessert, skip the prunes and the baked pears and go for the *mont blanc,* made with cream, whipped cream, and custard in a meringue covered with even more cream. Oh well, you won't have it every day!

**AREA**
Train station and opera

**TELEPHONE**
48-85-505

**OPEN**
Mon–Fri; Sat lunch only

**CLOSED**
Sun, Aug (3 weeks)

**HOURS**
Lunch noon–3:30 P.M., dinner 7–11 P.M.

**RESERVATIONS**
Not necessary

**CREDIT CARDS**
MC, V

**À LA CARTE**
L 38,000, beverage extra

**MENÙ TURISTICO**
L 25,000, 3 courses, cover and service included, beverage included

**COVER & SERVICE CHARGES**
Cover L 2,500, service included

**ENGLISH**
Yes, and *menù turistico* in English

## Restaurants in Trastevere

## (72) AL FONTANONE
### piazza Trilussa, 46 (Ponte Sisto)

Naturally, I recommend every entry in this book. I should know, I have been to them all, and in many cases, more than a few times. Some stand out more than others, and in Trastevere, Al Fontanone has always been one of my favorites. Joseph Pino, or Pino as everyone calls him, has been greeting guests at his popular restaurant for almost thirty years. The rustic interior with dried herbs and flowers hanging from the corners and along the wooden beams, the comfortable chairs placed around well-spaced yellow-clad tables, and Pino's heartfelt hospitality continue to make this a top pick.

I like to start my meal with a small sampling from the antipasti table, and then move on to the specialty of

**AREA**
Trastevere

**TELEPHONE**
58-17-312

**OPEN**
Mon, Wed–Sun

**CLOSED**
Tues, Aug 20–Sept 18, Christmas (1 week)

**HOURS**
Lunch 12:30–2:45 P.M., dinner 7:15–11:15 P.M.

**RESERVATIONS**
Advised

**CREDIT CARDS**
AMEX, MC, V

À LA CARTE
L 30,000, beverage extra

MENÙ TURISTICO
None

COVER & SERVICE CHARGES
Cover L 2,500, service included

ENGLISH
Yes, and English menu

the house, *fettuccine alla Fontanone,* a rich pasta with mushrooms, tuna, garlic, tomato, and fresh parsley. The noodles in this dish and all the other pastas are made right here. If you are going for a meat course, stellar choices are the *abbacchio al forno* (pink-roasted baby lamb), the strapping *osso buco* (veal shank with mushrooms or peas), or on a cold day, spicy sausage and polenta. In addition to the regular menu, wood-fired pizzas, *crostini,* and *bruschette* are available each evening. After two or three courses, the idea of dessert may seem almost impossible, but do order the house *tiramisù,* even if you share it or eat only a spoonful.

## (73) DA GIOVANNI OSTERIA E CUCINA
### via della Lungara, 41A

AREA
Trastevere

TELEPHONE
68-61-514

OPEN
Mon–Sat

CLOSED
Sun, Aug

HOURS
Lunch 12:30–3 P.M., dinner 7:30–10 P.M.

RESERVATIONS
Not accepted

CREDIT CARDS
None

À LA CARTE
L 18,000, beverage included

MENÙ TURISTICO
None

COVER & SERVICE CHARGES
Cover L 1,000, service included

ENGLISH
Minimal

For local color, Cheap Eats, and few other tourists, check out this hole-in-the-wall on via della Lungara, which runs along the Tiber River. It is definitely a family-run show. The padrone, Giovanni de Blasio, is a neighborhood fixture and his sister runs the *tabacceria* next door. Before opening at noon, grandchildren occupy some of the tables, while their mothers hurry about getting ready and writing out the daily menu.

There are two rooms. The front one has only nine tables and is "decorated" with coatracks, a clock, some dusty wine bottles, and copper pots with dried pasta sticking out of them. The green-and-white tablecloths are covered with paper. The small room in back is distinguished by hanging braids of garlic. Many regulars come in early to get their favorite table and catch up on local gossip. Be prepared to be squeezed next to a young student couple busy falling in love, a table full of boisterous workers in paint-spotted overalls downing their fourth glass of Chianti, or relatives of inmates from the Regina Coeli prison, which is nearby.

No one is here for inspirational cuisine. People eat here for the kind of simple, satisfying peasant food their grandmothers and mothers stopped cooking years ago. The handwritten menu is *almost* possible to decipher. To start, everyone orders a bowl of homemade egg fettuccine, lightly bathed in olive oil with a sprinkling of fresh herbs. Ambitious portions of roast veal, chicken, fresh fish, and grilled steaks follow, with the usual list of seasonal vegetables and salads available as extras. Dessert choices are narrow, so it is best to stay with the fresh fruit or the cake of the day if your sweet tooth insists.

## (74) LA GENSOLA
### piazza della Gensola, 15

Sicilian food prepared by two brothers and one of their wives—a sweet Polish lady who speaks English—has made this Trastevere trattoria a popular address.

If it is on the menu, try the *caponata,* a lusty mixture of eggplant, sweet peppers, olives, capers, celery, and clams. Another good beginning is the *alici marinati,* fresh anchovies marinated in lemon oil with parsley and chili pepper. If you are really an anchovy fan, order the *pasta con sarde* (pasta with anchovies) or the *alici alla Beccafino* (fresh anchovies stuffed with bread crumbs, Parmesan cheese, eggs, and a little garlic, then grilled). Veal lovers will appreciate the *scaloppine alla siciliana,* tender veal rounds lightly sautéed with olive oil, fresh tomatoes, and capers. Skip the ordinary house wine and select one of the reasonably priced bottles of Sicilian wine to best complement your meal. For dessert, order the *cassata alla siciliana,* a layered sponge cake flavored with liqueur and topped with pieces of candied fruit and icing. If you are too full for this, consider a glass of Sicilian sweet wine, either *vino alla mandorla* or *zibibbo di Sicilia,* which is slightly less sweet.

**AREA**
Trastevere
**TELEPHONE**
58-16-312
**OPEN**
Mon–Fri, Sat dinner only
**CLOSED**
Sun, Aug 15–31
**HOURS**
Lunch noon–3 P.M., dinner 8–11:30 P.M.
**RESERVATIONS**
Advised
**CREDIT CARDS**
None
**À LA CARTE**
L 33,000, beverage extra
**MENÙ TURISTICO**
None
**COVER & SERVICE CHARGES**
Cover L 2,000, service included
**ENGLISH**
Yes

## (75) MARIO'S
### via del Moro, 53/55

For serious budget dining in Trastevere, Mario's is a place that was discovered long ago by Cheap Eaters of all nationalities. Here you can forget all about imaginative dishes served with exotic sauces in elegant surroundings populated by beautiful people. Mario's is a remarkably plain, family-run restaurant where waitresses wear slippers and aprons tied around their middles and the prices have not kept pace with spiraling inflation.

For those who have yet to master the finer points of the Italian menu, it is printed in English. The *menù turistico* is a deal when you consider it includes three courses, wine, coffee, and the cover and service charges. For not much more, you can select from uncomplicated à la carte dishes, such as spaghetti with ricotta cheese and black pepper, *osso buco, scamorza ai ferri con prosciutto* (fried cheese with ham), or daily specials of gnocchi on Thursday, *baccalà* on Friday, and tripe on Saturday. In the winter, look for the apple cake made by Mario's sister-in-law.

**AREA**
Trastevere
**TELEPHONE**
58-03-809
**OPEN**
Mon–Sat
**CLOSED**
Sun, Aug
**HOURS**
Lunch noon–4 P.M., dinner 7 P.M.–midnight
**RESERVATIONS**
Not necessary
**CREDIT CARDS**
AMEX, MC, V
**À LA CARTE**
L 20,000–28,000, beverage included
**MENÙ TURISTICO**
L 18,000, 3 courses, cover and service included, beverage included
**COVER & SERVICE CHARGES**
Cover L 1,000, service included
**ENGLISH**
Yes, and English menu

## (76) PIZZERIA IVO
### via di San Francisco a Rippa, 157

**AREA**
Trastevere
**TELEPHONE**
58-17-082
**OPEN**
Mon, Wed–Sun
**CLOSED**
Tues, Aug
**HOURS**
Lunch noon–3 P.M., dinner
6 P.M.–1 A.M.
**RESERVATIONS**
Not accepted
**CREDIT CARDS**
None
**À LA CARTE**
L 15,000–20,000, beverage
included
**MENÙ TURISTICO**
None
**COVER & SERVICE CHARGES**
Cover L 2,000, service included
**ENGLISH**
Yes

If you go for lunch, you will miss the true spirit and fun of Ivo's. It is an evening place, full of thirty-somethings who like a lively, chaotic atmosphere with high-speed waiters and noisy elbow-to-elbow dining (and who do not mind standing in line waiting to get in). Inside, the walls are papered with photos of Italian soccer teams and the tables are jammed together. In the summer, tables are placed not only on the street but between parked cars. As you can imagine, the service out here is not brilliant.

So, what about the pizza? Not bad . . . and neither are the pastas. I would skip over the two or three meat dishes and plan on dessert elsewhere. A pizza along with a glass of wine or beer and a salad will get you out the door for not much more than L 18,000. While it won't have been a restful or romantic evening meal, you will have sampled a typical Roman favorite.

## (77) PIZZERIA PANATTONI
### viale Trastevere, 53/59 (beyond piazza Sonnino and McDonald's)

**AREA**
Trastevere
**TELEPHONE**
58-00-919
**OPEN**
Mon, Tues, Thur–Sun
**CLOSED**
Wed, Aug 8–28
**HOURS**
6 P.M.–2 A.M.
**RESERVATIONS**
Not accepted
**CREDIT CARDS**
None
**À LA CARTE**
L 12,000, beverage included
**MENÙ TURISTICO**
None
**COVER & SERVICE CHARGES**
No cover, service included
**ENGLISH**
Enough

The place may not look like much—in truth, it is known as *l'obitorio,* or "the morgue," because the tables are made of marble slabs. Despite the cold interior, it is the loudest, most crowded, and above all, cheapest pizzeria in Trastevere. If you time it right on a weekend night, you will be able to witness the pizza chefs turning out more than a hundred pizzas per hour to a loyal corps of young-at-heart diners who return often for the cheap food. As you can guess, service is casual, and the tables are smashed together in the interest of squeezing in as many people as possible. If pizza does not appeal, there are several bean dishes that are really good. Try the *fagioli di fiasco* (beans cooked in wine over an open fire), or the white beans with tuna, onions, or cabbage. Here is all the fiber and roughage you will need for a week! The uninspiring antipasti can be passed and so should the tired desserts.

## (78) TRATTORIA DA AUGUSTO
### piazza de'Renzi, 15

**AREA**
Trastevere
**TELEPHONE**
58-03-798

Trattoria da Augusto is a Trastevere institution that has been serving basic Roman food to legions of committed

Cheap Eaters for decades. It has been owned for fifty-plus years by Augusto, his wife, Leda, and their son, Sandro. Located on the piazza de'Renzi, it has no sign outside, absolutely no decor inside, and certainly no pretense anywhere.

The daily carbon-copied menu is handwritten in an Italian script that takes some detective work to decode. The locals know it by heart and thrive on the filling and predictable fare—big bowls of lentil soup on Monday, bean or vegetable soup on Wednesday, gnocchi on Thursday, and fish on Tuesday and Friday. Everything is washed down with large amounts of house wine, and a good time is had by all.

**OPEN**
Mon–Fri, Sat lunch only
**CLOSED**
Sun, Aug
**HOURS**
Lunch noon–3 P.M., dinner 8–11 P.M.
**RESERVATIONS**
Not accepted
**CREDIT CARDS**
None
**À LA CARTE**
L 18,000, beverage extra
**MENÙ TURISTICO**
None
**COVER & SERVICE CHARGES**
Cover L 1,000, service included
**ENGLISH**
Yes

## Restaurants near the Trevi Fountain

### (79) COLLINE EMILIANE
### via degli Avignonesi, 22

In major Italian cities, quality has its price. To discover what you will have to pay to eat a step or two above the ordinary, reserve a table at Colline Emiliane. Don't panic . . . prices aren't *that* high. Just remember: you get what you pay for and the days of the $5 meal with a great bottle of Chianti are over *forever*.

The decor here is not much, especially if you forget to make a reservation and get stuck in the back room, where it gets hot and smoky as the meal wears on. The Bolognese food makes up in spades for the lack of interior zing. All of the pastas are made by the owner's wife, and I'm sure you will agree that they are super. The *tagliatelle con porcini* (pasta with mushrooms) and the *tortelli di zucca* (pumpkin dumplings) are both worth a trip across town. To go all out, treat yourself to one of their truffle specialties, which range from a salad with truffles to veal cutlet and cheese fondue. All is fit for a king and priced accordingly. For the *secondi piatti* (main course) stay with any veal preparation or the mixed boiled meats served with green sauce.

Don't leave without trying the pear tart with raisins and pine nuts or the *budino al cioccolato,* a chocolate custard.

**AREA**
Trevi Fountain
**TELEPHONE**
48-17-538
**OPEN**
Mon–Thur, Sat, Sun
**CLOSED**
Fri, Aug
**HOURS**
Lunch 12:30–2:45 P.M., dinner 7:30–10:45 P.M.
**RESERVATIONS**
Essential
**CREDIT CARDS**
None
**À LA CARTE**
L 50,000–60,000, beverage extra
**MENÙ TURISTICO**
None
**COVER & SERVICE CHARGES**
Cover L 3,500, service included
**ENGLISH**
Yes, and English menu

## (80) GIOIA MIA
### via degli Avignonesi, 34

**AREA**
Trevi Fountain

**TELEPHONE**
48-82-784

**OPEN**
Mon–Sat

**CLOSED**
Sun, Aug

**HOURS**
Lunch 12:15–3 P.M., dinner
7–11 P.M.

**RESERVATIONS**
Advised

**CREDIT CARDS**
AMEX, DC, MC, V

**À LA CARTE**
L 35,000, beverage extra

**MENÙ TURISTICO**
None

**COVER & SERVICE CHARGES**
Cover L 2,500, 10% service
added

**ENGLISH**
Yes

Gioia Mia has a well-deserved reputation for consistently good food, service, and prices. When you arrive, the tantalizing smells and busy waiters serving the happy crowd tell you this will be great, and it is. The inside is typical trattoria, with hanging sausages and peppers, bowls of seasonally fresh fruit and vegetables in the window, wines displayed on high shelves, and for fun, a stuffed boar's head sporting red plastic glasses and in the back a clothesline with baby clothes clipped to it.

Smart diners often skip the antipasti table and begin their feast with one of the twenty-five or thirty pasta offerings. There is something here for everyone, from gnocchi, crêpes, cannelloni, risotto, and ravioli to their rich signature pasta—*pappardelle alla Gran Duca,* ham, mushrooms, tomatoes, cognac, and cream. Carnivores will be hard-pressed to decide between the beautifully grilled baby lamb chops or the *cuscinetto alla Gioa Mia,* veal and ham wrapped around cheese, served in a white wine cream sauce topped with mushrooms. Those with trencherman appetites can attack the one-pound *bistecca alla fiorentina*: an enormous grilled steak that is almost enough for three people.

The two desserts to keep in mind, if you can possibly do it, are the *mille foglie della casa* (a flaky pastry layered with thick cream, chocolate, and whipped cream) and the *pera alla Gioia* (a pear cake covered with whipped cream and chocolate). No one said this would be a meal for someone on Weight Watcher's!

## (81) PICCOLO ARANCIO
### vicolo Scanderbeg, 112 (off via del Lavatore)

**AREA**
Trevi Fountain

**TELEPHONE**
67-86-139, 67-80-766

**OPEN**
Tues–Sun

**CLOSED**
Mon, Aug

**HOURS**
Lunch 12:30–3 P.M., dinner
7 P.M.–midnight

**RESERVATIONS**
Advised for dinner and holidays

**CREDIT CARDS**
AMEX, DC, MC, V

Many restaurants near the Trevi Fountain have given in to the temptation to feed as many tourists as possible, serving barely adequate food at prices as high as the traffic will bear. You will find none of this at Piccolo Arancio, a popular location where Romans mix happily with the tourists. The Cialfi family also owns Settimio all'Arancio (see page 104) and Arancio d'Oro (see page 97). The menus are almost the same at all three locations.

From the outside, it looks just like dozens of others: white walls, beamed ceilings, a bouquet or two of flowers, and a posted menu. If you arrive early, you will see the family in action. Grandfather usually sits at a table shelling peas or stuffing zucchini flowers, which will later be deep fried. One of the daughters-in-law will be minding a baby or two, while another will be helping in the kitchen. The family approach carries over to the service, which is warm yet still professional.

The food is substantial. The *pappardelle al sugo di lepre* (fettuccine with rabbit sauce) and the pasta with zucchini flowers in a light curry cream sauce are still my favorites. On Tuesday and Friday the menu is devoted entirely to fish. The delicate sole with a lemon and wine sauce is always a sure bet. For a light, easy dessert, order the vanilla ice cream with strawberry sauce or the lemon mousse.

**À LA CARTE**
L 33,000, beverage extra

**MENÙ TURISTICO**
None

**COVER & SERVICE CHARGES**
Cover L 2,500, service included

**ENGLISH**
Yes, and English menu

## (82) TRATTORIA SCAVOLINO
### vocolo Scavolino, 72/74

A meal at Trattoria Scavolino will be pleasing to the eye, fulfilling for the stomach, and easy on the wallet. Tucked away on vocolo Scavolino near the Trevi Fountain, it is just enough away from the tourist trail to remain honest and local. The healthy cooking is light, and you can feel free to order as little as you want without incurring the wrath of snooty waiters or grumbling management.

The *paglia e fieno* (green and white noodles with mushrooms, peas, ham, and cream) or their specialty, Sardinian *gnocchetti* with tomato cream sauce, make terrific beginnings. An almost guilt-free lunch might be the big farmer's salad, bursting with seasonal greens, ripe red tomatoes, black olives, and almonds, along with a slice of the special house dessert, apple strudel cake. For a change of pace, try the assortment of typical Italian cheeses. When accompanied by a basket of fresh bread, a glass of wine, and your favorite person across the table . . . who could ask for anything more on a Roman holiday?

**AREA**
Trevi Fountain

**TELEPHONE**
67-90-974

**OPEN**
Mon–Fri, Sun

**CLOSED**
Sat

**HOURS**
Lunch 12:30–3 P.M., dinner 7–11 P.M.

**RESERVATIONS**
Not necessary

**CREDIT CARDS**
AMEX, MC, V

**À LA CARTE**
L 15,000–18,000, beverage extra

**MENÙ TURISTICO**
None

**COVER & SERVICE CHARGES**
No cover, 10% service added for dinner and on holidays

**ENGLISH**
Yes

# Restaurants near the Vatican and Piazza Cavour

## (83) DA MARCO FORMICHELLA
### via Silla, 26

Da Marco is not a special occasion destination in the mainstream of Rome's tourist beat. Therefore it has remained a genuine neighborhood trattoria catering to

AREA
Vatican

TELEPHONE
32-12-362

OPEN
Mon–Sat

CLOSED
Sun, Aug, Christmas and
New Year's

HOURS
Lunch 12:30–3 P.M., dinner
8–11 P.M.

RESERVATIONS
Essential, especially for dinner

CREDIT CARDS
AMEX, MC, V

À LA CARTE
L 35,000, beverage extra

MENÙ TURISTICO
None

COVER & SERVICE CHARGES
Cover L 3,000, 10% service
added

ENGLISH
Limited

regular diners who appreciate the consistently high quality of the food, from first course to last.

The white interior is decorated with a mixture of this and that—a collection of lighted Greek and Roman busts, mirrors, and paintings—while busy black-panted waiters zoom from one table to another.

The food is a bracing blend of Roman favorites that have real star appeal. Start by sharing the *antipasti assortiti,* a plate of quickly fried zucchini, shrimp, stuffed olives, and cheese and potato puffs. Lighter appetites can start with the tossed tomatoes and salad greens, but frankly, it is not as interesting as the antipasti mix. There are sixteen pastas, ranging from a plain spaghetti with *ragù* to a heady *linguine all'astice* (with lobster), several risottos, and for the undecided, a sampling of several of their pastas. A smattering of pizzas is available as well as a full roster of meats and sides of vegetables.

The best dessert is not listed, but ask for the dessert *misto,* a large assortment of bite-sized pieces of cheesecake, macaroons, various *biscotti,* and shelled nuts. It is just the right ending to a meal in a place you will want to keep to yourself so that it will be just the same every time you return.

### (84) GIRARROSTO TOSCANO
### via Germanico 58/60

AREA
Vatican

TELEPHONE
39-72-5717, 39-72-3373

OPEN
Tues–Sun

CLOSED
Mon, Aug 10–31

HOURS
Lunch 12:30–3 P.M., dinner
8 P.M.–midnight

RESERVATIONS
Essential as far in advance as
possible

CREDIT CARDS
AMEX, DC

À LA CARTE
L 50,000–60,000, beverage
extra

MENÙ TURISTICO
None

The area around the Vatican has been declared a dining wasteland by many because of all the tacky and overpriced tourists joints, which charge their one-time diners top dollar for bottom quality. You need not despair—there is a bright star on the horizon at Girarrosto Toscano. This is a marvelous find where the tables are packed with boisterous, gesticulating Italians, many of whom look like they have been firmly planted at the same table discussing the same gossip or politics for years.

The restaurant is so good and so popular that reservations are required at least one day in advance. Seating is in a large two-room space dominated by a huge exhibition kitchen and open grill. The specialties are the foods and wines of Tuscany.

I think it is best to get started by ordering the hand-cut prosciutto or a light soup to save room for a bracing veal or beefsteak grilled over the coals. As a garnish, consider forgoing the usual vegetables and ordering the *fagioli toscani all'olio,* white beans cooked in olive oil with a liberal lacing of garlic. They are so creamy and wonderful . . . I dream of having them right this minute. If you add a small salad and a bottle of good Chianti Classico, you are bound to be pleased. Another strong recommendation is the house dessert, which has been served since the day they opened. It is a cream cake with hot chocolate sauce poured over at the last minute. This is the perfect cap on your Big Splurge in Rome.

COVER & SERVICE CHARGES
Cover L 3,000, 15% service added
ENGLISH
Yes

## (85) HOSTARIA DEI BASTIONI
### via Leone IV, 29

Due to the constant influx of tourists to the Vatican, finding a decent meal at a fair price can become almost a mission here. All Cheap Eating hope is not lost, however, thanks to the Hostaria dei Bastioni, found through a tiny doorway below street level on the busy via Leone IV. Inside, the pine basement dining room is overshadowed by a large television set that is usually on. Red-and-white tablecloths, a shelf with wine bottles, and a kitchen to one side finish the decor. The appreciative diners are made up largely of businesspeople, contented neighborhood regulars, and smart visitors.

At this homey, hospitable eatery, you will find moderately priced seafood and a host of other familiar Roman dishes. The antipasti selection is limited. Just have a look at the display and see what looks best . . . it changes constantly. You can't go wrong with the *fettuccine alla Bastioni,* made with cream, bacon, fresh tomato, and a hint of orange. The risotto with seafood, the veal with potatoes, or the assorted roast meats, also served with potatoes, are safe bets if you do not go for a fish main course. The house *tiramisù* or a seasonal fruit make the best ending.

AREA
Vatican
TELEPHONE
39-72-30-34
OPEN
Mon–Sat
CLOSED
Sun, July 15–31
HOURS
Lunch noon–3 P.M., dinner 7–11:30 P.M.
RESERVATIONS
Advised
CREDIT CARDS
AMEX, MC, V
À LA CARTE
L 30,000, beverage extra
MENÙ TURISTICO
None
COVER & SERVICE CHARGES
No cover, 10% service added
ENGLISH
Yes, and English menu

## (86) PIZZA RUSTICA AL GRACCHI
### via dei Gracchi, 7

The pizza ovens work overtime here, as the chefs turn out the big trays of lip-smacking pizza as fast as they can sell it in this take-out pizza stand. Food prices along this strip of real estate near the Vatican tend to reach the outer limits of heaven, so it is nice to find a convenient pit stop for refueling before or after tackling the Vatican's "D" plan: a five-hour walking tour. When you order, you choose the type and size of your slice from twelve to fifteen varieties, which are then cut and sold by the

AREA
Vatican
TELEPHONE
37-23-733
OPEN
Mon–Sat
CLOSED
Sun, Aug
HOURS
10 A.M.–8 P.M., continuous service
RESERVATIONS
Not accepted

CREDIT CARDS
None
À LA CARTE
L 800–2,300 per 100 grams
MENÙ TURISTICO
None
COVER & SERVICE CHARGES
None
ENGLISH
Limited to none

weight. You will probably not snag either of their two red plastic chairs, so plan to take this one with you.

## (87) TAVOLA D'ORO
### via Marianna Dionigi, 37

AREA
Near Vatican and piazza Cavour
TELEPHONE
31-12-601
OPEN
Mon–Sat
CLOSED
Sun, Aug 15–Sept 15,
Christmas (2 weeks)
HOURS
Lunch noon–3 P.M., dinner
7–11:30 P.M.
RESERVATIONS
Advised
CREDIT CARDS
None
À LA CARTE
L 30,000, beverage extra
MENÙ TURISTICO
None
COVER & SERVICE CHARGES
Cover L 2,000, 20% service
added
ENGLISH
None

Tavola d'Oro is a mom-and-pop restaurant on a busy neighborhood shopping street across the Ponte Cavour from via Condotti. Everything is made in-house, from the pasta to the *gelato*. If you are lucky enough to have the right seat, you can watch Mamma in the kitchen performing magic on all she prepares. The food is Sicilian, and that means hot, spicy, and very, very good. The one drawback of this postage-stamp-size place is the service, which can be downright rude if, for reasons you will never fathom, they take a dislike to you. If you do not speak some Italian, or at least have a food dictionary with you, you will be at a big disadvantage because no one will make any attempt at English.

If you have never had Sicilian *caponata* (eggplant, capers, and black olives in extra-virgin olive oil), here is your best shot in Rome. The Sicilian sausage with cheese and coriander seeds is another worthy option, and so is the potato-based pasta topped with eggplant and tomato sauce. To get the full effect of the meal, order a bottle of Sicilian wine, and for dessert, promise me you will save room for the cannoli filled with whipped sweet cheese and dusted with powdered sugar and chocolate. It is melt-in-your-mouth wonderful.

**NOTE:** Just because the weekly closure day and hours of operation are posted does not mean that they are kept. To avoid finding them closed for no apparent reason, please call ahead to be sure they are open.

## (88) TRATTORIA DINO
### via Tacito, 80

AREA
Vatican, piazza Cavour
TELEPHONE
36-10-305
OPEN
Mon–Sat lunch only

For lire watchers in search of homecooking near the Vatican and piazza Cavour, the Marrocu's family-run jewel is a smart choice. Once I looked inside the tiny eight-table room and smelled the wonderful aromas floating from the tiny kitchen in back, I knew this was where I would eat lunch. The whitewashed, rough stucco walls are hung with wood carvings, braids of garlic, dried herbs, old cooking pans, and pretty baskets. Each day a new menu is handwritten on little pieces of scratch paper and placed on the tables. The good food appeals to those who love to tackle a serious meal, beginning with a filling bowl of gnocchi or lasagna, followed by roast chicken or rolled beef, stuffed and served with peas, and accompanied by a glass or two of the house Chianti. If all this is not enough, there is dessert—meringue cookies with lemon or a *crostata*—and all for a final tab everyone can appreciate.

**CLOSED**
Sun, Aug

**HOURS**
12:45–4 P.M.

**RESERVATIONS**
Not necessary

**CREDIT CARDS**
None

**À LA CARTE**
L 18,000–20,000, beverage extra

**MENÙ TURISTICO**
None

**COVER & SERVICE CHARGES**
Cover L 2,500, service included

**ENGLISH**
Sometimes

## (89) TRATTORIA MEMMO
### piazza Cavour, 14/15

Hearty cooking speaks to us all. You can always find it at Memmo's, a busy neighborhood trattoria with basic Italian food and courteous service from timeless waiters in long white aprons.

The food is much more tempting than the plain surroundings. The menu boasts an appealing array of seasonal specialties, as well as tried-and-true favorites that keep the regulars returning day after day. Everyone knows that on Tuesday and Friday the special will be *pasta alle vongole veraci*: spaghetti with fresh clams. On Wednesday, the chunky minestrone soup is the highlight, and on Thursday, of course, the most popular dish is potato gnocchi. On Saturday, tripe headlines the menu, and for the family Sunday lunch, big portions of lasagna and cannelloni are consumed. There are also delicious daily pastas and meat dishes and a guilt-laden selection of desserts.

**AREA**
Vatican, piazza Cavour

**TELEPHONE**
68-75-065

**OPEN**
Tues–Sun

**CLOSED**
Mon, Aug

**HOURS**
Lunch 12:30–3 P.M., dinner 7:30–11:30 P.M.

**RESERVATIONS**
Not necessary

**CREDIT CARDS**
DC, MC, V

**À LA CARTE**
L 33,000, beverage extra

**MENÙ TURISTICO**
None

**COVER & SERVICE CHARGES**
Cover L 2,000, 13% service added

**ENGLISH**
Yes

# Food Shopping in Rome

Rome has many food markets. The most central and interesting are listed here. Most districts also have their own local food markets that usually operate from 7 A.M. until 12:30 P.M.

## INDOOR/OUTDOOR MARKETS

### Campo de' Fiori

*Campo de' Fiori*
*Mon–Sat 8 A.M.–1 P.M.*

Campo de' Fiori has been a focus of Roman life since the sixteenth century. Today the outdoor market attracts loads of tourists and is probably the most charming.

### Mercato dei Fiori

*Via Trionfale, 47–49*
*Tues only 10:30 A.M.–1 P.M.*

An indoor wholesale flower market with bargain prices that is open to the public on Tuesday morning only.

### Piazza Cosimato

*Trastevere, three blocks west of piazza Santa Maria*
*Mon–Sat 7 A.M.–1 P.M.*

A smaller market but with a good selection.

### Piazza Testaccio

*Piazza Testaccio*
*Mon–Sat 8 A.M.–1 P.M.*

This is in a working-class neighborhood with market prices to match.

### Piazza dell'Unita

*Piazza dell'Unita, off via Cola di Rienzo at Vatican end of the street*
*Mon–Sat 8 A.M.–1 P.M.*

There are wonderful selections and good prices here.

### Piazza Vittorio Emanuele

*Piazza Vittorio Emanuele, a few blocks south of Santa Maria Maggiore*
*Mon–Sat 6:30 A.M.–1:30 P.M.*

This big and busy market has everything from fish and produce to dairy products, meat, and dry goods. Watch out for gypsies who cruise through in packs about an hour before the market closes.

### Via dell'Arancio

*Via dell'Arancio, off via Tomacelli at end of via di Ripetta*

*Mon–Sat 8 A.M.–1 P.M.*

This small market in a high-end neighborhood makes up in quality for what it lacks in size. The few stalls sell only prime produce. If you keep going back to the same stall, after four or five visits you will be treated like a regular.

## SUPERMARKETS

### Castroni

*Via Cola di Rienzo, 19*

*Mon–Sat 7:45 A.M.–8 P.M.*

*Credit Cards: MC, V*

This is a wonderland of regional specialties, plus it has the largest selection of imported food in Rome. They will pack but not ship. Prices are on the high side, but if you are having Skippy extra-chunk peanut butter withdrawal pangs, here is the place to satisfy your fix.

### Catena

*Via Appia Nuova, 9 (San Giovanni)*

*Mon 3:30–7:30 P.M.; Tues–Sat 9:30 A.M.–1:30 P.M., 3:30–7:30 P.M.*

*No credit cards*

This luxury grocery store has one of the largest supplies of wrapped candy, purchased by the 100 grams. You'll also find vintage wines and liquors, coffees, hams, and cheeses as well as regional specialties.

### Franchi

*Via Cola di Rienzo, 204*

*Mon–Sat 8 A.M.–9 P.M.*

*Credit Cards: AMEX, MC, V*

A rival to Castroni, Franchi has an enormous selection of ham and cheese. Its large deli section is handy for picnics.

### Standa

*Via Trastevere*

*Via Cola di Rienzo*

*Viale Regina Margherita*

*Mon 3:30–7:30 P.M., Tues–Sat 9 A.M.–7:30 P.M.*

*Credit Cards: MC, V*

A supermarket and a dimestore-quality department store, Standa is good if you need a few quick things. Most produce is prepackaged, but prices are good.

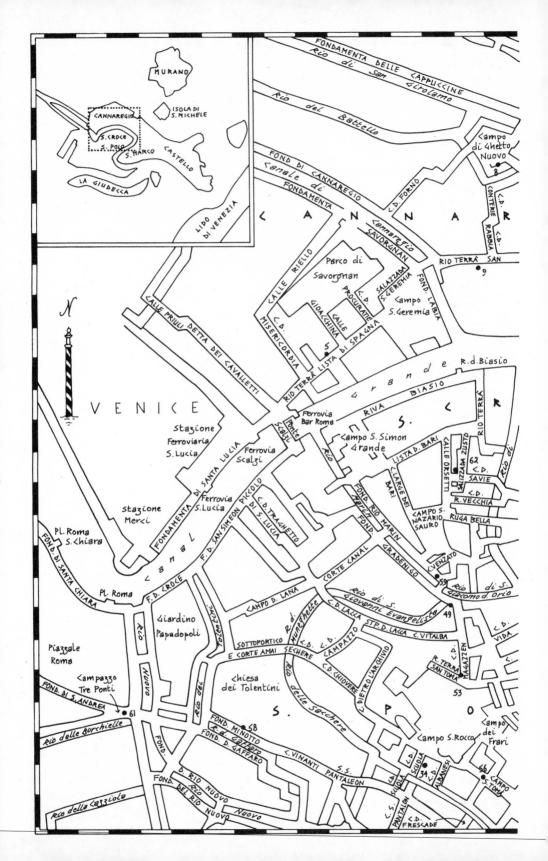

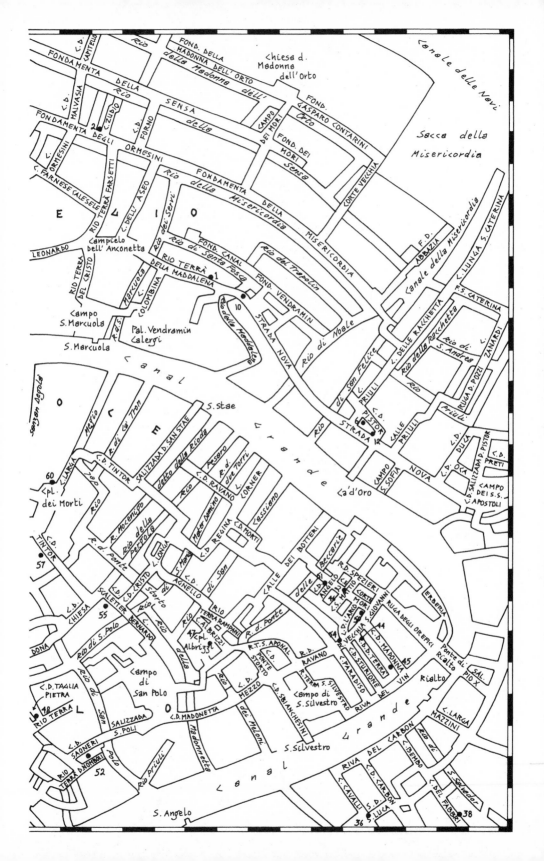

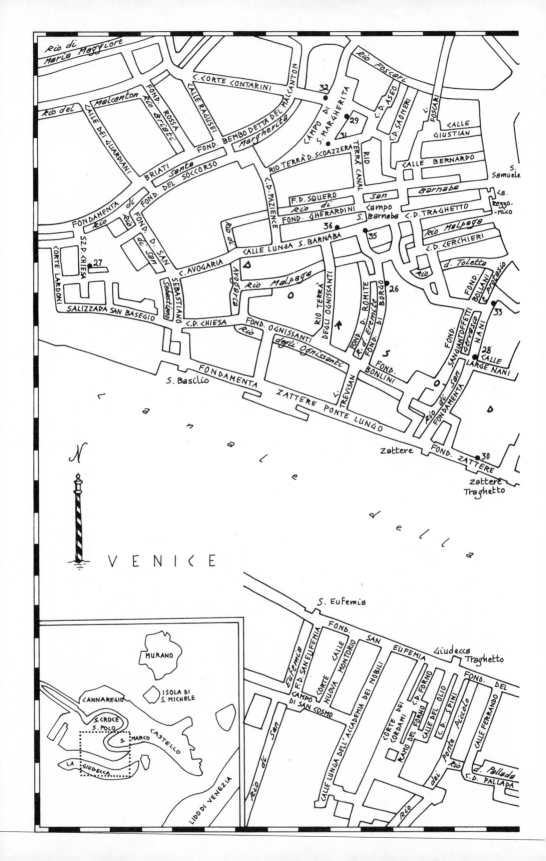

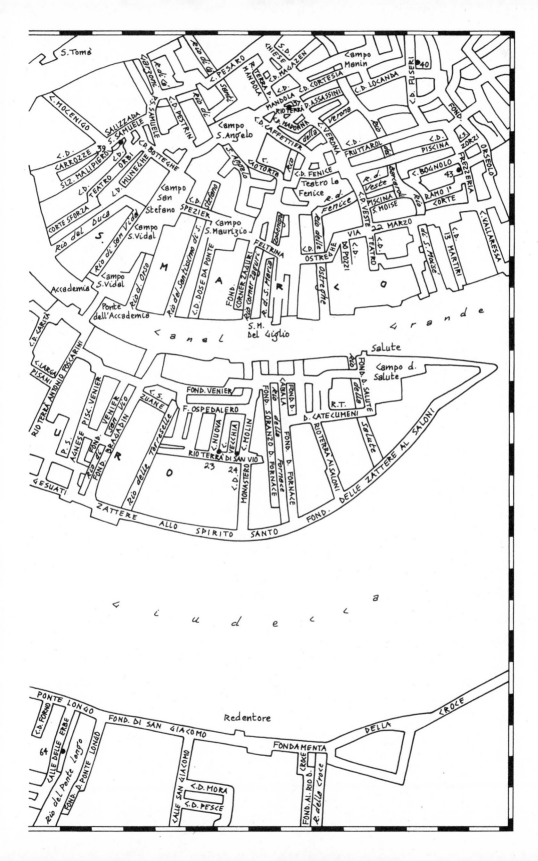

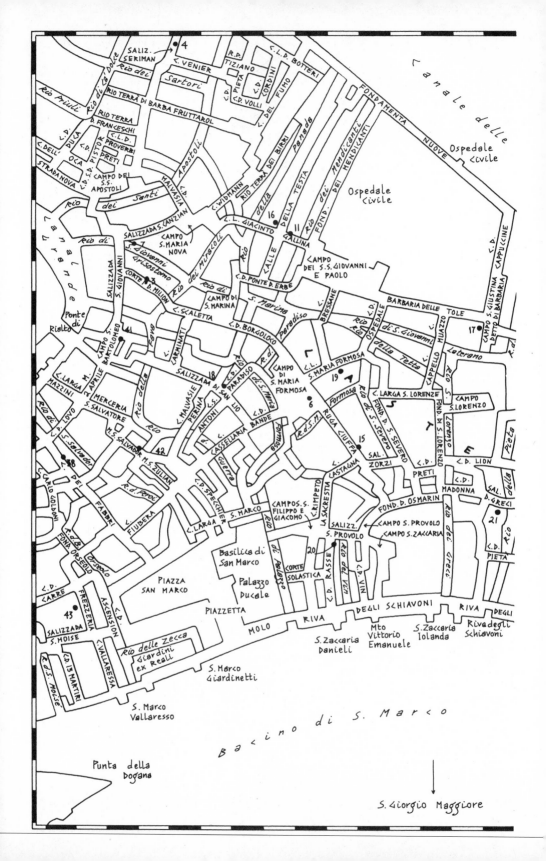

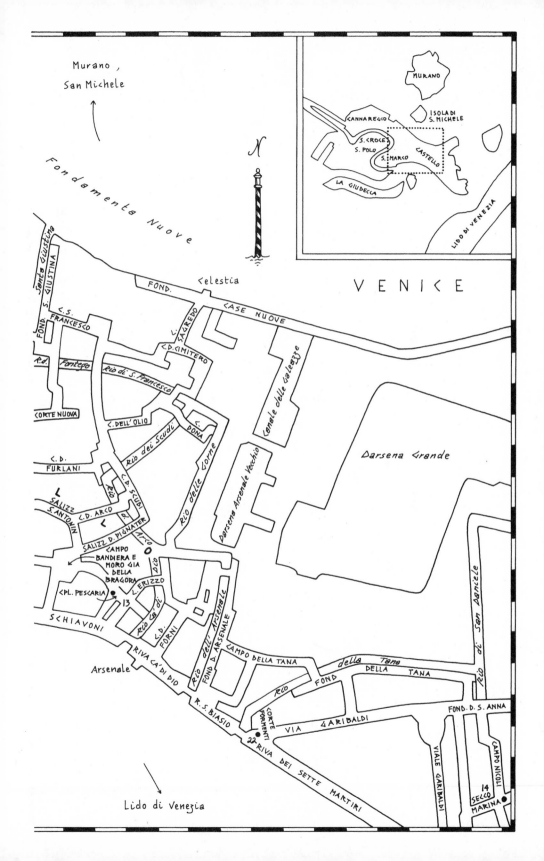

Murano,
San Michele

Fondamenta Nuove

VENICE

MURANO

ISOLA DI
S. MICHELE

CANNAREGIO

S. CROCE
S. POLO
S. MARCO
CASTELLO

LA GIUDECCA

LIDO DI VENEZIA

N

Celestia

FOND.

CASE NUOVE

Santa Giustina

C. S.
FRANCESCO

FOND. S.

FOND.

R.d.  Fontego

C. DELL'OLIO

CORTE NUOVA

C. D.
FURLANI

Rio di S. Francesco

Rio dei Scudi

V. SAGREDO

C.D. CIMITERO

C.
DONA

Canale delle Galeazze

Darsena Grande

Darsena Arsenale Vecchio

Rio delle Gorne

C. D. SCUDI

RIO

SALIZZ
S. ANTONIN

C.D. ARCO

SALIZZ. D. PIGNATER

CAMPO
BANDIERA E
MORO GIA
DELLA
BRAGORA

RIO

C. ERIZZO

L.
ARCO

RIO
D.

C. PL. PESCARIA

13

SCHIAVONI

Rio di
C. D.
FORNI

RIO
DELL'ARSENALE

FOND. D. ARSENALE

CAMPO DELLA TANA

della  Tana

FOND  DELLA  TANA

Rio di. San Daniele

RIVA CA' DI DIO

Arsenale

R. S. BIASIO

RIO

CORTE
FORMENTI

22

RIVA DEI SETTE MARTIRI

VIA  GARIBALDI

FOND. D. S. ANNA

VIALE
GARIBALDI

CAMPO NICOLI

14
SECCO
MARINA

Lido di Venezia

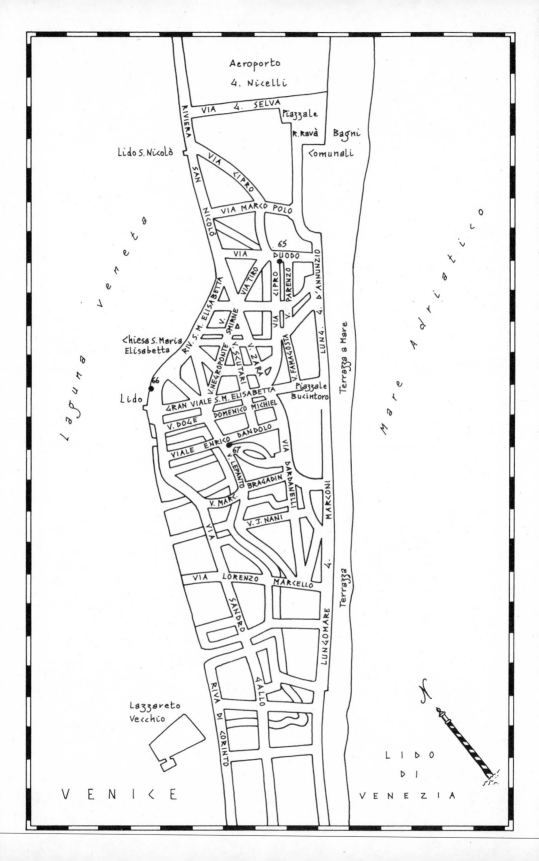

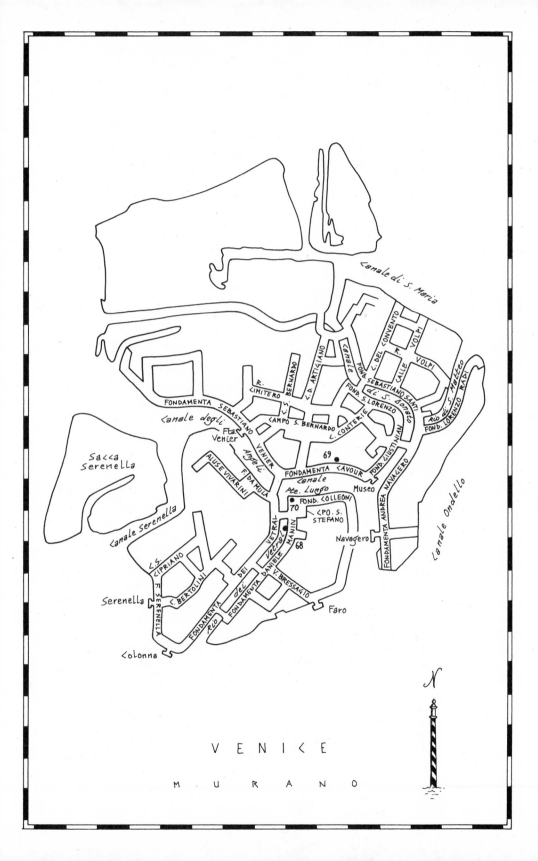

Canale di S. Maria

Canale di S. Maria

L. DEL CONVENTO

R. VOLPI

CALLE VOLPI

FOND SEBASTIANO SANTI

Rio di S. Matteo

R. CIMITERO

R. BERNARDO

L. D. ARTICIANO

canale

FOND di S. Donato

FOND. S. LORENZO

FOND. LORENZO RADI

FONDAMENTA SEBASTIANO

Canale degli

V. V.

CAMPO S. BERNARDO

L. CONTERIE

FOND. GIUSTINIAN

Fta Venier

VENIER

Angeli

69

FONDAMENTA CAVOUR

FONDAMENTA ANDREA NAVAGERO

Sacca Serenella

ALUISE VIVARINI

F. DA MULA

Canale

Museo

Canale Ondello

Pte. Lungo

FOND. COLLEONI

70

CPO. S. STEFANO

Canale Serenella

VETRAI

DEI

MANIN

68

Navagero

L. S. CIPRIANO

L. BERTOLINI

DANIELE

V. BRESSAGIO

F. SERENELLA

FONDAMENTA

RIO

FONDAMENTA DANIELE

Serenella

Faro

Colonna

V E N I C E

M U R A N O

N

# Venice

**Venetians . . . know all too well that they are picturesque, in Venice one never loses the sense that life is being staged for the onlooker.**

>—*Jonathan Raban,* Arabia through the Looking Glass, *1979*

**When I went to Venice, my dream became my address.**

>—*Marcel Proust, 1906*

Founded over fifteen hundred years ago on a cluster of mud flats, Venice came Europe's trading post between the East and West, reaching the height of its power in the fifteenth century. Although it no longer enjoys the same elite status, it remains a glorious reflection of its rich past, while depending for its income on the mass of visitors who arrive every year to marvel at her glorious relics.

In Venice, one always has the feeling of being suspended in time. Little has changed over the centuries to diminish the harmony of colors, lights, and sounds that float dreamlike over the canals and lagoons. Composed of more than 100 islets and 150 canals linked together by 400 bridges, it is little wonder that getting lost is so easy, even for a native. However, becoming hopelessly lost in the maze of *rios, campos, and campiellos* (see "Venetian Street Terms" below) will be one of the most pleasurable experiences of your visit to this romantic city on the Adriatic.

Since you cannot drive a car, hop a bus, or hail a cab, what you will do in Venice is walk, walk, and walk. To save yourself supreme confusion, it is necessary to become familiar with the six districts, or *sestieri,* that make up the city. They are San Marco, Castello, Cannaregio, San Polo, Dorsoduro, and Santa Croce. Addresses are usually given only by the district and number (i.e., Dorsoduro 3437), often omitting the name of the street. All of the listings in the Venice section of *Cheap Eats in Italy* include the name of the street, the number, and the district (i.e., calle dell' Oro, 5678, Dorsoduro). This will help, but you may still get lost; street names may repeat in more than one district, some buildings have more than one set of numbers, and addresses close to one another mathematically may indicate buildings at opposite ends of the district, since within *each* district there are some six thousand numbers with no clearcut sequence. It is just as bizarre as it sounds, and it often leads to hair tearing and extreme frustration, especially when you try to use logic.

Though you may be lost . . . *do not panic.* Look for the yellow signs posted throughout the city to find the direction you want. For example: Look for the sign saying Rialto, the bridge that connects the San Marco district with San Polo, when you are going to shop at the Rialto Bridge. Accademia is your direction if you want to see the Guggenheim collection. If you are going back to get your car parked on land, watch for signs saying Piazzale Roma. If your destination is St. Mark's Square, look for signs pointing to San Marco. If you are leaving Venice on the train, go in the direction marked *ferrovia* (train station).

Venice celebrates a number of holidays (*feste*). The most important is Carnivale, held during the ten days before Lent and ending on Shrove Tuesday with a masked ball for the elite and dancing in St. Mark's Square for the rest of us. Crowds during this time defy description. Unless you enjoy elbow-to-elbow, pushing mob scenes and the-sky-is-the-limit prices in hotels and restaurants, it is best to avoid this time in Venice.

If you think food is expensive in Florence and Rome, you have not yet eaten in Venice, where even for Italians used to runaway inflation dining out is considered expensive. While Venice is a city of romantic enchantment, the high cost of living here and the endless flow of tourists keep the prices in the stratosphere. The best word-of-mouth recommendation for a Venetian restaurant is that the prices are not *too* high. My own feeling is that the short-term visitor to Venice should seriously consider casting aside thoughts of great economy and take the philosophical view that he or she may never pass this way again. This is not to say that good-value restaurants do not exist, because they do and I have found many wonderful ones. I am just warning you that you will probably spend more for food in Venice than you want to.

One good way to shave food costs is to lunch at a snack bar. Most Venetians do, and many order a plate of *cicchetti*: little appetizers similar to Spanish tapas. Another option is a plump *tremezzino*: a sandwich filled with almost anything you can think of. The Cheapest Eat will be a picnic you make up yourself from foods bought at a market or deli.

Venetian cuisine often comes from the sea, such as *granseole* (spider crabs), *molecche* (soft-shell crabs), and *seppie in nero* (squid cooked in its own black ink and usually served with pasta or polenta). When ordering at a restaurant, remember that on Sunday and Monday the Rialto Fish Market is closed, so any fish served on these days will not be fresh that day. Risotto is the favored starch, sauced with delicate seafood or tender seasonal vegetables. Polenta appears not only with fish but with the famous *fegato alla veneziana*: calves' liver with onions. Pastries and sweets abound. Try the ring-shaped cookies called *bussolai,* which are the specialty of Burano. Particular foods are traditional to eat on certain feast days. During Carnivale you will see small doughnuts known as *frittelle,* which come plain, with fruit (*con frutta*), or cream (*con crema*). When you buy a bagful, be sure to eat them almost on the spot because they do not keep well.

While most restaurants in other cities take their annual holidays in either July or August, in Venice the most popular months to close, in addition to July and August, are December, January, and February until the beginning of Carnivale, when the dampness and all-embracing cold of Venice subside.

Venice is also home to a group of independent restaurateurs called Ristoranti della Buona Accoglienza. This organization pledges a proper price-to-quality ratio, the use of fine products, and fine service in an agreeable atmosphere. Most of these restaurants are Big Splurges, but you are virtually guaranteed a wonderful meal. If you have any complaints about the food or service in any of the member restaurants, please call 52-39-896, or write to them at Castella Postale No. 624, 30100 Venezia, Italy. The members listed in *Cheap Eats in Italy* are:

Ai Gondolieri, page 154
Al Covo, page 147
Alla Madonna, page 165
Caffè Orientale, page 167
Fiaschetteria Toscana, page 144
Ignazio, page 169
Osteria da Fiore, page 171

**Venetian Street Terms**

| | |
|---|---|
| *Calle* | main alleyway |
| *Campo* | square, usually with a church on it with the same name as the square |
| *Campiello* | small square |
| *Corte* | courtyard |
| *Fondamenta* | pavement along a section of water |
| *Piscina* | former pool |
| *Ramo* | small side street |
| *Rio* | canal |
| *Riva* | major stretch of pavement along water |
| *Ruga* | main shopping street |
| *Salizzada* | sometimes spelled *salizada,* the main street of a district |
| *Sestiere* | district |
| *Sottoportico* | small alley running beneath a building |

## RESTAURANTS IN VENICE
### Cannaregio

*Restaurants marked with an asterisk (*) are considered Big Splurges.

# Restaurants in Cannaregio

## (1) ALLA MADDALENA
### rio Terra della Maddalena, 2348

Where to go when you find yourself stranded in the dining desert around the train station and do not want to settle for the unappetizing tourist food that is the rule rather than the exception here? One answer is Alla Maddalena, a fine place to come for a sandwich, a plate of rigatoni, *tagliatelle,* or the daily hot special. All the food is made fresh daily and in some cases in limited supply, so when they run out of roast beef or pasta of the day, you are out of luck. Desserts are brought in, so I recommend going to the *gelateria* across the street and having a scoop or two.

At Alla Maddalena, you can enjoy your repast standing at the bar and kibitzing with the friendly bartenders or sitting on a tall stool by the window and watching the foot traffic hustle by.

**AREA**
Cannaregio
**TELEPHONE**
72-07-23
**OPEN**
Mon–Sat bar and lunch only
**CLOSED**
Sun, Aug
**HOURS**
7:30 A.M.–9 P.M.; hot lunch 12:30–2 P.M.
**RESERVATIONS**
Not accepted
**CREDIT CARDS**
None
**À LA CARTE**
From L 6,000, beverage extra
**MENÙ TURISTICO**
None
**COVER & SERVICE CHARGES**
No cover, service included
**ENGLISH**
Limited, as the barman said, "We don't speak English, only Venetian."

## (2) ALL' ANTICA MOLA
### fondamenta degli Ormesini, 2800

Venice exists today because of the huge influx of tourists who spend over $100 million a year here. A visitor to Venice can easily become a sitting duck for dining rip-offs. With a little extra effort and some ingenuity, venturing off the beaten tourist track can yield not only better food but a great increase in value. Sitting along a canal on the edge of the ghetto is All' Antica Mola, where you will be assured of a close encounter with the natives along with a decent meal at a fair price. It is an unassuming place, but you will be able to spot it as you approach: it is the one with the flags flying beside the canalside tables (cross the bridge at rio Terrà Farsetti and turn left).

Time and tradition stand behind the food and the dowdy atmosphere. The two inside rooms, hung with old copper, postcards from regulars, and signed drawings on napkins, are in need of redecorating, but no one is thinking of doing anything like that anytime soon. The most satisfying meal lire will be spent on the simple pastas and second courses based on fish. If dessert is part

**AREA**
Cannaregio
**TELEPHONE**
71-74-92
**OPEN**
Daily April–Nov; Mon, Tues, Thur–Sun Dec–Mar
**CLOSED**
Wed from Dec–Mar; July–Aug (6 weeks)
**HOURS**
Noon–midnight, continuous service
**RESERVATIONS**
Advised
**CREDIT CARDS**
AMEX, DC, MC, V
**À LA CARTE**
L 30,000, beverage extra
**MENÙ TURISTICO**
None
**COVER & SERVICE CHARGES**
Cover L 2,500, service included
**ENGLISH**
Yes

of your plan, look at the fruit-topped custard tarts or the orange cake. House wines are good . . . and cheap. Another bonus: The food is served nonstop from noon to midnight every day except Wednesday from November to March, and daily from April to November.

## (3) AL MILION
### corte al Milion, 5841 (in back of San Giovanni Criostomo Church)

AREA
Cannaregio

TELEPHONE
52-29-302

OPEN
Mon, Tues, Thur–Sun

CLOSED
Wed, Aug

HOURS
Lunch noon–2 P.M., dinner 6–10 P.M.

RESERVATIONS
Recommended; not accepted on Sat

CREDIT CARDS
None

À LA CARTE
L 45,000, beverage extra

MENÙ TURISTICO
None

COVER & SERVICE CHARGES
Cover L 2,000, service included

ENGLISH
Yes

"We spoil our guests," says Mario, the longtime manager of Al Milion, a friendly *osteria* and trattoria that is reliably good, always busy, and known and loved by almost everyone in Venice. You can join old-timers and gondoliers at the bar, or sit at one of the three tables near the bar, and have a glass of good wine and a plate of *cicchetti*. Full meals are served in the dining room; tables are covered with red-and-white checked tablecloths with white paper overlays.

Feel free to order as much or as little as you want, and if you do not see what you want on the handwritten menu, ask for it and chances are they can prepare it. Fish, cooked with skill and restraint, is the backbone of the main-course roster. There is salmon, fried scampi and calamari, and the ever-present filet of sole. Other dishes that earn high marks are the liver, veal steak served with potatoes, and the homemade desserts, especially the almond cake, *tiramisù*, and *sorbetto al limone*. On Saturday, you can't call for reservations because they do not take them, so to avoid a wait on Saturday, arrive early during the meal service.

## (4) ANTICA TRATTORIA DA NINO
### salizada Seriman, 4858

AREA
Cannaregio

TELEPHONE
52-85-266

OPEN
Mon–Fri; Sat lunch only

CLOSED
Sun, Jan

HOURS
Bar 9 A.M.–9 P.M.; lunch 11 A.M.–2:30 P.M., dinner 6:30–8:30 P.M.

RESERVATIONS
Not accepted

CREDIT CARDS
AMEX, MC, V

Every once in a while, we need a port in a storm, and this little trattoria is just that. It is certainly nothing to write home about, or worth a special trip, but if you are en route to take the boat to Murano, and need a little sustenance, this is an answer. The key is to remember where you are and not to expect gourmet renderings from a sophisticated chef. Order what can be prepared at the moment and you will do fine. The interior used to be cluttered with collections of soccer scarves, plastic plants, and assorted posters. But the walls have been repainted white, sporting only framed sailor's knots and pictures of Venice. The only piece of true kitsch left is the big wristwatch clock hanging over the bar.

The best Cheap Eat is the simple *menù turistico*. Start with spaghetti in a *ragù* or tomato sauce, and order either the mixed fish fry or roast pork for the main course. The vegetables are truly awful . . . canned. Instead have a mixed salad and for dessert a scoop of *gelato*. With a quarter liter of the house *vino,* you will have had a filling meal and be on your way without having put a major dent in your budget.

**NOTE:** Please take a minute while you are in this area to look into Chiesa di S. Maria Assunta (Gesuiti) with works by Tintoretto. The church is located down the street from the restaurant and is open from 10 A.M. to noon and from 4 to 6 P.M. Mass is at 5:30 P.M.

**À LA CARTE**
L 28,000, beverage extra

**MENÙ TURISTICO**
L 20,000, 3 courses, cover and service included, beverage extra

**COVER & SERVICE CHARGES**
Cover L 2,500, service included

**ENGLISH**
Yes, and English menu

## (5) BELLA VENEZIA
### lista di Spagna, 129

Bella Venezia is a bright spot along this touristy strip of real estate leading from the train station on lista di Spagna. Owner Armando Raccanello is on hand daily, keeping an eagle eye on everyone, from the bus boy to the chef and his kitchen staff. Specializing in fresh fish, Bella Venezia offers a time-honored combination of food that is well-cooked, generously served, and affordable. The interior of the restaurant is delightful, with bouquets of flowers, candles on the tables at night, and pictures of old Venice on the walls. White-coated waiters help with menu selections, pointing out specials and seasonal favorites.

The hot mixed-vegetable antipasti or the gratin of black mussels, clams, and scallops flavored with cognac ushers in a memorable meal. In autumn and spring, the spider crabs or the fish soup with shellfish and white fish is another marvelous beginning. Still more fish specialties include the *tagliolini* with shrimp, the spaghetti with lobster sauce, and the fresh salmon or sole. Carnivores will love the beef filet pan-fried in butter and topped with a cream sauce made with Gorgonzola cheese. After concentrating on the rest of the meal, the best dessert will be the house zabaglione or a dish of *sorbetto*.

**AREA**
Cannaregio

**TELEPHONE**
71-52-08

**OPEN**
Mon–Wed, Fri–Sun

**CLOSED**
Thur, Jan 6–Feb 1 (dates vary), July (last 2 weeks)

**HOURS**
Lunch 11:30 A.M.–3 P.M., dinner 6:30–10 P.M.

**RESERVATIONS**
Advised on holidays

**CREDIT CARDS**
AMEX, DC, MC, V

**À LA CARTE**
L 40,000, beverage extra

**MENÙ TURISTICO**
L 26,000, 3 courses, cover and service included, beverage extra

**COVER & SERVICE CHARGES**
Cover L 2,800, 12% service added

**ENGLISH**
Yes, and English menu

## (6) DA BEPPI
### salizzada D. Pistor, 4550

One hundred years ago this was a rough-and-ready watering hole for the workers who cleaned the canals. Today, only the beamed ceiling remains as a reminder of those rowdy days. Inside this modest little trattoria near

**AREA**
Cannaregio

**TELEPHONE**
52-85-031

**OPEN**
Mon, Wed–Sun

**CLOSED**
Tues, Jan–Feb (till Carnivale)
**HOURS**
Lunch noon–3 P.M., dinner
7–10 P.M.
**RESERVATIONS**
Advised for weekends
**CREDIT CARDS**
MC, V
**À LA CARTE**
L 32,000, beverage extra
**MENÙ TURISTICO**
None
**COVER & SERVICE CHARGES**
Cover L 2,500, service included
**ENGLISH**
Yes

Ca' d'Oro are two wood-paneled rooms with the usual paintings of Venice hanging about. In front is a shaded patio that is perfect for combining warm-weather dining with people-watching. The food at Da Beppi is good because the mother and son who own it and do the cooking create the type of Venetian homestyle cooking everyone knows and loves.

Daily specials depend on the season and whatever they find fresh at the market. No matter what time of year it is, you can expect to find *baccalà* (creamed salted cod), marinated sardines, liver and onions, and a wonderful homemade chocolate almond cake with creamy chocolate frosting. The pastas are served in generous portions with a basket of crusty bread on the side to lap up the last drops of sauce.

### (7) FIASCHETTERIA TOSCANA
### salizzada San Giovanni Grisostomo, 5719

**AREA**
Cannaregio
**TELEPHONE**
52-85-281
**OPEN**
Mon, Wed–Sun
**CLOSED**
Tues, one week before or after
Carnivale, July
**HOURS**
Lunch 12:30–2:30 P.M., dinner
7:30–10:30 P.M.
**RESERVATIONS**
Essential for downstairs seating
**CREDIT CARDS**
AMEX, DC, MC, V
**À LA CARTE**
L 45,000–55,000, beverage
extra
**MENÙ TURISTICO**
None
**COVER & SERVICE CHARGES**
Cover L 3,000, 12% service
added
**ENGLISH**
Yes, and English Menu
**MISCELLANEOUS**
A member of Ristoranti della
Buona Accoglienza; see page
138 for details.

Fiaschetteria Toscana is the top choice of many Venetians for a celebration meal. The trick is to be sure to reserve a table downstairs, where the Murano wall lights and candles cast a soft and romantic aura in the evenings. Here the air is cooler, the tables farther apart, and the service better. The brightly lit, beamed upstairs room is hot, smoky, and crowded with tables so closely spaced that only models could wedge into them.

No matter where you are seated the food will be good. The fish is always excellent, but the price tags on most of these dishes could send the bill quickly into triple digits. Better to start with warm artichoke hearts or a plate of designer greens, and then order the pasta or the day—maybe gnocchi with bacon and radicchio or ravioli with sea bass. If you are going on to a second course, the mixed grill is sufficient for any stevedore. Veal scallops with Marsala wine, lemon, and mushrooms should allow you to at least share a dessert, which I think is important to do here. The caramel apple cake with a scoop of vanilla ice cream is my favorite, but if there is a piece of the dense almond cake available, I am always torn.

### (8) I QUATTRO RUSTEGHI
### campo Ghetto Novo, 2888

**AREA**
Cannaregio
**TELEPHONE**
52-40-635

Cheap Eaters in Venice who show a copy of this book will receive a 10 percent discount at Luis Chicchini's new restaurant in the ghetto area of Venice. For lunch, the meal is only cafeteria-style self-service and sells for one low price. The menu repeats itself every fifteen days, and it includes two courses, vegetable, fruit, and coffee. Wine or mineral water is extra. If you want only one dish, you will pay around L 12,000.

At dinner, the menu is all à la carte, but your meal, excluding beverage, will not add up to more than L 25,000 or L 30,000. The food is basic, but the quality is good.

The freshly appealing restaurant looks like a southern California cafe, with peach-colored walls and sea-blue inserts. The lovely lights match the wall coloring and were made especially for the restaurant, in Murano. Even the pink-tiled bathrooms are appealing, especially if you have been out sightseeing all day and need a place to freshen up a bit. Seating on the campo is in the planning stages.

**OPEN**
Tues–Sun

**CLOSED**
Mon

**HOURS**
Lunch noon–3 P.M., dinner 7:30 P.M.–midnight

**RESERVATIONS**
Not accepted

**CREDIT CARDS**
AMEX, MC, V

**À LA CARTE**
Dinner only, L 25,000–30,000, beverage extra

**MENÙ TURISTICO**
Lunch only, L 20,000, 2 courses, beverage included

**COVER & SERVICE CHARGES**
None for lunch or dinner

**ENGLISH**
Yes, and English menu

## (9) L'ISOLA DEL GELATO
### rio Terra San Leonardo, 1525 (just before campo San Leonardo)

The strip of real estate leading from the *ferrovia* (train station) on rio Terra di Spagna, across campo S. Geremia and along rio Terra San Leonardo, is full of tourist traps. You really need to know what you are doing here to avoid getting your budget soaked by poor quality restaurants and greedy shopkeepers selling mostly garish junk. As you may have already guessed, this is not my favorite Venice neighborhood. However, you may find yourself here, and if so, there are a few redeeming places worthy of a stop. L'Isola del Gelato is one of them. From 9 A.M. until midnight, 365 days a year, you can indulge in cones, cups, sundaes, banana splits, and other ice cream treats, made with delicious *gelato* manufactured on the premises. With a nod toward the health conscious customers, low-fat yogurt is also available and so are zero-fat and -sugar soya ices, including chocolate. While not worth a *vaporetto* trip from St. Mark's Square, this is worth a stop if you are in the neighborhood.

**AREA**
Cannaregio

**TELEPHONE**
52-40-454

**OPEN**
Daily

**CLOSED**
Never

**HOURS**
9 A.M.–midnight

**RESERVATIONS**
Not accepted

**CREDIT CARDS**
None

**À LA CARTE**
*Gelato* from L 1,250–7,500

**MENÙ TURISTICO**
None

**COVER & SERVICE CHARGES**
None

**ENGLISH**
Limited

## (10) RISTORANTE AL PONTE
### rio Terra alla Maddalena, 2352

Ristorante al Ponte is within easy walking distance to the *ferrovia* (railway station), but it's just far enough away to elude the touristy dining nightmare that surrounds it.

**AREA**
Cannaregio

**TELEPHONE**
72-07-44

**OPEN**
Wed–Mon

**CLOSED**
Tues, June or July

**HOURS**
Lunch 12:30–2:30 P.M., dinner
6:30–10 P.M.

**RESERVATIONS**
Advised

**CREDIT CARDS**
AMEX, MC, V

**À LA CARTE**
L 32,000, beverage extra

**MENÙ TURISTICO**
L 20,000, 2 courses, cover and
service included, beverage extra

**COVER & SERVICE CHARGES**
Cover L 3,000, 12% service
added

**ENGLISH**
Limited, but English menu

This is a quiet spot, tucked next to a bridge along the rio Terra alla Maddalena. The best tables are those by the window, where diners can watch the ever-changing characters in the passing parade. The service by uniformed waiters is dignified and formal. The lighting is subdued with candles at night on well-spaced tables. It all adds up to a restaurant that is a favorite with first-time visitors and romantics alike.

The impressive antipasti display of salads and tempting starters tells you good things are ahead. The pastas concentrate on fish with sauces made from tuna, crab, shrimp, and cuttlefish. Always ask what fish is fresh that day because they do serve some frozen fish, and in Venice, you don't need to eat frozen fish *ever*. If you are having meat, the tender veal scallop with lemon and the filet steak in wine sauce are two solid choices. For the vegetable garnish, I like the grilled red chicory or the mixed vegetables vinaigrette. Desserts are from a local pastry shop and really quite good, but there is always a nice selection of fresh fruit and excellent cheeses if you do not want a high-calorie, sweet finish.

### (11) RISTORANTE VEGETARIANO—L'ARCA DI NOÈ
### calle Larga Giacinto Gallina, 5401

**AREA**
Cannaregio, near Castello

**TELEPHONE**
52-38-153

**OPEN**
Mon–Fri; Sat dinner only

**CLOSED**
Sun, Aug, Dec (dates vary)

**HOURS**
Lunch noon–2:30 P.M., dinner
7–10:30 P.M.

**RESERVATIONS**
Required for Indian dinner
Tues

**CREDIT CARDS**
AMEX, MC, V

**À LA CARTE**
L 20,000–28,000, beverage
extra

**MENÙ TURISTICO**
Tues only, L 22,000, Indian
dinner, beverage extra

**COVER & SERVICE CHARGES**
No cover, service included

**ENGLISH**
Yes

It used to be that vegetarians in Venice had a tough time of it if they wanted something more imaginative than a tomato-based pasta primavera or a salad. Now there is hope. Laura and Paolo Rossetti are passionate about their vegetarian restaurant and their authentic, healthy cooking, which is winning daily converts.

Of course, they use only fresh foods; nothing is frozen or zapped in the microwave. From their kitchen come savory pasta sauces, rich quiches, tofu-based main courses, interesting salads, and whole-grain breads. In addition, they offer sugarless desserts and biological wines, herb teas, and apple cider. Tuesday night they devote to a set-price Indian meal with seven dishes: soup, salad, two vegetables, rice, samosa, and a light dessert. The rustic two-room restaurant sits right alongside a canal, and there are several tables overlooking the waterway. The casual service encourages lingering, especially in the evening as the tempo builds and the tables fill. There is a piano in one corner for guests who are so inclined.

## (12) TRATTORIA CA' D'ORO, OSTERIA DALLA VEDOVA
**calle del Pistor and ramo Ca' d'Oro, 3912–3952 (off strada Nova)**

The name on the business card reads: Trattoria Ca' d'Oro—Ostaria dalla Vedova. The sign on the front says: Birra Dreher Trattoria. But on the window, it's simply La Vedova, which is how it's known by all its loyalists.

This spot has been in the same family for 125 years, and judging from the inside, very little has changed in that time. The two rooms are filled with what looks like original furniture, a marvelous collection of copper pots hanging from the ceiling, and pretty antique white-shaded lights. Anytime you go you will find the owners, Lorenzo and Mirella, his sister, mixing and mingling with an interesting sampling of area regulars, who sit at the plain wooden tables sharing a bottle of *vino rosso* and arguing about Sunday's soccer scores or the latest Italian political scandal.

Even though there is no proper menu and they do not serve dessert, this is a good place to keep in mind for a light lunch or dinner. Find out what the chef has prepared for that day, maybe a pasta with fresh clams or a hearty soup, and pair that with the plate of antipasti, a few chunks of bread, and a sturdy wine, and you will be all set. Service has been known to be cool, but after a few glasses of wine, your Italian should improve, and you will feel more welcome.

**AREA**
Cannaregio

**TELEPHONE**
52-85-324

**OPEN**
Mon–Wed, Fri–Sat; Sun dinner only

**CLOSED**
Thur, 2 weeks after Carnivale, Aug–Sept (dates vary)

**HOURS**
Lunch 11:30 A.M.–3 P.M., dinner 6:30–11 P.M.

**RESERVATIONS**
Advised

**CREDIT CARDS**
None

**À LA CARTE**
L 15,000–25,000, beverage extra

**MENÙ TURISTICO**
None

**COVER & SERVICE CHARGES**
Cover L 1,500, service not included

**ENGLISH**
Most of the time

# Restaurants in Castello

## (13) AL COVO
**campiello della Pescaria, 3968**

People often ask me, If you had only one meal to eat in a city, where would it be? In Venice the answer is simple: I would go to Al Covo for dinner. It was opened in 1987 by Diane and Cesare Benelli, a dynamic American/Italian couple who know and appreciate good food. The popularity of Al Covo is due to the excellence of its cuisine, prepared by Cesare, and the warm atmosphere created by Diane using their impressive collection of artwork. At night, fresh flowers and candles adorn the tables, which are formally set with floral-patterned china, heavy cutlery, and gleaming crystal.

**AREA**
Castello

**TELEPHONE**
52-23-812

**OPEN**
Mon, Tues, Fri–Sun

**CLOSED**
Wed, Thur, Jan, Aug (2 weeks)

**HOURS**
Lunch 12:45–2:15 P.M., dinner 7:45–10:15 P.M.

**RESERVATIONS**
Essential

**CREDIT CARDS**
Dinner only, MC, V

**À LA CARTE**
Lunch from L 20,000; dinner
L 60,000; beverage extra
**MENÙ TURISTICO**
Lunch only, L 35,000, 2
courses, cover and service
included, beverage extra
**COVER & SERVICE CHARGES**
Cover L 5,000, service not
included
**ENGLISH**
Yes, and English menu
**MISCELLANEOUS**
A member of Ristoranti della
Buona Accoglienza; see page
138 for details.

While looking over the menu, a glass of complimentary champagne and some nibbles are brought to your table. The assorted breads are served with iced butter curls, a treat unknown in other Venetian restaurants. All of their dishes are prepared to order, using what the market offers each day and what products are in season. No frozen or canned foods are used, and neither do they use glutamates in making sauces. The fresh seafood is prepared without the use of butter or other animal fats. At dinner, fish and seafood dominate the menu, but other tastes are graciously accommodated if you call ahead.

Their new lunch offer has taken off like wildfire. In the tradition of wine *osterias,* they have a special menu consisting of a daily pasta, main dish, and generous side salad. If you do not want this large of a meal, platters of mixed cheeses or vegetables, appetizers, soups, or just a bowl of pasta will be available. The atmosphere is casual, with bare tables, paper napkins, and quick service geared to a repeat crowd of locals who have a limited time for lunch.

Whenever you eat at Al Covo (and I know readers who have found it and eaten *all* of their meals here while in Venice), you absolutely must promise me to try at least one or two of Diane's homemade desserts. If the pear and prune cake with grappa sauce is available, have it for sure. It is so good it was featured in *Gourmet* magazine. The other choices are endless: chocolate chip or oatmeal cookies to dip in sweet wine, a bitter chocolate cake, walnut cake with caramel sauce, spiked with aged run, or *panna cotta* with dark chocolate sauce.

Service by the English-speaking staff is attentive and helpful. While the lunch prices will fit into most budgets, the dinner prices are definitely not for budgeteers, so reserve this special occasion for a last night in Venice with someone you love.

## (14) ALLA LAMPARA
### secco Marina, 738

**AREA**
Castello
**TELEPHONE**
52-37-102
**OPEN**
Mon, Tues, Thur–Sun
**CLOSED**
Wed, Christmas (1 week)

Alla Lampara occupies small but vibrant quarters that are further in spirit from tourist central than they are in kilometers. Located a block off via Garibaldi, about a twenty-minute walk east of piazza San Marco, this neighborhood gathering place is run by Paolo and his English wife, Jackie, who also shares the cooking responsibilities. Jackie did not start out to be a chef. On a lark, she left her native Cornwall at age seventeen and came to the Lido, where she taught pony riding to children. She worked her way up, finally becoming well-known as a trainer for the top Italian show jumpers. Along the way she met Paolo, who was a waiter at Harry's Bar, and the rest is history: they married, had two children, and bought this restaurant, which they run with another couple. Pictures of their children hang on the left wall in the room beyond the bar.

At noon, blue-collar workers troop in for Jackie's specials and her *pasta della casa,* an imaginative mix of vegetables, scampi, and shrimp tossed with spaghetti and a spoonful of cream. This makes a nice meal, accompanied by one or two of her homemade crusty rolls, an *insalata mista,* and a glass of the house red wine, which is an excellent Pinot Nero. In the evening, pizza is featured, and the diners are a sampling of the area's younger residents.

**NOTE:** When you go, don't look for a sign saying Alla Lampara. For reasons known only to obscure Italian bureaucrats and lovers of red tape, the sign outside says Trattoria dei Tosi. It has been decreed a historical sign and therefore cannot be moved, painted, or restored. Why the owners changed the name is another story . . . but just so you remember to look for the trattoria sign, not one saying Alla Lampara.

If you go for lunch, be sure to take the time to see the oldest church in Venice, which is quite close by. The San Pietro di Castello is open daily from 8 A.M. to noon and 3 to 6 P.M., and on holidays from 8 A.M. to noon and 4:30 to 7:30 P.M.

**HOURS**
Lunch noon–3 P.M., dinner 6:30–11 P.M.

**RESERVATIONS**
Not necessary

**CREDIT CARDS**
MC, V

**À LA CARTE**
L 20,000–25,000, beverage extra; pizza L 6,500–10,000

**MENÙ TURISTICO**
None

**COVER & SERVICE CHARGES**
Cover L 2,500, 12% service added

**ENGLISH**
Yes

## (15) AL TUCANO
### ruga Giuffa, 4835

The bar at Al Tucano serves as a private fraternity for the locals in this pocket of Venice. For the rest of us, it is a place to go if you want to eat well without having to dress up or spend a lot. The best seats in the house are in the front by the bar. That way you can not only watch the bar scene but be in a better position to flag down service, which varies from peppy and bright to bored and disinterested, depending on your luck of the draw.

Start with a pitcher of the house white wine; avoid the red unless you like it tart and chilled. Skip the *insalata* in favor of the asparagus served just warm and

**AREA**
Castello

**TELEPHONE**
52-00-811

**OPEN**
Mon–Wed, Fri–Sun

**CLOSED**
Thur, Jan (1 week), other times throughout year (dates vary)

**HOURS**
Lunch noon–3 P.M., dinner 7–11 P.M.

**RESERVATIONS**
Not necessary

bathed in a light vinaigrette. The food is all cooked to order, so don't think you are going to zip through this one. Pastas are good—try the gnocchi with shrimp and rucola. The mixed grill features Scottish beef, and the assorted fish fry is done in extra-virgin olive oil. Also available for dinner is a well-chosen selection of pizzas. House desserts worth the calorie blitz are the two cakes: either the fresh strawberry or the pear with cream.

**CREDIT CARDS**
AMEX, MC, V
**À LA CARTE**
L 35,000–40,000, beverage extra; pizza from L 8,000
**MENÙ TURISTICO**
None
**COVER & SERVICE CHARGES**
Cover L 3,000, only L 2,000 for pizza; service included
**ENGLISH**
Most of the time

## (16) CIP CIAP
### calle del Mondo Nuovo, 5799 (at Ponte del Mondo Nuovo)

If you want a slice of good pizza, a bulging calzone, or an assortment of minipizzas to munch on for a quick snack, do not miss this busy little corner establishment off the campo Santa Maria Formosa. This is Italian fast food and I love it. It was located close to my Venetian flat, and I will admit, I was a regular customer.

You can eat here if you want to stand along the calle del Mondo Nuovo, or better, have your slices packaged to go. Dole out a worthwhile L 3,000 or so per slice and a little more for the calzone, take your feast over to the campo Santa Maria Formosa, and sit on a bench and watch the neighborhood at work and at play. It is a good way to feel Italian and have a satisfying Cheap Eat in the bargain.

**AREA**
Castello
**TELEPHONE**
52-36-621
**OPEN**
Mon, Wed–Sun
**CLOSED**
Tues, Dec (dates vary)
**HOURS**
9 A.M.–9 P.M., continuous service
**RESERVATIONS**
Not accepted
**CREDIT CARDS**
None
**À LA CARTE**
Slices from L 3,000, pizzas from L 10,000
**MENÙ TURISTICO**
None
**COVER & SERVICE CHARGES**
No cover, service included
**ENGLISH**
Sometimes

## (17) HOSTARIA AE DO PORTE
### San Giustina, 6492

You are right. This is one no one would ever try unless they were told about it. I would never have given it a second glance had my distinguished Venetian landlady not recommended it. She told me that she and her husband considered it "our canteen" while they were redoing her parents' top-floor flat, which I subsequently occupied. The flat is another story (see *Cheap Sleeps in Italy*), and so is this rather scruffy trattoria where the lunchtime clientele is about as local as you will find.

Rotund, blue-overalled workers, who have not had a nodding acquaintance with a diet or a scale for years, stream in before noon for bowls of pasta with clams or heavy meat sauce, heaping plates of thin beefsteak with olive oil, the daily special, and fish every Friday. They also never miss eating a side order of the best white beans

**AREA**
Castello
**TELEPHONE**
52-08-842
**OPEN**
Mon, Wed–Sun
**CLOSED**
Tues, Aug, Dec 28–Jan 10
**HOURS**
Lunch 11:30 A.M.–2:30 P.M., dinner 6 P.M.–midnight
**RESERVATIONS**
Not necessary
**CREDIT CARDS**
MC, V
**À LA CARTE**
L 28,000, beverage extra

you will taste. Big ceramic pitchers of house wine keep their cheeks and noses a rosy red well into the afternoon. No one seems to mind the service, which is almost nonexistent: plates of food are placed on a glass antipasti case, and diners are expected to retrieve them and take them to their tables. Salads? Desserts? *Please.* If you are still in the mood for dessert, stop by the Pasticceria-Bar Domenegati at 6645 Barbaria delle Tolle, not far from the restaurant. This is the neighborhood address for beautiful cakes and other pastries. They also serve coffee.

### (18) LA BOUTIQUE DEL GELATO
### salizzada San Lio, 5727

Italians know good *gelato* when they taste it, and nowhere is it much better than here. It's easy to find: just look for the line that weaves down the narrow salizzada San Lio, which begins when they open around 10 A.M. and lasts until closing at 8:30 P.M. Run by an energetic trio—Sandra and Silvio Calvaldoro and her brother, Paolo—this tiny operation has been doing an amazing business since it opened a year or so ago. They are smart: they offer a few knockout flavors sold by the cone or cup, or packaged to go. There is no seating at all and no beverages available. I passed the shop coming and going to my flat each day, and every time it was all I could do not to stop in for a scoop of *nocciolosa* (a creamy chocolate *gelato* laced with nuts) or their specialty (and secret recipe) the *millefoglie.* Sandra and Silvio both speak English and have friends in San Francisco who they often visit. If you are anywhere near their Venice *gelateria,* please have a scoop or two for me.

### (19) OSTERIA AL MASCARON
### calle Lunga Santa Maria Formosa, 5225

To get almost anyplace I wanted to go during my two month stay in Venice, I had to walk by Al Mascaron, a bustling *osteria* that never seemed to have an empty seat or space at the bar. When I finally got in, I found out why. Not only is the food good and the prices right, it is great fun and one of the liveliest places in town. Even the menus are super: black ink caricatures and drawings of food done on folded placemats with the day's offerings on either side.

The chef comes up with an almost new menu daily, based on whatever fresh fish he can find at the Rialto Market. Big spenders will want to try his spaghetti with

---

**MENÙ TURISTICO**
L 25,000, 2 courses, cover and service included, beverage extra

**COVER & SERVICE CHARGES**
Cover L 2,000, service included

**ENGLISH**
None

---

**AREA**
Castello

**TELEPHONE**
52-23-283

**OPEN**
Daily

**CLOSED**
Jan

**HOURS**
10 A.M.–8:30 P.M.

**RESERVATIONS**
Not accepted

**CREDIT CARDS**
None

**À LA CARTE**
*Gelato* from L 1,500

**MENÙ TURISTICO**
None

**COVER & SERVICE CHARGES**
None

**ENGLISH**
Yes

---

**AREA**
Castello

**TELEPHONE**
52-25-995

**OPEN**
Mon–Sat

**CLOSED**
Sun, July (2 weeks), Dec 15–Jan 15

**HOURS**
Lunch 12:30–2:30 P.M., dinner 7:30–10:30 P.M.

**RESERVATIONS**
Advised

---

CREDIT CARDS
None
À LA CARTE
L 35,000, beverage extra
MENÙ TURISTICO
None
COVER & SERVICE CHARGES
Cover L 2,000, 15% service added
ENGLISH
Yes

lobster sauce. Other mere mortals will be nicely satisfied with the fresh clams or scampi ladled over their pasta. Portions are huge. The counter display of antipasti brings in the lunch bunch, who appreciate the many good wines poured by the affable owner, Gigi. The two rooms have a rustic interior and the original faded tile floor. The close seating on hard wooden benches around bare wooden tables will encourage you to get to know your neighbor.

NOTE: Newly opened by the same owner is the Enoteca Mascareta, down the street (calle Lunga Santa Maria Formosa, 5183). This is a great watering hole, perfect for a glass of wine in the early evening along with a plate of sliced ham and assorted cheeses. No meals as such are served, but it is good for something light, or to tide you over if dinner will be late. It's open from 5 P.M. to 1 A.M. from Monday to Saturday, and prices begin around L 3,000.

## (20) TRATTORIA ALLA RIVETTA
### ponte San Provolo, 4625 (off campo S.S. Filipino e Giancomo)

AREA
Castello
TELEPHONE
52-87-302
OPEN
Tues–Sun
CLOSED
Mon, Aug (dates vary)
HOURS
10 A.M.–10 P.M., continuous service
RESERVATIONS
Not necessary
CREDIT CARDS
None
À LA CARTE
L 35,000, beverage extra
MENÙ TURISTICO
None
COVER & SERVICE CHARGES
Cover L 2,000, 12% service added
ENGLISH
Some, and English menu

Trattoria alla Rivetta, squeezed in on the right side just before the ponte San Provolo, is a genuine and reasonable alternative to the many other very touristy alternatives that plague this area of Venice. A good sign, as always, is that the locals know about it and eat here in droves, filling every seat in the house almost as soon as it is open. You will see everyone from gondoliers on their breaks grabbing a snack at the bar and a glass of *vino della casa* to women out for a gossipy afternoon with their friends. The menu is printed in English, and the restaurant serves full meals from 10 A.M. to 10 P.M., two distinct advantages for Venetian visitors.

Portions are not for the light eater. In fact, the bowl of mussels ordered as a first course will be plenty if you add a salad and the fresh bread that comes with every Italian meal. Growing boys and other hungry diners can start with the *tagliolini ai granchio,* pasta with fresh crab, or a time-honored spaghetti with meat sauce. The squid cooked in its own black ink, served with polenta, and the grilled jumbo shrimp are delicious entrées. There is also a full line of meats, including Venetian liver and onions, veal chops, and boiled beef with pesto sauce. Desserts are run-of-the-mill except for the house *tiramisù,* that heavenly rum-spiked cake layered with triple-cream cheese and dusted with chocolate.

## (21) TRATTORIA DA REMIGIO
### salizzada dei Greci, 3416

At da Remigio, any choice of appetizer, pasta, and fish or meat course will be a happy one. For a new twist on an old dish, try the *gnocchi alla pescatora,* potato-based pasta puffs with fish. Always pay close attention to the handwritten daily specials and check the display of the day's glistening catch for the best seafood results. Desserts will have you doing penance on a thighmaster when you get home.

Arrive late and you will need a shoehorn to get in. The restaurant enjoys the fiercely devout patronage of Venetians, and they virtually pack it out both day and night, so get your name in for a reservation and be on time.

**AREA**
Castello
**TELEPHONE**
52-30-089
**OPEN**
Wed–Sun; Mon lunch only
**CLOSED**
Tues, Jan, Aug
**HOURS**
Lunch 12:30–2:30 P.M., dinner 7:30–10:30 P.M.
**RESERVATIONS**
Essential
**CREDIT CARDS**
AMEX, MC, V
**À LA CARTE**
L 35,000, beverage extra
**MENÙ TURISTICO**
None
**COVER & SERVICE CHARGES**
Cover L 2,500, 12% service added
**ENGLISH**
Limited

## (22) TRATTORIA TOFANELLI
### rio Terra Garibaldi, 1650

"I was born right here and that makes me older than the street," said Micole Tofanelli when I asked how long she and her sister, Nella, had been serving homespun food at their corner location, a twenty-minute stroll east of Saint Mark's Square. As you can imagine, the trattoria is as old as the hills, and nothing has been done to bring it into the nineties, let along the fifties. But it is tidy and very appealing in its own way. Inside are eight tables with brown-and-white tablecloths, an old-fashioned ice box in the corner, and green plants sitting everywhere all needing various amounts of TLC.

The small handwritten menu features meat and pasta, with fresh fish making only a cameo appearance. The sisters are best known for their *bigoli*—fresh egg pasta with anchovies and salsa—and veal scaloppine in Marsala sauce. None of the food hits the high notes of gourmet cuisine, but it is filling and the portions are ample. The best part is that the prices are about as old-fashioned as the setting, a real plus for any Cheap Eater in Venice.

**NOTE:** The sisters also operate a small hotel in connection with the restaurant. See *Cheap Sleeps in Italy* for details.

**AREA**
Castello
**TELEPHONE**
52-35-722
**OPEN**
Mon, Tues, Thur–Sun
**CLOSED**
Wed, Jan 4–Feb 15 (til Carnivale)
**HOURS**
Lunch noon–3 P.M., dinner 6–9 P.M.
**RESERVATIONS**
Not accepted
**CREDIT CARDS**
None
**À LA CARTE**
L 23,000, beverage extra
**MENÙ TURISTICO**
L 20,000, 3 courses, cover and service included, beverage extra
**COVER & SERVICE CHARGES**
No cover, service included
**ENGLISH**
None

# Restaurants in Dorsoduro

## (23) AI CUGNAI
### san Vio, 857

Those in search of a Cheap Eat near the Peggy Guggenheim Museum will do well to eat at Ai Cugnai. This cheapie, not too far from the Accademia vaporetto stop, has been run for almost forty-five years by two sisters, their brother, and their combined families. Elegant it is not, but the down-home atmosphere makes for an authentic Venetian experience. As you enter, you will find a cluster of neighbors standing at the bar, comparing notes on their day. Eventually, they will go on their way or sit at one of the tables in back to have a meal.

The food is far from fancy, but it is surprisingly good, especially the daily specials and their renditions of fresh crab, when it is in season. If you want to keep your check in the Cheap Eat department, you will unfortunately have to forgo the fresh fish and go for the *menù turistico,* which allows you to select from certain dishes on the à la carte menu and includes not only the beverage and dessert but cover and service charges. Be sure to ask which of the vegetables are fresh; you don't want canned spinach. For dessert, I would not miss another piece of their velvety chocolate cake for anything, but if it is all gone, try the almond cake . . . it is special, too.

## (24) AI GONDOLIERI
### rio Terra San Vio, 366 (off campo San Vio, near Peggy Guggenheim Museum)

When reserving your table at Ai Gondolieri, ask to be in the main dining room, where you will sit at blue-linen-covered tables set with smart china and crystal, fresh flowers, and glowing candles in the evening. The other narrow room, off the bar, has the same pretty place settings but has uncomfortable wooden benches along the wall and serves as a corridor for restaurant patrons coming and going.

The food at Ai Gondolieri is more expensive than some, and that is why it should be saved for a Big Splurge. The best buy is definitely the *menù degustazione,* since it includes all of the chef's special dishes from appetizer to dessert. Coffee comes with it, but wine does not. You will start with three or four antipasti choices, including snails in Burgundy wine sauce, an unusual treatment of polenta cooked with smoky bacon, or a baby artichoke torte. Next will be homemade pasta, perhaps early spring asparagus tossed with buttery egg noodles, or tortellini with truffles. The main course might be a tender guinea hen garnished with seasonal vegetables, steak with mushrooms, or the chef's daily special. Wrapping it all up is a choice of such luscious homemade desserts as strawberry cream cake or a slice of warm apple pie, lightly dusted with cinnamon.

## (25) AL PROFETA
**calle Lunga San Barnaba, 2689**

Compared to many of its soggy cousins across the Atlantic, pizza in Italy has been raised to an art form. Ask Italians who know and love their pizza and they will tell you that thin, crisp crusts are in, thick crusts are out. Regulars at Al Profeta know to ignore most of the regular menu and order one of the chef's eighty varieties of pizza. The most popular choice is the *capriociosa*—tomatoes, mozzarella cheese, ham, mushrooms, and artichokes. For groups who can agree, there are king-size pizzas to fill four hungry souls. To go with your pizza, there are five large salads, all perfect candidates for sharing.

This popular student hangout sits on the campo Santa Margherita at the San Barnaba end. It boasts a covered winter garden, an outside terrace, and a nonsmoking section.

## (26) ANTICA LOCANDA MONTIN
**fondamenta Eremite, 1147**

Reservations are essential at this seventeenth-century inn, where the large dining room looks as if it has kept every piece of furniture and painting accumulated during the past forty years. The paintings were donated by or purchased from many renowned patrons, including Modigliani, Mark Rothko, Jackson Pollock, and virtually every other artistic figure who has passed through Venice since the end of World War II. The arbor-covered garden in back is a popular warm-weather place to dine and to experience the real Venice.

Although the quality of the food and service can be erratic, the chef's versions of Venetian standards are all wonderful, such as marinated sardines, *spaghetti alle seppie*

**MENÙ TURISTICO**
L 60,000, 3 courses, cover and service included, beverage extra
**COVER & SERVICE CHARGES**
Cover L 5,000, 10% service added
**ENGLISH**
Yes
**MISCELLANEOUS**
A member of Ristoranti della Buona Accoglienza; see page 138 for details.

**AREA**
Dorsoduro
**TELEPHONE**
52-37-466
**OPEN**
Tues–Sun
**CLOSED**
Mon, Jan
**HOURS**
Lunch noon–3 P.M., dinner 7–10:30 P.M.
**RESERVATIONS**
Advised on weekends for outside table
**CREDIT CARDS**
AMEX, DC, MC, V
**À LA CARTE**
Pizza and a salad, L 20,000, beverage extra
**MENÙ TURISTICO**
None
**COVER & SERVICE CHARGES**
Cover L 2,000, 12% service added
**ENGLISH**
Yes

**AREA**
Dorsoduro
**TELEPHONE**
52-27-151
**OPEN**
Mon, Thur–Sun; Tues lunch only
**CLOSED**
Wed, Jan 1–20, Aug 1–10
**HOURS**
Lunch 12:30–2:30 P.M., dinner 7:30–10 P.M.
**RESERVATIONS**
Essential, especially in summer
**CREDIT CARDS**
AMEX, DC, MC, V

(with squid), *rigatoni ai quattro formaggi* (with four cheeses), liver with onions and polenta, and Adriatic fish either deep-fried or grilled. The desserts, so loaded with butter, cream, and sugar that they should carry health warnings, include a *semifreddo* with strawberries and a rich chocolate torte slathered in whipped cream.

**NOTE:** The Locanda also has hotel rooms. See *Cheap Sleeps in Italy* for details.

### (27) ANZOLO RAFFAEL
**campo Angelo Raffaele, 1722**

In tourist terms, Anzolo Raffael is located a block beyond Mars, and it certainly should not be thought of as destination dining. But for Cheap Eaters *no-matter-what* who are looking for fresh fish at a price that will not reduce them to a diet of beans and bread for the next few meals, this is one answer. Tucked on a campo across from a church, it boasts true local color: the waitress, wearing a porch-dress and slippers, serves an aging clientele who show up every day, wearing the same suits and probably telling the same stories. There is no proper menu; they will tell you what's cooking. Generally speaking, the menu consists of fish. All the favorites are here, it just depends on what is in season and the mood of the chef. Veggies, salads, and desserts are afterthoughts. House wine is not and is enthusiastically consumed by all who eat here.

### (28) CANTINA GIÀ SCHIAVI
**fondamenta Nani, 992**

Beginning with Giaccomo, three generations of the Schiavi family have kept up a 110-year-old tradition of selling fine wines worldwide from this canalside location. Every family member has a specific role to play, right down to the black, house mascot dog Lupo, who proudly rides with her master in the motorboat when he delivers wine orders. In addition to selling wines by the bottle and case, it has become a favorite local wine bar selling sandwiches and snacks at lunch. In fact, Alessandra, the wife of the owner, makes over three hundred sandwiches *per day,* which sell out by 2 P.M. When you multiply that by the week, month, and year, you know they have a hit. If you are looking for something unusual to give as a gift, try a bottle of their

---

**À LA CARTE**
L 40,000, beverage extra
**MENÙ TURISTICO**
None
**COVER & SERVICE CHARGES**
Cover L 4,000, 12% service added
**ENGLISH**
Yes

**AREA**
Dorsoduro
**TELEPHONE**
52-37-456
**OPEN**
Wed–Sun
**CLOSED**
Mon, Tues, Aug
**HOURS**
Lunch 12:30–2:30 P.M., dinner 7:30–9 P.M.
**RESERVATIONS**
Not necessary
**CREDIT CARDS**
None
**À LA CARTE**
L 25,000, beverage extra
**MENÙ TURISTICO**
None
**COVER & SERVICE CHARGES**
Cover L 2,000, 12% service added
**ENGLISH**
None

**AREA**
Dorsoduro
**TELEPHONE**
52-30-034
**OPEN**
Mon–Sat
**CLOSED**
Sun, Aug–Sept (2 weeks)
**HOURS**
Bar 8:30 A.M.–2:30 P.M., 3:30–8:30 P.M.; sandwiches noon–2:30 P.M.
**RESERVATIONS**
Not accepted
**CREDIT CARDS**
None
**À LA CARTE**
Sandwiches from L 3,500

*Fagolina Bianco* (strawberry wine), which you can sample by the glass and buy by the half liter.

When you arrive, don't be confused because the sign outside reads "Vini Al Bottegon"—you're at the right place.

## (29) DUE TORRI
### campo Santa Margherita, 3408

No one has thumbed through fat-free cookbooks, called an interior decorator, or ever considered changing a thing here—in this local pit stop, English is not tolerated and the cooking is as rough-hewn as the characters inhabiting it. It is basically a no-frills lunchtime gathering place for ruddy workers, who sit around oil-cloth-covered tables telling the same old war stories and polishing off a few glasses of red before digging into their pasta and fresh fish lunch. There is no menu, no dessert served, and no rules about smoking. Even the waiters may smoke on the job, but no one notices or minds because they are busy puffing their brains out, too. I recommend this place because the plain food is honest, filling, and cheap, and above all, the restaurant provides a visitor with a look into the real lives of everyday Venetians.

**AREA**
Dorsoduro
**TELEPHONE**
52-38-126
**OPEN**
Mon–Sat, bar and lunch only
**CLOSED**
Sun, Christmas to New Year's, Aug
**HOURS**
Bar noon–8 P.M.; lunch noon–2:30 P.M.
**RESERVATIONS**
Not accepted
**CREDIT CARDS**
None
**À LA CARTE**
L 15,000–22,000, beverage extra
**MENÙ TURISTICO**
None
**COVER & SERVICE CHARGES**
No cover, service included
**ENGLISH**
None

## (30) GELATI NICO
### Zattere ai Gesuati, 922

The Zattere is the southernmost promenade in Venice and is especially popular with families who spend their Sunday afternoons strolling along the walkway that borders the Giudecca Canal. Along the way, there are several *gelaterie,* but Nico is far and away the best and most popular. I was first here on a freezing April afternoon during a driving rainstorm, and there were ten people ahead of me in line waiting to dig into their specialty, a *gianduiotto*: a large slice of dense chocolate hazelnut ice cream buried in whipped cream and served in a cup. You can eat here, but Cheap Eaters will certainly order their *passeggio* to go, because it will be only L 3,500. To have it served at a tiny table inside, or on the deck overlooking the canal, will set you back L 6,000. The same man has been dipping out *gianduiottos* for almost three decades; others have tried to imitate him, but none have ever equaled his version. There are other ice cream treats

**AREA**
Dorsoduro
**TELEPHONE**
52-25-293
**OPEN**
Mon–Wed, Fri–Sun
**CLOSED**
Thur, Dec 15–Jan 15
**HOURS**
7 A.M.–10 P.M., continuous service
**RESERVATIONS**
Not accepted
**CREDIT CARDS**
None
**À LA CARTE**
Gianduiotto to go, L 3,500, at a table, L 6,000; other ice cream from L 2,000
**MENÙ TURISTICO**
None
**COVER & SERVICE CHARGES**
None

**MENÙ TURISTICO**
None
**COVER & SERVICE CHARGES**
No cover, service included
**ENGLISH**
Usually

available, from sundaes to frappés, but about the only thing anyone orders here is the famous *gianduiotto*.

### (31) IL DOGE GELATERIE
### campo Santa Margherita, 3058 A

**AREA**
Dorsoduro
**TELEPHONE**
52-34-607
**OPEN**
Daily in summer; Tues–Sun in winter
**CLOSED**
Mon in winter; Nov–Jan
**HOURS**
Summer, 10 A.M.–1 A.M.; winter, 10:30 A.M.–8 P.M.
**RESERVATIONS**
Not accepted
**CREDIT CARDS**
None
**À LA CARTE**
*Gelato* from L 2,500
**MENÙ TURISTICO**
None
**COVER & SERVICE CHARGES**
None
**ENGLISH**
Limited

I must confess, I adore Italian *gelato*. Nowhere in Venice is it any better than at Il Doge Gelaterie, a shrine to this scrumptious treat located on the campo Santa Margherita. All the ice cream is made here by Giovanni Mladovan and his family. Helping out with the constant flow of customers is Ardit Graziella, and greeting them as they arrive is the friendly dog Alice. Giovanni has more than forty-seven superb flavors in his repertoire, including black-and-white coffee, rum, Amaretto, *marron glace, tiramisù,* and English trifle. He also makes countless fruit *sorbettos* in the summer and, to keep insistent dieters happy, several low-fat yogurts. However, this is the place to put your diet on hold because there is one flavor you positively cannot miss, and that is his special *panna cotta del Doge,* a custard-based ice cream swirled with ribbons of caramel. It sounds rather pedestrian, but let me assure you, after one taste you will agree that it is anything but. Just thinking about it makes me wish I was there right now eating another scoop or two of this celestial *gelato*.

### (32) L'INCONTRO
### campo Santa Margherita, 3062 A (near Ponte dei Pugni across rio Terra Canal)

**AREA**
Dorsoduro
**TELEPHONE**
52-22-404
**OPEN**
Tues–Sun
**CLOSED**
Mon, July
**HOURS**
Lunch 12:30–3 P.M., dinner 7:30–11 P.M.
**RESERVATIONS**
Advised
**CREDIT CARDS**
AMEX, MC, V
**À LA CARTE**
L 35,000, beverage extra
**MENÙ TURISTICO**
None

L'Incontro is just the kind of place you always hope will be just around the corner, and it was for me. The first time I researched Venice for *Cheap Eats in Italy,* I lived on campo Squellini, near the campo Santa Margherita in Dorsoduro. Naturally, I tried every Cheap Eat candidate in the vicinity, and L'Incontro topped my list of favorites. I liked it because it was local and extremely popular; it served dependable, well-priced food; and it was, until now, totally undiscovered. During my last stay in Venice, while working on the second edition, I ate here several times, and I am happy to say I still love this restaurant.

The small establishment is composed of two rooms, with a bar dividing them. The low-beamed ceilings, lacy window curtains, flowered tablecloths, baskets on the walls, and strawflower arrangements create a cozy, old-world atmosphere. If you go for dinner, give it a chance to fill up with other diners, and arrive about 8:30 or 9 P.M. When planning your meal, forget the long printed menu and stay strictly with the handwritten daily one. The owner, Luciano, is Sardinian, so the dishes reflect his love for the cooking of this region. The specials include generous servings of homemade pastas, including wonderful versions of gnocchi dressed in *pecorino* cheese sauce or with artichokes. The chef does not prepare any fish, but concentrates instead on wild game in season and grilled, roasted, or stewed beef and pork. You can always count on finding Angus beefsteak. The desserts are adequate, but not thrilling, so I always pass on the sweet course and walk over to Il Doge Gelaterie for a scoop of my favorite *gelato* (see above). The house wine is light and refreshing.

**NOTE:** When I first discovered L'Incontro, there was no sign. Now there is, but that does not mean it is going to be a snap to locate. It's toward the left end of the campo Santa Margherita as you head to campo Santa Barnaba and the floating vegetable market. At lunch and dinner you will see the daily menu taped to a small window to the left of the door. The restaurant is next to a mask shop. When all else fails, ask a shopkeeper. Everyone knows it.

**COVER & SERVICE CHARGES**
Cover L 3,000, service included
**ENGLISH**
Yes

## (33) TAVERNA SAN TROVASO
### fondamenta Priuli, 1016

The Taverna San Trovaso is small and very popular. You *must* call ahead for reservations and arrive on time if you expect to get a table. Readers of *Cheap Eats in Italy* as well as smart Venetians know and recommend it as a restaurant where a good, uncomplicated meal can be had for a moderate price. Restful and relaxing it is not, but typical, full of happy locals having a good time and raising the noise level by the minute, it is.

The *menù turistico* is a good value and offers enough choices not to be boring. The à la carte menu is varied and includes pizzas noon and night, so it should appeal to everyone. Servings are tremendous, thus it is imperative to arrive hungry in order to do justice to it all.

**AREA**
Dorsoduro
**TELEPHONE**
52-03-703
**OPEN**
Tues–Sun
**CLOSED**
Mon, Dec 31–Jan 2
**HOURS**
Lunch noon–2:30 P.M., dinner 7–9:30 P.M.
**RESERVATIONS**
Essential (and don't be late)
**CREDIT CARDS**
AMEX, MC, V
**À LA CARTE**
L 35,000, beverage extra; pizza from L 6,000
**MENÙ TURISTICO**
L 22,000, 3 courses, cover included, beverage included
**COVER & SERVICE CHARGES**
Cover L 2,000, service not included
**ENGLISH**
Yes, and English menu
**MISCELLANEOUS**
There is a nonsmoking section.

## (34) TONOLO
### salizzada San Pantalon, 3764

AREA
Dorsoduro

TELEPHONE
52-37-209

OPEN
Tues–Sun

CLOSED
Mon, Feb (1 week), Aug

HOURS
8 A.M.–9 P.M., continuous service

RESERVATIONS
Not accepted

CREDIT CARDS
None

À LA CARTE
Pastries from L 1,400

MENÙ TURISTICO
None

COVER & SERVICE CHARGES
None

ENGLISH
Very limited

You will undoubtedly be the only tourist when you join the students, blue-haired dowagers, well-dressed businessfolk, and shopkeepers at Tonolo, the most popular spot to have a cappuccino and pastry in the San Pantalon area of Venice. Before arriving, sharpen your elbows and your determination to better edge your way to the counter, where the young women somehow miraculously keep straight all the early morning orders as they are shouted. Open from 8 A.M. until 9 P.M., this constantly crowded bakery makes some of the best high-calorie treats in Venice, and everyone knows it. There are no tables, so you must eat standing or have your order packaged to go. In the morning, indulge in a fresh cream-filled doughnut, a plain or almond topped *cornetto* (croissant), raisin pound cake, or buttery brioche. At lunch, try two or three little pizzas. In the late afternoon, any one of their indulgent pastries or cakes will make you even happier that you are in Venice.

## (35) TRATTORIA DA BRUNO
### calle Lunga Santa Barnaba, 2754 A

AREA
Dorsoduro

TELEPHONE
52-06-978

OPEN
Mon–Sat

CLOSED
Sun, Aug 14–30, Dec 20–Jan 8

HOURS
Lunch 11:30 A.M.–3 P.M., dinner 5:30–10:30 P.M.

RESERVATIONS
Not necessary

CREDIT CARDS
None

À LA CARTE
L 25,000, beverage extra

MENÙ TURISTICO
L 17,000, 2 courses, cover and service included, beverage extra

COVER & SERVICE CHARGES
Cover L 1,500, service included

ENGLISH
Limited

Trattoria da Bruno has been serving budget-priced Venetian food longer than anyone cares to remember. The forty-nine seats in the two plain rooms are filled for lunch and dinner with pensioners, starving students, and anyone else on a hard-core budget in Venice. The food is not imaginative, there is no decor, and the service rarely smiles. What you get is a filling meal with absolutely no ruffles or flourishes.

The *menù turistico* includes a first and second course with vegetable, but no dessert or beverage. Another approach, if you are not ravenous, is to order just one course and a salad from the à la carte menu, sticking with the specials, since they will be the freshest items to come out of the kitchen. You can skip the fish because it is all frozen, and the desserts are packaged, so you do not need these either. The industrial strength house red or white wine is very low-priced. You can have a half liter here for almost what a glass would cost at home.

# Restaurants in San Marco

## (36) LEON BIANCO
### salizzada San Luca, 4153 (between campo San Luca and campo Manin)

When you want a snack or light meal and cannot face another slice of street pizza, try Leon Bianco, the type of place Venetians patronize day after day. Terrific *cicchetti* (finger-food snacks) and *tramezzini* (sandwiches) are served throughout the day, but hot food is offered only between noon and 3:30 P.M.

Rice or cheese croquettes, grilled shrimp, and roasted vegetables are only a few of the *cicchetti* you can pluck with a toothpick and pop into your mouth. There are always two or three hot dishes, and if you want to sample more than one, they will serve half portions. The *tramezzini*—toasted or plain bread filled with prosciutto, *funghi* (mushrooms), tomatoes, tuna, egg, shrimp, roast beef, or pork—were some of the best I tried in Venice. You can rub shoulders standing at the marble counters and bar, or if you want to take a more relaxed approach to your meal, you can sit on small benches around long tables and still not have any cover or service added to your bill. When you are finished eating, be local and take your dishes back up to the bar.

**AREA**
San Marco

**TELEPHONE**
52-21-180

**OPEN**
Mon–Sat

**CLOSED**
Sun

**HOURS**
Snacks 8 A.M.–8 P.M., hot food noon–3:30 P.M.

**RESERVATIONS**
Not accepted

**CREDIT CARDS**
None

**À LA CARTE**
*Cicchetti* from L 900, sandwiches from L 3,500, hot dishes from L 5,000

**MENÙ TURISTICO**
None

**COVER & SERVICE CHARGES**
No cover, service included

**ENGLISH**
None

## (37) OSTERIA AI ASSASSINI
### rio Terra dei Assassini, 3965

For years this was only a place to buy wine by the bottle or case. Then Giuseppe Galardi turned it into an *enoteca* (wine bar), and it has enjoyed popularity with the locals, probably because they are the only ones who can find it.

Actually, you can find it . . . if you have an abundance of determination and patience and are armed with the best street map of Venice money can buy. To add to the fun of the hunt, there is no name outside. Just look for the yellow light over the door, which is turned on when the place is open.

Ever day the long wooden tables and benches are filled with people having lunch or *cicchetti* while sipping a glass or two of the wide variety of wines available. *Cicchetti* are little snacks similar to Spanish tapas, ranging from a piece of bread with a slice of prosciutto to meatballs, deep-fried veggies, and whipped salt cod. For many, a few *cicchetti* with a glass of nice wine to go with

**AREA**
San Marco

**TELEPHONE**
52-87-986

**OPEN**
Mon–Fri; Sat dinner only

**CLOSED**
Sun, Aug (2 weeks)

**HOURS**
Lunch 11:30 A.M.–3 P.M., dinner 6:30 P.M.–midnight

**RESERVATIONS**
Not accepted

**CREDIT CARDS**
None

**À LA CARTE**
*Cicchetti* from L 3,500, meals for L 15,000, beverage extra

**MENÙ TURISTICO**
None

it can easily substitute for lunch or a light supper. The hot specials change daily, featuring a certain dish on each day of the week: Monday you will have soup, Tuesday stew, Wednesday *pasta e fagioli,* Thursday boiled meat or *baccalà,* Friday fish, and Saturday whatever the chef feels like cooking. The only dessert is a plate of *biscotti* to dip in sweet wine.

### (38) OSTERIA A LA CAMPANA
### calle dei Fabbi, 4720

**AREA**
San Marco

**TELEPHONE**
52-85-170

**OPEN**
Mon–Fri, Sun

**CLOSED**
Sat

**HOURS**
Lunch 10 A.M.–3 P.M., dinner 6:30–11 P.M.

**RESERVATIONS**
Not necessary

**CREDIT CARDS**
Not accepted

**À LA CARTE**
*Cicchetti* from L 2,000, 2-course meal for L 18,000, beverage extra

**MENÙ TURISTICO**
None

**COVER & SERVICE CHARGES**
No cover, service included

**ENGLISH**
Yes

"Where do you go for a good, cheap lunch in this neighborhood?" I asked Nellie, the friendly owner of one of my favorite Cheap Sleeps in Venice (see Locanda Casa Petrarch in *Cheap Sleeps in Italy*). "I go to La Campana on calle dei Fabbi," she said. Once found, you, too, will go back to this small, homey place with a dark wood interior that can charitably be called rustic. For the best selection at lunch, get there early when the *cicchetti* are at their picture-perfect best. You can always find rice balls with a mozzarella cheese pocket inside, tuna or potato puffs, braised vegetables, frittatas, and chunks of cheese all displayed along a counter. For an even Cheaper Eat, have your *cicchetti* standing at the bar and you can deduct about L 500 per item.

If you want something more substantial, ask what the chef prepared that morning. There is a posted menu but no one bothers looking at it. Fish is the Friday special, and on other days look for bean soup, hearty stews, and assorted risottos and pastas.

### (39) OSTERIA AL BACARETO
### salizzada S. Samuele, 3447

**AREA**
San Marco

**TELEPHONE**
52-89-336

**OPEN**
Mon–Fri; Sat lunch only

**CLOSED**
Sun, Aug

**HOURS**
Lunch noon–3 P.M., dinner 7–10 P.M.

**RESERVATIONS**
Advised

**CREDIT CARDS**
AMEX, MC, V

The house wine is good, the welcome always warm, the other diners interesting, and the prices fair. In short, this is a winner. Everyone seems to know each other at this comfortable family *osteria,* where you may see the neighborhood dogs sitting patiently by the door waiting for their masters to finish eating. At lunch, in order to feel part of the action, order a plate of *cicchetti* or a sandwich and a glass of the featured wine. Remember, if you stand at the bar to eat, you will save both the cover and the service charges. For dinner, reserve one or more of the sixteen places at any of the outside tables for a ringside seat on the evening *passeggiata.* If you stay with the chef's versions of Venetian dishes, the food will not disappoint. For example, the *risotti vari* (rice mixed with peas, squid, vegetables, or seafood) or the *bigoli in salsa* (wholemeal pasta with anchovy and onion sauce) are surefire first courses. Move on to the excellent seafood offerings and close with your choice of the three house desserts: *Buranelli biscotti* (Venetian cookies from Burano dipped in dessert wine), *tiramisù,* or Amaretto mousse.

**À LA CARTE**
*Cicchetti* from L 2,000, full meals from L 45,000, beverage extra

**MENÙ TURISTICO**
None

**COVER & SERVICE CHARGES**
Cover L 3,000, 12% service added

**ENGLISH**
Yes, and English menu

## (40) PREMIATA LATTERIA VENEZIANA ZORZI
### calle dei Fuseri, 4359-4352

It looks from the outside like dozens of other bars selling assorted sandwiches and packaged goodies, but the difference is the dining room in back and another, larger one upstairs with a nonsmoking section. The downstairs dining is considered to be part of the bar, so there is no cover charge to sit and eat here. Eating upstairs will add L 1,000 cover charge per person to the bill. For anyone looking for lighter fare with light price tags to match, this vegetarian restaurant is one answer. Here you will mingle with office workers, young mothers with their babies in tow, students, and smart tourists eating *crostini* (toasted bread with different toppings), spinach or pumpkin crêpes, spaghetti with soya *ragù,* rice with vegetables, and lovely salads. Freshly squeezed juices and toasted sandwiches are always available, but hot food is served only at lunchtime.

**AREA**
San Marco

**TELEPHONE**
52-25-350

**OPEN**
Mon–Sat bar and lunch only

**CLOSED**
Sun, July (dates vary)

**HOURS**
Bar and sandwiches 7:30 A.M.– 8:30 P.M., lunch noon–3 P.M.

**RESERVATIONS**
Not accepted

**CREDIT CARDS**
MC, V

**À LA CARTE**
Sandwiches from L 4,000, hot dishes L 6,500–14,000

**MENÙ TURISTICO**
None

**COVER & SERVICE CHARGES**
Downstairs, L 500 bread charge per piece; Upstairs, cover L 1,000; service not included

**ENGLISH**
Limited

## (41) ROSTICCERIA S. BARTOLOMEO
### calle della Bissa, 5424 (on campo S. Bartolomeo, near the Rialto Bridge)

Cheap Eaters do not go to the upstairs restaurant here. Instead they stay downstairs, go through the self-service line, and take their food to one of the long bar-tables by the window, thus avoiding the cover, service, and higher prices for almost the same food served upstairs. The downstairs cafeteria is a popular refueling stop for those who want a proper meal. Featured each day are good selections of salads, pastas, and hot dishes that include the Venetian specialties of *baccalà alla Vicentina* (salt cod simmered in milk and herbs), deep-fried mozzarella, *seppie con polenta* (squid in its own black ink sauce), and all the usual desserts. For around

**AREA**
San Marco

**TELEPHONE**
52-23-569

**OPEN**
Tues–Sun

**CLOSED**
Mon

**HOURS**
Lunch 10 A.M.–2:30 P.M., dinner 5–9 P.M.

**RESERVATIONS**
Not accepted

**CREDIT CARDS**
AMEX, DC, MC, V

**À LA CARTE**
L 20,000–25,000, beverage included

**MENÙ TURISTICO**
L 16,000, 2 courses, cover and service included, beverage included

**COVER & SERVICE CHARGES**
No cover, service included

**ENGLISH**
Some

**MISCELLANEOUS**
Prices quoted are for downstairs dining

L 16,000 or so, you will get a two- or three-course meal and a glass of house wine, and in Venice, this is definitely a Cheap Eat.

## (42) SEMPIONE
### ponte Baretteri, 578

**AREA**
San Marco

**TELEPHONE**
52-26-022

**OPEN**
Mon, Wed–Sun

**CLOSED**
Tues, Dec–Jan

**HOURS**
Lunch 11:30 A.M.–3 P.M., dinner 6:30–10 P.M.

**RESERVATIONS**
Advised for dinner

**CREDIT CARDS**
AMEX, MC, V

**À LA CARTE**
L 45,000, beverage extra

**MENÙ TURISTICO**
None

**COVER & SERVICE CHARGES**
Cover L 3,000, 12% service added

**ENGLISH**
Yes, and English menu

The beautiful canalside setting, good service, and tempting Venetian cuisine draw me back to this restaurant time after time. Its privileged location near St. Mark's Square and some of the city's most luxurious shops makes it an ideal stop for a leisurely lunch or dinner. The best tables, naturally, are by the leaded windows overlooking the canal and the gondolas quietly floating by. The food is simple, with unfussy preparations and a lavish use of olive oil. *Pennette* (small penne) tossed with a well-flavored *amatriciana* sauce of tomatoes and sweet red peppers is a hit. So is the pasta with spider crab and the *spaghetti Sempione* with prawns, mussels, and octopus. Finish every drop, but save room for the heaping platter of scampi and squid, the calamari, or the filet of *S. Pietro* cooked in butter. Meat lovers will be pleased to find liver and onions served with polenta, steaks, veal dishes, and roast chicken. For a pleasant ending, I like to have a bowl of fresh strawberries or a slice of pineapple.

## (43) TRATTORIA DA NICO
### Frezzeria, 1702

**AREA**
San Marco

**TELEPHONE**
52-21-543

**OPEN**
Mon–Sat

**CLOSED**
Sun, Aug 1–15

**HOURS**
Lunch noon–2:30 P.M., dinner 7–10:30 P.M.

**RESERVATIONS**
Advised for dinner

**CREDIT CARDS**
AMEX, DC, MC, V

Da Nico, not too far from piazza San Marco, is always crowded early in the evening with regulars and their families who show up for the simple, well-prepared traditional cuisine offered by owner-chef Donato. It is a comfortable restaurant, with salmon-colored tablecloths, half-wood walls, bright lights, and abstract paintings. The waiters are serious and helpful, and the welcome offered by Leonella, Donato's pretty daughter, is always genuinely friendly.

Among the first-course pastas, the popular favorite is the house specialty: *tagliatelle alla boscaiola,* a subtle interplay of mushrooms, tomatoes, and smoky bacon with a light dusting of freshly grated Parmesan cheese.

Fish fanciers will be pleased to find Adriatric sole lightly cooked in butter, grilled scampi, and a platter of mixed fried fish. Meat eaters will enjoy the sautéed chopped calf's liver with onions or the *petto di pollo alla "Nico,"* a breast of chicken served in a light mushroom sauce and garnished with vegetables. For dessert, either the fresh fruit tart or the delicious nut cake are the best choices.

**NOTE:** Prices here can quickly climb into the Big Splurge category, so unless your budget is flexible, reserve a table here for a late-night dinner or another special occasion.

**À LA CARTE**
L 55,000, beverage extra
**MENÙ TURISTICO**
None
**COVER & SERVICE CHARGES**
Cover L 4,000, 12% service added
**ENGLISH**
Yes, and English menu

## Restaurants in San Polo

### (44) ALIANI GASTRONOMIA
### ruga Vecchia S. Giovanni, 654-655 (main street leading to Rialto Bridge)

For fast, flavorful, and fabulous deli-style takeout, one of the best and most central spots is Aliani Gastronomia near the Rialto Bridge. The shop, owned and operated by Bruno Aliani and his charming wife, who tends the cash register, has been doing business in this location for twenty-six years and only gets better with time. Fresh daily pastas, roast meats, seasonal vegetables, a wide variety of Italian hams and cheeses, and bottles of wine from the Veneto keep customers returning. There are no tables or bar areas for dining here, and no beverages sold by the glass, so it is best to purchase drinks somewhere along this busy street and take your gourmet picnic elsewhere to enjoy.

Though the deli section is open for business on Monday, hot food is available only from Tuesday to Saturday.

**AREA**
San Polo
**TELEPHONE**
52-24-913
**OPEN**
Tues–Sat; Mon morning only
**CLOSED**
Sun, Aug
**HOURS**
8 A.M.–1 P.M., 5–7:30 P.M., continuous service
**RESERVATIONS**
Not accepted
**CREDIT CARDS**
None
**À LA CARTE**
Between L 8,000–15,000, beverage extra
**MENÙ TURISTICO**
None
**COVER & SERVICE CHARGES**
None
**ENGLISH**
Yes, the owner speaks English

### (45) ALLA MADONNA
### calle della Madonna, 594 (near Rialto Bridge)

Alla Madonna is in a pivotal location on a narrow street on the San Polo side of the Rialto Bridge. Almost every guidebook on Venice lists it as one of the restaurants you *must* visit, and for good reason. The fresh fish is always delicious and reasonable, and the atmosphere is typical and pleasing. The unadorned tables are filled every day with a good mix of chattering Venetians and visitors. If you arrive without reservations after about 12:15 for lunch or 7:30 for dinner, you can expect to

**AREA**
San Polo
**TELEPHONE**
52-23-824
**OPEN**
Mon, Tues, Thur–Sun
**CLOSED**
Wed, Aug 1–15, Dec 20–Jan 31
**HOURS**
Lunch noon–3 P.M., dinner 7–9:30 P.M.

wait up to an hour for a table, so beware. Service by white-coated waiters, some of whom have been on the job since time began, can be brusque, but given the number of tables they have to serve, it is easy to see why patience can run thin during the crunch.

From appetizer to pasta and main course, the star of the show is always fresh fish. As you enter, you will pass an iced display of only some of the many delicacies awaiting you. The specialties are seafood rice, spaghetti with black squid, squid with polenta, fried cuttlefish, mixed fish fry, and grilled sole. Add a salad or fresh vegetable and a slice of Madonna cake (cream-filled sponge cake), and you will be in seventh heaven, or close to it.

**RESERVATIONS**
Absolutely essential
**CREDIT CARDS**
AMEX, MC, V
**À LA CARTE**
L 35,000, beverage extra
**MENÙ TURISTICO**
None
**COVER & SERVICE CHARGES**
Cover L 2,500, 12% service added
**ENGLISH**
Yes, and English menu
**MISCELLANEOUS**
A member of Ristoranti della Buona Accoglienza; see page 138 for details

### (46) ALL' ANTICO PIZZO'
### San Mateo, 814 (near Rialto Market)

The Rialto fish and produce market is one of the top tourist attractions in Venice, and I recommend it highly. Today the old commercial meeting-place along the quay is a lively and colorful outdoor market crowded with countless stalls and shouting hawkers selling everything that is seasonally fresh. Housewives and chefs come early each morning for the best food available, and visitors wander through eager to soak up the local color and take advantage of the many interesting photo opportunities.

Whenever you are in this area, a good target for lunch is Antico Pizzo'. The two rooms with simply laid tables are filled every day with regulars, who come for the fine fish offered by Vittorio Marcolin and his two brothers, Mario and Fabio. As you enter, the fresh fish and anti-pasti display will tempt you. Fish is number one here, prepared simply and without fanfare. Start with the fish risotto or the lasagna layered with fish. For the main course, I suggest the *fritto misto dell' Adriatico* (assorted fried Adriatic fish) or the *coda di rospo ai ferri* (grilled angler fish). Always ask what the daily specials are because they are bound to be winners. Landlubbers can settle for an omelette, liver with onions, or veal scaloppine, but frankly, the order of the day here should be fish. Desserts are not a high priority with the chef.

**AREA**
San Polo
**TELEPHONE**
52-31-575
**OPEN**
Tues–Sat; Sun lunch only
**CLOSED**
Mon, Jan (2 weeks), Aug (dates vary)
**HOURS**
Lunch 12:30–2:30 P.M., dinner 7:30–10 P.M.
**RESERVATIONS**
Not necessary
**CREDIT CARDS**
None
**À LA CARTE**
L 45,000, beverage extra
**MENÙ TURISTICO**
None
**COVER & SERVICE CHARGES**
Cover L 3,000, service included
**ENGLISH**
Yes, and English menu

### (47) ANTICHE CARAMPANE
### rio Terra de le Carampane, 1911

Almost everything from the formal atmosphere to the reliably good food remains unchanged at Antiche

**AREA**
San Polo
**TELEPHONE**
52-40-165

Carampane, reported to be one of the oldest taverns in Venice. For a dress-up meal designed to impress your boss, difficult mother-in-law, or important date, this should do very well, provided everyone likes fish, since that is all they serve. To help casual guests not "in the know," there is a sign posted outside stating that they do not serve pizza, lasagne, or pasta with *ragù* sauce. They should also add there is no printed menu. The food you eat depends on what looked best that day at the Rialto Market. The selections for each course are priced the same: antipasti L 15,000, *primi piatti* L 15,000, *secondi piatti* either L 20,000 or L 25,000, vegetables or a salad L 5,000, and the homemade desserts on the house. So are the *biscotti* served with after-dinner coffee. This is a Big Splurge designed for the old-school person who avoids life in the fast lane.

**OPEN**
Tues–Sat, Sun lunch only

**CLOSED**
Mon, Aug

**HOURS**
Lunch noon–3:30 P.M., dinner 7–11 P.M.

**RESERVATIONS**
Advised

**CREDIT CARDS**
AMEX, DC, MC, V

**À LA CARTE**
L 55,000–60,000, beverage extra

**MENÙ TURISTICO**
None

**COVER & SERVICE CHARGES**
Cover L 3,500, service included

**ENGLISH**
No

### (48) CAFFÈ DEI FRARI
**fondamenta dei Frari, 2564 (foot of ponte dei Frari after leaving campo dei Frari)**

At this rambunctious *caffè* near the campo dei Frari, you will find yourself sitting with Venetian students, men quaffing a third glass of Chianti far too early in the day, and elderly women jump-starting their trip to the market with a latte or cappuccino. There is always neighborly service and made-to-order savory sandwiches served from dawn to dusk by owners Giorgio and Dodo and their casual back-up crew. I like to go around noon and order a pocket-bread sandwich filled with slices of *prosciutto crudo* (air-dried salt-cured ham) and thin slices of provolone or *mozzarella di bufala* cheese. For the best people-watching, sit downstairs at one of the six round tables along the padded banquette, or in summer, at one of the tables outside facing the canal.

**AREA**
San Polo

**TELEPHONE**
52-41-877

**OPEN**
Mon–Sat

**CLOSED**
Sun, Aug 1–10

**HOURS**
7:30 A.M.–9 P.M., continuous service

**RESERVATIONS**
Not accepted

**CREDIT CARDS**
None

**À LA CARTE**
Sandwiches from L 3,500

**MENÙ TURISTICO**
None

**COVER & SERVICE CHARGES**
None, but prices higher for table service than at the bar

**ENGLISH**
Some

### (49) CAFFÈ ORIENTALE
**rio Marin, 2426 (at Fondamenta d. Late and calle dell' Olio o del Caffettier)**

Caffè Orientale is a special restaurant to save for a Big Splurge. It is located in a picturesque, upscale corner of Venice laced with quiet canals. On a warm day or balmy evening you want to sit on the terrace at a table along the water. Otherwise, request a table in the second room, away from the kitchen.

**AREA**
San Polo

**TELEPHONE**
71-98-04

**OPEN**
Tues–Sat; Sun lunch only

**CLOSED**
Mon, Jan, Aug (dates vary)

Lunch 12:30–2:30 P.M., dinner 7:30–10:30 P.M.

**RESERVATIONS**
Essential for terrace, advised otherwise

**CREDIT CARDS**
AMEX, DC, MC, V

**À LA CARTE**
L 55,000, beverage extra

**MENÙ TURISTICO**
Non

**COVER & SERVICE CHARGES**
No cover, service included

**ENGLISH**
Yes

**MISCELLANEOUS**
A member of Ristoranti della Buona Accoglienza; see page 138 for more details.

Christina Dellatoffola has been running this oasis of quiet, good service and reliable food for over ten years. Her attention to detail and imagination is first evident in the whimsical front window display of an elaborately dressed oriental potentate looking at a menu. Inside there is another full-size figure in the corner, complete with turban and robes. The rest of the interior is dignified, with correct table settings, waiters in black pants who speak some English, and black-and-white drawings of Venetian waterways.

The menu selections are first-rate and rotate with each season. Some specialties you'll always find. The *prosciutto crudo,* boiled shrimps, grilled scallops, and sole marinated with onions are appetizer favorites of the stylishly well-dressed regulars. Seafood pastas make up the bulk of the first courses, and for the second, the fresh catches of the day dominate. Meat eaters are not completely forgotten as there are several beef dishes and the ever-present liver and onions. I think the most satisfying dessert is the *semifreddo di Torrone,* a creamy smooth, soft nougat ice cream. Coffee is served with a plate of Venetian cookies.

### (50) CANTINA DO MORI
### calle do Mori, 429 (off ruga Vecchia S. Giovanni)

**AREA**
San Polo

**TELEPHONE**
52-25-401

**OPEN**
Mon–Sat bar and lunch only; Wed lunch only

**CLOSED**
Sun, July 15–Aug 15

**HOURS**
Bar 8:30 A.M.–1:30 P.M., 5–8:30 P.M.; lunch noon–1:30 P.M.

**RESERVATIONS**
Not accepted

**CREDIT CARDS**
None

**À LA CARTE**
Cicchetti from L 2,500, sandwiches from L 4,000

**MENÙ TURISTICO**
None

**COVER & SERVICE CHARGES**
None

**ENGLISH**
No, but the owner speaks French and German

For a glimpse of where the Rialto Market traders, delivery boys, and local office workers go for wine and camaraderie in a decidedly male-dominated atmosphere, look no further than Cantina do Mori. Inside it is long, narrow, dark, and smoky. Hams hanging from low beams, a stand-up bar (there are no tables at all), great *cicchetti,* platters of local salami and prosciutto, enormous sandwiches, and more than sixty wines sold by the glass are part of this traditional wine bar. In existence since 1462, this *enoteca* is now run by knowledgeable sommelier Roberto Biscontin. He will be happy to advise you on which wines you should drink with whatever you are eating. For instance, if it is salt cod, it should be a glass of Prosecco. With winter sausage and beans, you will need a robust Cabernet.

## (51) CANTINA DO SPADE DA GIORGIO
### calle do Spade, 860

Cantina do Spade is almost lost in the Venetian laby-rinth under the archways of the Do Spade Bridge just south of the Rialto Market. Don't look for a sign, be-cause there isn't one. Look for two lanterns and two wine barrels on each side of the entrance at 860 calle do Spade; a blackboard with the day's specials handwritten on it is hanging to the right. These will be the only indications that this is the place you are looking for.

For more than two decades, Giorgio Lanza and his family have been pouring wine while dispensing good cheer, wonderful snacks and sandwiches, and a lineup of hot dishes at noon to their multitude of dedicated re-turnees, many of whom consider this to be their semipri-vate club. There are over 220 wines available by the glass. And you will never run out of sandwich choices— try wild boar ham, salted cod, rabbit, elk, deer and the Do Spade Sandwich, spicy ham covered with fresh herbs and piled onto crusty bread. Arrive early to sample their hot dishes, such as *baccalà* with polenta, risotto with pumpkin, and their he-man dish called *musetto,* which is sausage with beans and polenta. Probably not for the Jenny Craig followers in your group, but good for those brave enough to withstand the calorie overload.

**AREA**
San Polo
**TELEPHONE**
52-10-574
**OPEN**
Mon–Sat bar and lunch only; Thur half day only
**CLOSED**
Sun, Aug
**HOURS**
Bar and sandwiches 9 A.M.–2:30 P.M., 4:30–8:30 P.M., hot lunch noon–2:30 P.M.
**RESERVATIONS**
Not accepted
**CREDIT CARDS**
None
**À LA CARTE**
Sandwiches from L 2,000, daily specials from 6,000
**MENÙ TURISTICO**
None
**COVER & SERVICE CHARGES**
Cover from L 300–1,000 (depending on order), 10% service added
**ENGLISH**
Some
**MISCELLANEOUS**
No coffee is served

## (52) IGNAZIO
### calle Saoneri, 2749

Ignazio is named after Florenzo Scroccaro's father, who began this fine family-run restaurant in 1951. Then as now, it serves some of the best food in Venice. Just ask anyone who has ever eaten there and they will agree . . . I know I do.

Everything is impressive, from the host's warm greet-ing to the last forkful of dessert. Great pains are taken to lay a handsome table using delicate china and attractive glass and silverware. In the summer, there is an added bonus of a leafy green outdoor garden for alfresco dining. The English-speaking waiters carry out their duties with professionalism.

One taste of the food, prepared by three hardworking female chefs, including Ignazio's wife, and you will know you are in the hands of talented women. It is clear that they are all an important part of this extended family. When I was last there for lunch, one of the owner's daughters ran through the restaurant, heavy

**AREA**
San Polo
**TELEPHONE**
52-34-852
**OPEN**
Mon–Fri, Sun
**CLOSED**
Sat, 2 weeks before Carnivale, July (last two weeks)
**HOURS**
Lunch noon–3 P.M., dinner 7–10 P.M.
**RESERVATIONS**
Essential
**CREDIT CARDS**
AMEX, DC, MC, V
**À LA CARTE**
L 50,000, beverage extra
**MENÙ TURISTICO**
None

**COVER & SERVICE CHARGES**
Cover L 2,500, 12% service
added
**ENGLISH**
Yes, and English menu
**MISCELLANEOUS**
A member of Ristoranti della
Buona Accoglienza; see page
138 for details.

book bag in tow, and headed straight for the kitchen, where all work came to a halt and the girl was warmly greeted with kisses and hugs from everyone.

The meal begins with an assortment of antipasti, perhaps huge prawns bathed in lemon oil dressing or the mixed seafood plate. For the first course, I recommend their special *spaghetti alla trapanese*: egg pasta tossed with a mixture of eggplant, peppers, tomatoes, and garlic in a light cream sauce. Although fish is king here, with grilled sole or sea crab heading the list, meat eaters can order the Venetian-style sautéed liver and polenta or the veal scallop prepared "as you wish." Desserts, so often the least distinguished part of an Italian meal, are excellent, especially the homemade *tiramisù*, that rich favorite made with Mascarpone, a sweet triple-cream cheese, Prices at Ignazio tend to run a little high, so if cost is a factor, select this one for a special occasion.

## (53) MENSA UNIVERSITA CANTEEN
### calle Magazen, 2480

**AREA**
San Polo
**TELEPHONE**
71-80-96
**OPEN**
Mon–Sat; Sun lunch only
**CLOSED**
School holidays, Aug
**HOURS**
Lunch 11:45 A.M.–2:30 P.M.,
dinner 6:30–8:30 P.M.; Sunday
noon–2 P.M.
**RESERVATIONS**
Not accepted
**CREDIT CARDS**
None
**À LA CARTE**
None
**MENÙ TURISTICO**
L 6,000, 3 courses, cover and
service included, beverage
included
**COVER & SERVICE CHARGES**
Both included
**ENGLISH**
Yes, usually
**MISCELLANEOUS**
Open only to university
students

The Mensa Universita Canteen is open to any student who can show a current I.D. card from his or her university. When I commented on what a Cheap Eat I thought this is, I was sternly told that this is expensive by some students' standards. In the south of Italy (they didn't say where), the same food goes for between L 500 and L 1,000. Nevermind, this is Venice, and for this expensive city, this must be the Cheapest Eat on the island.

Here is what you get: a three-course meal starting with soup, rice, or pasta, followed by a meat course garnished with seasonal vegetables or a salad, bread, and dessert, cheese, or fruit. Included is a bottle of either plain or carbonated mineral water, a soft drink, wine, or beer. Almost any place else, food dished out at these giveaway prices would cause a stampede. But it is all quite civil here, with seating at long communal tables where you can brush up on your Italian with your fellow students.

**NOTE:** There is a second university canteen with the same charitable prices. It is along the rio Novo in Dorsoduro, near campo Santa Margarita (tel: 52-41-268).

## (54) OSTERIA ANTICO DOLO
### ruga Vecchia San Giovanni, 778 (ruga Rialto)

For good wine and food near the Rialto Bridge, stop by Antico Dolo, a picture-postcard version of a typical wine bar frequented by neighborhood residents and shopkeepers.

The front half is the wine bar, and ten tables are squeezed into the restaurant section in back, which is decorated with pots hanging on beams and a lazy ceiling fan slowly moving the air. The size does not seem to deter the faithful, including gondoliers, who swear by the chef's dishes of country sausages, hearty seafood pastas, locally caught fish, and tripe with Parmesan cheese. The wine selections are better than the dessert options, of which there are two: *biscotti* or *gelato*.

**AREA**
San Polo
**TELEPHONE**
52-26-546
**OPEN**
Mon–Sat
**CLOSED**
Sun, Feb, Aug (middle 10 days)
**HOURS**
Lunch 10:30 A.M.–2 P.M., dinner 6:30–10:30 P.M.
**RESERVATIONS**
Advised
**CREDIT CARDS**
None
**À LA CARTE**
L 25,000–35,000, beverage extra
**MENÙ TURISTICO**
None
**COVER & SERVICE CHARGES**
Cover L 2,000, service included
**ENGLISH**
Yes

## (55) OSTERIA DA FIORE
### calle del Scaleter, 2202

Everyone has a favorite fish restaurant in Venice, and this one is mine. Run by a charming man and his wife, who is the capable chef, it has been in operation since 1978. Since that time it has built an enviable reputation for serving only the best and freshest seasonal seafood available. The well-designed interior is beautiful in its overall simple elegance. A vase of flowers graces each well-spaced table, set with soft yellow linen, large wine glasses, and shining cutlery. Formally dressed waiters are versed in explaining the menu and suggesting appropriate wines. Please note that meat is not served, and only one pasta does not contain fish.

For delicious openers, you can always count on a seafood salad or a delicate fish soup. According to the time of year, you might see imaginative dishes featuring octopus, scallops, or razor clams. First courses include a very light consommé with scampi and ravioli filled with a light white fish. Be sure to save adequate room to do justice to the main courses, which also vary with the season. Look for grilled eel, filet of striped bass splashed with balsamic vinegar, turbot baked in a potato crust, and soft-shelled crab served with polenta. For dessert, the lemon *sorbetto* or the vanilla ice cream in a wine soaked pear are light finishes to this lovely meal. Yes, this is definitely a Big Splurge, but one I hope you will agree is worth it.

**AREA**
San Polo
**TELEPHONE**
72-13-08
**OPEN**
Tues–Sat
**CLOSED**
Sun, Mon, Dec 15–Jan 6
**HOURS**
Lunch 12:30–2:30 P.M., dinner 7:30–10:30 P.M.
**RESERVATIONS**
Essential as far in advance as possible
**CREDIT CARDS**
AMEX, DC, MC, V
**À LA CARTE**
L 60,000, beverage extra
**MENÙ TURISTICO**
None
**COVER & SERVICE CHARGES**
Cover L 5,000, service included
**ENGLISH**
Yes
**MISCELLANEOUS**
A member of Ristoranti della Buona Accoglienza; see page 138 for details

## (56) TRATTORIA PIZZERIA SAN TOMÀ
### campo San Tomà, 2864 A

**AREA**
San Polo

**TELEPHONE**
52-38-819

**OPEN**
Mon, Wed–Sun

**CLOSED**
Tues, Feb 1–15, Nov 15–
Dec 15 (dates can vary)

**HOURS**
Lunch noon–3 P.M., dinner
7:30–10:30 P.M. (till 11 P.M. for
pizza)

**RESERVATIONS**
Advised for weekends and
holidays

**CREDIT CARDS**
AMEX, DC, MC, V

**À LA CARTE**
Pizza L 6,000–14,000, one-plate
meals from L 15,000, full meals
from L 40,000, beverage extra

**MENÙ TURISTICO**
L 20,000, 3 courses, cover and
service included, beverage extra
(L 45,000 for Venetian
specialties)

**COVER & SERVICE CHARGES**
Cover L 2,000, 12% service added

**ENGLISH**
Yes, and English menu

Good pizza (with regular or whole wheat crusts),
delicious homemade pastas and bread, a better-than-
average *menù turistico,* friendly waiters offering good service, a beautiful lighted garden, and an outside dining
terrace on a piazza that is perfect for people-watching all
work together to create a memorable dining experience
at Bernardo Di-Zio's trattoria. If you don't order a pizza
or plate of pasta, consider his very special paella. When
you order this, you get to keep the bib that protects
your clothing from this juicy dish. Also on the menu
are the usual Venetian standards of marinated sardines,
fried fish, and liver with polenta. In a nod to Bernardo's
French wife, they serve a wonderful homemade beef
*tartare.* Because all the food servings are so big, dessert is
kept to a minimum, with the emphasis on *sorbetto, tartufo,*
or fruit.

The only drawback is the cover and service charges,
which can bump the price over the edge for many Cheap
Eater budgets. The good news is that a full, three-course
meal is *not* necessary. You can order one of the large
meal-size salads or a *piatto unico*—a one-plate dish of
goulash with pasta, lasagna, and salad or chicken and
fries—and still be treated as though you were ordering
the works.

## Restaurants in Santa Croce

## (57) AE OCHE
### calle del Tentor, 1552 A-B

**AREA**
Santa Croce

**TELEPHONE**
52-41-161

**OPEN**
Tues–Sun

**CLOSED**
Mon, Jan, Aug, Dec (dates vary)

**HOURS**
Lunch noon–3 P.M., dinner
7–11:30 P.M.

**RESERVATIONS**
Not accepted

**CREDIT CARDS**
MC, V

Ae Oche is young, fun, cheap, and good. This popular
gathering ground for the Italian fast-food generation is
*never* empty. I have yet to find a way to beat the Sunday
crowd of contented families who arrive for one of the
sixty-one varieties of crisp pizza and calzones. You can
dine outside on a little deck, in a tented garden in the
back, or at one of inside booths with bench seats crafted
from bed headboards.

Fire-eaters will love pizza No. 15, the *mangiafuoco*
featuring spicy salami, pepperoni, paprika, and tabasco
sauce. Tamer taste buds will appreciate No. 18, the
*capricciosa* topped with prosciutto, mushrooms, and

hearts of artichokes. The *disco volante* (flying saucer), two pizzas put together sandwich style, is not a stellar choice, and neither is the house wine. You are better off with something from their long international beer list, which offers brews from Australia and Mexico to the United States and Spain. There is also a regular trattoria menu with all the familiar antipasti, pastas, meats, and side dishes. A word of caution if you order from this part of the menu: many things are frozen, and these items are marked with an asterisk. Best to avoid these dishes.

**NOTE:** There are two streets named calle del Tentor, and it can be spelled Tentor or Tintor. On the map it is Tintor, on the street, Tentor. You want the one that leads into campo S. Giacomo dell'Orio.

**À LA CARTE**
Pizza from L 6,000, full meal from L 28,000, beverage extra

**MENÙ TURISTICO**
None

**COVER & SERVICE CHARGES**
Cover L 2,000, 12% service added

**ENGLISH**
Yes

## (58) BRODO DI GIUGGIOLE
### fondamenta Minotto, 158

Longtime restaurateur Irina Freguia took a tired old spot not far from piazzale Roma and turned it into an eye-catching winner that reminds me of someplace in California. The stark white walls, yellow tablecloths, black brentwood chairs with cane seats, white china, fresh flowers, nonsmoking section, and huge outside dining patio create a casually appealing atmosphere. This is enhanced by the informally dressed waiters, whose upbeat attitudes make everyone feel welcome.

The food is an imaginative mix of Venetian standbys with fish as the highlight. To begin, I suggest sharing a selection of regional fish and shellfish or an order (in season) of sautéed clams. The pastas are a step or two above the ordinary. I liked the spaghetti in a fresh tomato sauce with a taste of curry and the *tagliolini* with crab and zucchini. For the main course, any fresh fish is reliable, or try their special beef fondue Bourguignonne. For dessert everyone adores the *brodo di Giuggiole,* floating island in a sea of soft custard, or the chocolate fondue with fresh and dried fruits for dipping. As with most Venetian restaurants, if you order any of the fresh fish specialties, prices are no longer such a Cheap Eat deal. Therefore, it is best to save this for a time when your budget is more flexible.

**NOTE:** For a Cheap Sleep, be sure to see Irina's one-star hotel next door, Locanda Salieri. For more details, see *Cheap Sleeps in Italy.*

**AREA**
Santa Croce

**TELEPHONE**
52-42-486

**OPEN**
Tues–Sun

**CLOSED**
Mon

**HOURS**
Lunch noon–2:30 P.M., dinner 7:30–10:30 P.M.

**RESERVATIONS**
Advised for weekends

**CREDIT CARDS**
AMEX, MC, V

**À LA CARTE**
L 40,000–50,000, beverage extra

**MENÙ TURISTICO**
None

**COVER & SERVICE CHARGES**
Cover L 2,000, service included

**ENGLISH**
Yes, and English menu

**MISCELLANEOUS**
There is a nonsmoking section

## (59) LA BOUTIQUE DEL DOLCE
### rio Marin, 890

AREA
Santa Croce

TELEPHONE
71-85-23

OPEN
Mon, Tues, Thur–Sun

CLOSED
Wed, Aug

HOURS
6:30 A.M.–8 P.M., continuous service

RESERVATIONS
Not accepted

CREDIT CARDS
None

À LA CARTE
Pastries from L 3,000, individual pizzas and sandwiches from L 2,000

MENÙ TURISTICO
None

COVER & SERVICE CHARGES
None

ENGLISH
None

On my way to lunch at Caffè Orientale (see page 167), I walked by the large picture window of a bakery kitchen, where a corps of hardworking women were busy pulling trays of pastries from the ovens, putting the finishing touches on decorated cakes, and filling individual tarts with fresh fruit. It was an impressive operation. After asking around, I found that this was the kitchen for a well-known Venetian pastry shop just across the canal. Of course, I rushed right over, and I can tell you I liked what I found.

La Boutique del Dolce is owned by Gino Viviani, who worked for twenty years as an artisan glassblower on Murano. He also lived in Montreal, Canada, but does not admit to speaking English. His welcome is brusque and rather sharp. Maybe it is because his feet hurt and he feels overworked . . . who knows. It doesn't matter because, despite this, he sells some of the best pastries in Venice, and let me assure you, the competition is stiff. All of the products are made using only pure ingredients without coloring or additives. Whenever you go, expect a crowd, especially on Sundays around noon, when handsome fathers with several young children walk here to purchase dessert for their midday meal. In the morning, order several fruit-filled croissants. Later on, vegetable-based puff pastries, individual pizzas, and sandwiches made on their own breads go like hotcakes. In the afternoon, stop in for coffee and an airy rum meringue dusted with chocolate, or pick up a bag of their cookies or a box of hand-dipped chocolates for a special treat. Even if you don't buy a thing (a guaranteed impossibility), do go by to admire . . . and to smell.

## (60) LA ZUCCA
### San Giacomo dell'Orio, 1762 (by the ponte del Megio)

AREA
Santa Croce

TELEPHONE
52-41-570

OPEN
Mon–Sat

CLOSED
Sun

HOURS
Lunch 11 A.M.–3:30 P.M., dinner 7 P.M.–midnight

RESERVATIONS
Advised for dinner and holidays

Collectors of unusual cuisine take note: this may be your only chance to sample pumpkin pasta or pumpkin soup, two tasty treats from which this appealing little trattoria takes its name. Unfortunately, you will have to time your visit in the fall or winter, since these dishes are only available seasonally. The rest of the food shows a degree of originality, and while not everything works all the time, most of it does. The menu changes almost daily, and the young and enthusiastic owners strive to please a savvy group of youthful habitués, many of whom are vegetarians and appreciate the interesting ways the chef has with fresh vegetables.

Aside from the pumpkin creations, thin pasta tossed with mushrooms and rucola and the round *orecchietti* mixed with broccoli, smoked ricotta cheese, and spicy peppers are the first-course front-runners. The chicken and pork "Chinese-style" leaves one wondering, but not the white wine sausage served with savoy cabbage or the lamb with fennel in a *pecorino* cheese sauce. Veggie admirers will want to try the carrots cooked with lemon and seasoned with curry, small onions simmered in Prosecco wine, or the potato and cauliflower gratinée. For dessert, the *panna cotta* with honey and nuts on top and the chocolate cream torte are first class in their simplicity.

I think the best seating is toward the back at a window table on the rio delle Megio canal rather than up front in the bar area where the shoulder-to-shoulder crowd can get a little loud at times. When you go, be sure to take a good look at the modern paintings of pumpkins in every guise imaginable lining the oak-paneled walls.

**CREDIT CARDS**
AMEX, MC, V

**À LA CARTE**
L 38,000, beverage extra

**MENÙ TURISTICO**
None

**COVER & SERVICE CHARGES**
Cover L 2,500, service included

**ENGLISH**
Yes

## (61) TRATTORIA ALLE BURCHIELLE
### Tre Ponti, fondamenta Burchielle, 393

Trattoria alle Burchielle was founded on this site in 1503 and is considered one of the oldest in continuous operation in Venice. Eighty-five years ago, Pagin Bruno's uncle took charge, and now, under Bruno and his niece Serena's direction, it is still going strong—a local favorite best known for its treatment of fresh fish. The restaurant is along a pretty canal in a picturesque corner of Venice, not too far from piazzale Roma. On a summer evening, it is wonderful to sit outside under the Venice moon and watch the boats drifting by while enjoying textbook examples of traditional Venetian preparations of fish.

Noteworthy among the first courses are the seafood lasagna and the spaghetti with whole clams. The most popular main courses are the *soglicla ai ferri* (grilled sole) and the giant prawns in a lemon, garlic, and olive oil marinade. There are a few meat dishes, but they are not the reason to eat here. Sweets adorn the pastry cart, but they are not made in-house. A nice change of pace for dessert is a selection of Italian cheeses. The menu is

**AREA**
Santa Croce

**TELEPHONE**
52-31-342

**OPEN**
Tues–Sun

**CLOSED**
Mon, Jan

**HOURS**
Lunch noon–3 P.M., dinner 7–10 P.M.

**RESERVATIONS**
Advised

**CREDIT CARDS**
AMEX, DC, MC, V

**À LA CARTE**
L 32,000, beverage extra

**MENÙ TURISTICO**
L 20,000, 3 courses, cover and service included, beverage extra

**COVER & SERVICE CHARGES**
Cover L 1,700, 10% service added

**ENGLISH**
Yes, and English menu

translated into English, but if you can understand restaurant Italian at all, ask for the Italian version and the list of daily specials. There is also a "hidden" *menù turistico*—you have to know to ask for it because it is not automatically handed out.

### (62) TRATTORIA ANTICA BESSETTA
### salizzada de Ca' Zusto, 1395

**AREA**
Santa Croce

**TELEPHONE**
72-16-87

**OPEN**
Mon, Thur–Sun

**CLOSED**
Tues, Wed, July 15–Aug 15

**HOURS**
Lunch 12:30–2:30 P.M., dinner 7:30–9:30 P.M.

**RESERVATIONS**
Essential for Sunday lunch, advised otherwise

**CREDIT CARDS**
None

**À LA CARTE**
L 45,000, beverage extra

**MENÙ TURISTICO**
None

**COVER & SERVICE CHARGES**
Cover L 3,000, service included

**ENGLISH**
Very limited

**MISCELLANEOUS**
No large groups are accepted

For a slice of real Venetian homecooking without pretense, you can hardly get more authentic than this well-known and much-loved trattoria in Santa Croce run by Nereo Volpe and his wife, Mariuccia. The only problem is finding it. If you have a detailed map, good walking shoes, and infinite patience, you will be fine, since chances are excellent that you will get lost at least once before you find it (see below for directions).

The two rooms remind me of a granny's parlor, with lifelong collections and displays of beloved bric-a-brac. Here are antique copper pots and irons mixed in with old mirrors and dubious-quality paintings. Baskets of fresh fruit and produce are displayed along with a wagonwheel clock and a Mexican sombrero. Tables are traditionally set with linens and candles or a small lamp on each. Best time to go? I like it on Sunday for lunch, when it fills with extended families enjoying a part of Venetian life that is too rapidly vanishing.

From Mariuccia's kitchen come wonderful pastas, veal dishes, roast chicken, and simple desserts, all based on seasonal market shopping. The Volpes produce their own wines, a light pinot blanc and a lusty red cabernet. The restaurant is always crowded, making reservations essential, especially for Sunday lunch.

**NOTE:** To get there, look for the Riva di Biasio vaporetto stop. Take calle Zen and follow it to campo Riello, cross it, continuing in the same direction, and you will be on salizzada de Ca' Zusto.

## *Restaurants on Burano*

### (63) TRATTORIA AL GATTO NERO
### via Giudecca, 88

**AREA**
Burano

**TELEPHONE**
73-01-20

The gaily painted, multicolored houses, tranquil canals, and clusters of picturesque locals make Burano a giant photo opportunity. Most visitors come to Burano from Venice for two reasons: one, to buy the handmade lace, and two, to eat fish. Most tourists rarely stray from the via Baldassare Galuppi, which is lined with shops selling linen and lace and a selection of overpriced eating places featuring greasy fried fish guaranteed to induce acute heartburn. Just beyond all of this is the most attractive part of Burano, one blissfully free of fellow travelers. It is here that you will find Al Gatto Nero, named after its first boss, who was a fascist about 160 years ago.

Now it is one of the best trattorias on the island with plenty of charm and character, not to mention good food at moderate prices. It is the most crowded at lunchtime, when local residents order the *menù turistico,* which includes two courses and wine. You may want to skip the broiled eel, but not the fresh prawns, broiled sardines, or fresh sole. Desserts do not play a starring role, so you can concentrate fully on the rest of the meal. Of course, you will skip the meat dishes; they are real understudies.

**OPEN**
Tues–Sun

**CLOSED**
Mon, Jan, Nov (last 10 days)

**HOURS**
Lunch noon–3 P.M., dinner 6:30–9:30 P.M.

**RESERVATIONS**
Advised

**CREDIT CARDS**
AMEX, DC, MC, V

**À LA CARTE**
L 40,000, beverage extra

**MENÙ TURISTICO**
L 30,000, 2 courses, cover and service included, beverage included

**COVER & SERVICE CHARGES**
Cover L 3,000, service included

**ENGLISH**
Yes, and English menu

## Restaurants on La Guidecca

### (64) ALTANELLA
### calle delle Erbe, 268–270 (at rio de Ponte Lungo)

Altanella has what Italians call a *buona forchetta* ("a good fork") and a *buon bicchiere* ("a good glass"). Buried halfway down a narrow street on Guidecca Island, the Stradella family restaurant has been in business since the turn of the century preparing *only* fish. It looks undiscovered, but it is firmly on the map. Hemingway was a customer in his day, and now, François Mitterand eats here whenever he is in Venice. However, fame has not gone to anyone's head . . . the food is still marvelous.

During warm weather, reserve a table on the irresistibly romantic terrace overlooking the island's central canal. Otherwise, you can sit at one of the tables inside, where there are pictures of the restaurant in its early days and a photo of the founder over the kitchen door. Dishes I look forward to having again are the risotto with fish, the pasta with cuttlefish or mussels and sweet peppers, the grilled sea bream, and the flavorful tuna. The desserts are made here, so be sure to plan on a piece of the lush chocolate cake or the unusual pumpkin cake.

**AREA**
La Giudecca

**TELEPHONE**
52-27-780

**OPEN**
Wed–Sun

**CLOSED**
Mon, Tues, Jan–Carnivale, Aug 10–20

**HOURS**
Lunch 12:30–2 P.M., dinner 7:30–9 P.M.

**RESERVATIONS**
Essential in summer, advised rest of the year

**CREDIT CARDS**
None

**À LA CARTE**
L 45,000, beverage extra

**MENÙ TURISTICO**
None

**COVER & SERVICE CHARGES**
Cover L 2,500, 10% service added

**ENGLISH**
Yes, and English menu

# Restaurants on Lido

## (65) FAVORITA
### via Francesco Duodo, 33

The regulars at Favorita come for the good wine and the dependable fish preparations turned out by a hardworking squad of chefs. In addition, I like it because of its location: hidden in a pretty residential district about a twenty minute walk from the vaporetto stop.

Summer seating on the vine-covered terrace is always in demand, but the seats are hard plastic without cushions, and thus not many deals are made or romances begun while sitting here. The inside is more comfortable, and it is air-conditioned, a real bonus during the sizzling Venetian summers. The two large rooms have great atmosphere, with heavy beams, a nice collection of country furniture, liberal use of green plants and fresh flowers, and soft pink table linens.

The kitchen does not feature daily specials; instead it concentrates on doing a superb job with everything listed on the sensible menu. The emphasis is on fish. In fact, if you are not a fish eater you have two entrée choices: steak either plain or with peppers. The gnocchi with crab is perfect, and so is the spaghetti with fresh clams. Grilled eel, filet of sole, bass, a mixed grilled fish platter, and turbot make up the bulk of the main courses. The wine list is exceptional, listing only regional wines in all price categories. If something sweet is called for at the end of your meal, sip the vodka-lemon-Prosecco smoothie.

**AREA** Lido
**TELEPHONE** 52-61-626
**OPEN** Tues–Sun
**CLOSED** Mon, Jan
**HOURS** Lunch 12:30–2:30 P.M., dinner 7:30–10:30 P.M.
**RESERVATIONS** Essential
**CREDIT CARDS** AMEX, DC, MC, V
**À LA CARTE** L 45,000, beverage extra
**MENÙ TURISTICO** None
**COVER & SERVICE CHARGES** Cover L 3,000, service included
**ENGLISH** Yes, and English menu

## (66) RISTORANTE BELVEDERE E TAVOLA CALDA
### piazalle la Santa Maria Elisabetta, 4

If you are visiting the Lido for the day, chances are you will want to eat. Unless you know where to go, most of the food is overpriced tourist pizza or deadly dull and ludicrously expensive hotel dining; there does not seem to be much middle ground. Enter the Ristorante Belvedere and its Tavola Calda snack bar next door, which are part of the Hotel Belvedere (see *Cheap Sleeps in Italy*).

Everyone agrees that some of the best food to be had in this tourist mecca is at the Belvedere, right across the street from the vaporetto stop from Venice. At the restaurant, Cheap Eaters will order the *menù turistico,* a L 30,000 value that includes three courses, cover and service charges, and the beverage. The food, which

**AREA** Lido
**TELEPHONE** 52-60-115, 52-60-164
**OPEN** Tues–Sun
**CLOSED** Mon; Ristorante only, Nov–April
**HOURS** Lunch noon–2:30 P.M., dinner 7–9 P.M.
**RESERVATIONS** Advised for Ristorante, not accepted at Tavola Calda
**CREDIT CARDS** AMEX, DC, MC, V

features marvelous fresh fish, is served on a pretty street-side terrace or in the formal hotel dining room with big picture windows.

Confirmed card-carrying Cheap Eaters will skip the *ristorante* side completely and head straight for the Tavola Calda that adjoins it, which is just the answer for the visitor with lots on the agenda and no time or desire for a fancy meal. The same kitchen is used for both places, but the prices here are much lower. Every day there are pastas, roast chicken, fish, and an excellent selection of vegetables, salads, and made-to-order sandwiches. Another benefit is that it is open year round, while the hotel restaurant is closed from November to April.

**À LA CARTE**
Tavola Calda, L 18,000–22,000, beverage included; Ristorante, L 50,000, beverage extra

**MENÙ TURISTICO**
L 30,000, 3 courses, cover and service included, beverage included

**COVER & SERVICE CHARGES**
Tavola Calda, none; Ristorante, cover L 3,500, service included

**ENGLISH**
Yes, and English menu at Ristorante

### (67) TRATTORIA ANDRI
**via Lepanto, 21**

Trattoria Andri is in a pretty neighborhood only a five- or ten-minute stroll from the usual tourist trail on the island of Lido. There are ninety places outside on a covered terrace and maybe fifty more inside this lovely old villa. The interior is open and airy, featuring white walls hung with modern, abstract paintings and brass platters. Silk flowers are on each table, and a fresh bouquet is on the bar. The same family has been serving Lido residents for thirty years.

The best first course is the house specialty: *spaghetti Andri,* featuring fat shrimp. Grilled turbot or filet of sole sautéed in butter make good main course selections. Dessert calls for something light and the best choice, in my opinion, is not listed on the menu and does not have a name. Ask for the *limone digestif*—a frothy, refreshing mix of lemon, ice, sparkling wine, and vodka blended together like a milkshake and served in a champagne flute.

**AREA**
Lido

**TELEPHONE**
52-65-482

**OPEN**
Wed–Sun

**CLOSED**
Mon, Tues, Jan, Feb

**HOURS**
Lunch noon–3 P.M., dinner 7:30 P.M.–midnight

**RESERVATIONS**
Advised

**CREDIT CARDS**
V

**À LA CARTE**
L 40,000, beverage extra

**MENÙ TURISTICO**
None

**COVER & SERVICE CHARGES**
Cover L 2,500, 12% service added

**ENGLISH**
Yes, and English menu

## Restaurants on Murano

### (68) AI VETRAI
**fondamenta Manin, 29**

Forty-seven years ago Sergio Scarpa and his wife, Luisa, opened Ai Vetrai. Then it was a small restaurant with only a few tables, serving fresh fish. The years have changed things. Now there are seats for two hundred people in several rooms and on an outside terrace facing a canal. In the back room overlooking the garden, be sure

**AREA**
Murano

**TELEPHONE**
73-92-93

**OPEN**
Mon–Wed, Fri–Sun; Winter, lunch

**CLOSED**
Thur, Jan

to notice the framed artist's sketches done on the restaurant's napkins.

When you arrive, you will generally be met by the official greeter: Lea, a big, multilingual dog with a wagging tail. The menu is printed in four languages, and most of the waiters speak at least two. While he has expanded his operation, Sergio has not changed his goal: to provide reliable service and the best fresh meat and fish at fair and reasonable prices. The two-course *menù turistico* at L 22,000 is one of the best Cheap Eats on Murano. Daily specials, in addition to seasonally fresh fish, may include ravioli with spinach and ricotta cheese, spaghetti with whole clams, and *risotto de pesche* (rice with fish). In the summer there is continuous food service from 11:30 A.M. until 11 P.M., a real boon to visitors with different meal schedules.

**HOURS**
11:30 A.M.–11 P.M., continuous service; winter, 11:30 A.M.–5 P.M.

**RESERVATIONS**
Not necessary

**CREDIT CARDS**
AMEX, DC, MC, V

**À LA CARTE**
L 40,000–50,000, beverage extra

**MENÙ TURISTICO**
L 22,000, 2 courses, cover and service included, beverage extra

**COVER & SERVICE CHARGES**
Cover L 2,000, service included

**ENGLISH**
Yes, and English menu

### (69) ANTICA TRATTORIA MURANESE
fondamenta Cavour, 20

**AREA**
Murano

**TELEPHONE**
73-96-10

**OPEN**
Sun–Fri lunch only

**CLOSED**
Sat

**HOURS**
Noon–8 P.M., hot lunches noon–3 P.M.

**RESERVATIONS**
Not necessary

**CREDIT CARDS**
AMEX, MC, V

**À LA CARTE**
L 35,000, beverage extra

**MENÙ TURISTICO**
L 25,000, 3 courses, cover and service included, beverage extra

**COVER & SERVICE CHARGES**
Cover L 2,500, 12% service added

**ENGLISH**
Some

Situated on the canal about halfway down from the Venice vaporetto stop is the Antica Trattoria Muranese, a reliable bet for an unassuming seafood lunch in Murano. Thanks to the tourists who arrive by the boatload from Venice, Murano stays in business selling its famous glass. There are no real "local" spots, but at least here the food is honest and cheap . . . for Murano. There is a summer garden in back with tables and umbrellas. In the cooler months, seating is inside two steamy rooms with very little in the way of interior decoration.

Cheap Eaters are going to want the *menù turistico,* but you will have to ask for it because it is not usually displayed or offered. Haute cuisine is not one of the kitchen's strengths, so for maximum results, think simple. Rely on what has to be prepared to order, such as grilled fish or whatever they are pushing as the special. The uninteresting bakery desserts make it easy to bypass this course. House wine is okay, but a beer is probably better. Once the hot lunch is over around 3 P.M., sandwiches are served.

### (70) TRATTORIA BUSA ALLA TORRE DA LELE
campo S. Stefano, 3

**AREA**
Murano

**TELEPHONE**
73-96-62

Welcome to Lele and Christina's trattoria, where knowledgeable Venetians eat when they visit the island of Murano. More expensive, yes, but certainly worth the extra cost. Lele, a big man with red hair and a twinkle in his eye, is a Murano fixture who meets and greets his guests with gusto. His wife, Christina, keeps things moving from behind the bar. Waiters offer casual service, but time should not be a top priority on your visit here. There are two rooms inside the thirteenth-century building, but if weather permits, sit outside. Settle in at one of the terrace tables on the campo by the clock tower and enjoy a romantic, leisurely lunch, accompanied by a nice bottle of Venetian wine . . . and be glad you are not home having to mow the lawn.

The food probably will not sweep you off your feet with exotic or nouvelle interpretations. The kitchen does know, however, how to turn out classic dishes with finesse and just the right amount of dash. You will have the best success if you stick to any of the fresh fish offerings, paying close heed to whatever the chef has on for the daily special. The pasta with fresh clams, a brimming fish soup, and *tagliolini* with crab are only a few of the regular first courses. Fourteen main courses feature local fish, or you can order omelettes, beef, or veal. But, what for? Here you eat fish.

**OPEN**
Daily lunch only; winter, Tues–Sun

**CLOSED**
Mon in winter, Jan 10–30

**HOURS**
Noon–3:30 P.M.

**RESERVATIONS**
Advised

**CREDIT CARDS**
AMEX, DC, MC, V

**À LA CARTE**
L 45,000, beverage extra

**MENÙ TURISTICO**
None

**COVER & SERVICE CHARGES**
Cover L 2,000, 12% service added

**ENGLISH**
Yes, and English menu

# Food Shopping in Venice

## OUTDOOR MARKETS

Open-air markets selling fruits, vegetables, and flowers are set up in various squares every day but Sunday. They are all open in the mornings and sometimes in the afternoon. You will find them at Santa Maria Formosa (Castello), Santa Margherita (Dorsoduro), campiello dell'Anconetta (Cannaregio), rio Terrà San Leonardo (Cannaregio), and on a barge off campo Santa Barnaba (Dorsoduro). Generally speaking, hours are from Monday to Saturday 8:30 A.M. to 12:30 P.M., and afternoons, except Wednesday, from 3:30 to 7:30 P.M.

The market to end all markets is the famous Rialto Market next to the Rialto Bridge (San Polo). The hawker stalls lining the bridge sell everything from T-shirts and glassware to fake and real lace. These sellers are open from around 9 A.M. until 6 P.M. in the winter and later in the summer. The vegetable market (*erberia*) is the best, least expensive, and most colorful in Venice. It is open *only* in the morning from Monday to Saturday, 8 A.M. to 1 P.M. The fish market (*pescheria*) is one of the finest in Europe. Here you will see every known variety of fresh fish, and some you never knew existed. This is worth a trip, and don't forget your camera. Open Tuesday to Saturday from 8 A.M. to 1 P.M.

## SUPERMARKETS

Big supermarkets do not exist in Venice, and most of the so-called supermarkets are well hidden. Hours are usually from 8:30 A.M. to 12:30 P.M. and 3:30 to 7:30 P.M. from Monday through Saturday, except Wednesdays, when they are closed in the afternoon. Sunday, of course, is a full day of rest.

### Standa

*Strada Nuova, 3660, at campo San Felice*
*Cannaregio*
There is a second location on Lido on via Corfù.

### SMALLER MARKETS INCLUDE
### Car

*Zattere al Ponte Lungo, 1491*
*Dorsoduro*
They have a good liquor section.

### Minimarket
*Campo Santa Margherita, 3019/3112*
*Dorsoduro*

### Dogal
*Calle del Pistor, 3989*
*Castello*

### SuVe
*Corner of salizzada San Lio and calle Mondo Nuovo,*
*5812*
*Castello*

This is the most central market, and it has a good meat and cheese selection.

# Glossary of Words, Phrases, and Menu and Food Terms

This glossary is broken down into two main sections: the first half gives Italian equivalents for some general words and phrases you might need to use while ordering in a restaurant. The second half gives English translations of Italian words you might find as you read a menu. Many restaurants have English menus, but invariably they do not include the daily specials, which most often are the best items to order. This glossary is designed to help you make sure there will not be a difference between what you want to eat and what you actually order.

## GENERAL COURTESIES

| | |
|---|---|
| Hello (telephone) | *pronto* |
| Hello/goodbye (familiar) | *ciao* |
| Good morning | *buon giorno* |
| Good afternoon | *buon pomeriggio* |
| Good evening | *buona sera* |
| Good night | *buona notte* |
| Goodbye | *arrivederci* |
| Please | *per favore* |
| Thank you | *grazie* |
| You are welcome | *prego* |
| Yes/No | *si/no* |
| Excuse me | *mi scusi* |
| I am sorry | *mi dispiace* |
| Do you speak English? | *parla inglese?* |
| I don't speak Italian | *non parlo italiano* |
| I understand | *capisco* |
| I don't understand | *non capisco* |
| Where are the restrooms? | *dov'è la toilette [per signore (women), per signori (men)]* |
| How much is it? | *quanto costa?* |

**185**

| | |
|---|---|
| a little/a lot | *poco/tanto* |
| more/less | *più/meno* |
| enough/too much | *abbastanza/troppo* |
| open/closed | *aperto/chiuso* |
| Please telephone for a taxi | *per favore, telefoni per un tassi* |
| No smoking | *vietato fumare* |
| I am hungry | *ho fame* |
| I am diabetic | *ho il diabete* |
| I am on a diet | *sono a dieta* |
| I am vegetarian | *sono vegetariano (a)* |
| I cannot eat | *non posso mangiare* |
| It is hot/cold | *è caldo/freddo* |
| Please give me | *per favore, mi dia* |
| today, tonight, tomorrow, yesterday | *oggi, stastera, domani, ieri* |

## DAYS OF THE WEEK

| | |
|---|---|
| Monday | *lunedì* |
| Tuesday | *martedì* |
| Wednesday | *mercoledì* |
| Thursday | *giovedì* |
| Friday | *venerdì* |
| Saturday | *sabato* |
| Sunday | *domenica* |

## NUMBERS

| | |
|---|---|
| 1 | *uno* |
| 2 | *due* |
| 3 | *tre* |
| 4 | *quattro* |
| 5 | *cinque* |
| 6 | *sei* |
| 7 | *sette* |

| | |
|---|---|
| 8 | *otto* |
| 9 | *nove* |
| 10 | *dieci* |
| 11 | *undici* |
| 12 | *dodici* |
| 13 | *tredici* |
| 14 | *quattrodici* |
| 15 | *quindici* |
| 16 | *sedici* |
| 17 | *diciasette* |
| 18 | *diciotto* |
| 19 | *diciannove* |
| 20 | *vente* |
| 21 | *ventuno* |
| 30 | *trenta* |
| 40 | *quaranta* |
| 50 | *cinquanta* |
| 60 | *sessanta* |
| 70 | *settanta* |
| 80 | *ottanta* |
| 90 | *novanto* |
| 100 | *cento* |

## RESTAURANT BASICS

| | |
|---|---|
| waiter/waitress | *cameriere/cameriera* |
| breakfast | *colazione* |
| lunch | *pranzo* |
| dinner | *cena* |
| The menu, please | *la lista, per favore* |
| The wine list, please | *la lista dei vini, per favore* |
| The bill, please | *il conto, per favore* |
| service charge | *servizio* |

| | |
|---|---|
| cover charge | *pane e coperto* |
| Is the service included? | *il servizio è incluso?* |
| Service is included | *il servizio è compreso/incluso* |
| Service is not included | *il servizio non è compreso/incluso* |
| appetizers | *antipasti* |
| first courses | *primi piatti* |
| second courses | *secondi piatti* |
| side dishes | *contorni* |
| dessert | *dolce* |
| fixed-price menu | *menù turistico/prezzo fisso* |
| dish of the day | *piatto del giorno* |
| specialty of the house | *specialità della casa* |
| in season | *di stagione* |
| | |
| I need a: | *ho bisogno di* |
|    knife |    *un cotello* |
|    fork |    *una forchetta* |
|    spoon |    *un cucchiaio* |
|    cup |    *tazza* |
|    plate |    *piatto* |
|    ashtray |    *portacenere* |
|    chair |    *sedia* |
|    table |    *tavola* |
|    napkin |    *il tovagliolo* |
| | |
| I would like: | *vorrei* |
|    a cup of |    *una tazza di* |
|    a glass of |    *un bicchiere di* |
|    a bottle of |    *una bottiglia di* |
|    a half-bottle of |    *una mezza bottiglia di* |
|    a carafe of |    *una caraffa di* |
|    a liter of |    *uno litro di* |

| | |
|---|---|
| I would like it: | *vorrei essa/esso* (fem/mas) |
| barbequed | *alla brace* |
| boiled | *bolliot/lesso* |
| cooked | *cotto* |
| cooked in wine | *brasato* |
| firm, not overcooked (as in pasta) | *al dente* |
| fried | *fritto* |
| frozen | *surgelato* |
| grilled | *alla griglia/ferri* |
| on the spit | *allo spiedo* |
| rare | *al sangue/poco cotto* |
| raw | *crudo* |
| roast | *arrosto* |
| smoked | *affumicato* |
| steamed/stewed | *al vapore/umido* |
| stuffed | *ripieno* |
| well-done | *ben cotto* |

## READING THE MENU
### Types of Pasta

| | |
|---|---|
| *agnolotti* | filled pasta |
| *bigoli* | round, solid pasta (Venice) |
| *bucatini* | hollow spaghetti |
| *cannelloni* | stuffed pasta tubes |
| *capelli d'angelo* | angel hair pasta |
| *conchiglie* | pasta shells |
| *crespelle* | crêpes |
| *farfalle* | butterfly-shaped pasta |
| *fettuccine* | long, thin flat pasta |
| *fusilli* | spiral-shaped pasta |
| *gnocchi* | small potato dumplings |
| *lasagne* | large, flat noodles layered with ingredients and baked |

| | |
|---|---|
| *maccheroni* | macaroni |
| *orecchiette* | ear-shaped pasta |
| *paglia e fieno* | green and yellow tagliatelle |
| *pappardelle* | wide noodles |
| *pasta verde* | spinach noodles |
| *pasticcio* | baked pasta pie with cheese, vegetables, and meat |
| *penne* | narrow, diagonally cut macaroni |
| *ravioli* | filled pasta squares |
| *rigatoni* | large macaroni |
| *risotto (ai funghi, alla Milanese)* | rice (with mushrooms, saffron) |
| *rotelle* | spiral-shaped pasta |
| *tagliatelle* | thin, flat egg pasta ribbons |
| *taglierini* | thin pasta ribbons |
| *tagliolini* | thin, flat noodles |
| *tonnarelli* | square-shaped spaghetti |
| *tortelli* | ravioli with a filling of potato or spinach and ricotta cheese |
| *tortellini* | small meat-filled pasta dumplings |
| *tortellone* | large tortellini |
| *vermicelli* | thin spaghetti |
| *zite, ziti* | short, wide, tube-shaped pasta |

**Pasta Sauces**

| | |
|---|---|
| *aglio e olio (e peperoncino)* | tossed in garlic, olive oil (hot peppers) |
| *al burro (e salvia)* | with butter (and sage) |
| *amatriciana* | bacon, tomatoes, onion, hot pepper |
| *arrabbiata* | spicy tomato sauce with chilies |
| *bolognese* | meat sauce |

| | |
|---|---|
| *bucaniera* | seafood, tomato, garlic, parsley, oil |
| *cacciatora* | tomato, onion, peppers, mushrooms, garlic, herbs, wine sauce |
| *carbonara* | cream, ham or bacon, egg, Parmesan cheese |
| *frutta di mare* | seafood |
| *funghi* | mushroom |
| *panna* | cream |
| *parmigiano* | Parmesan cheese |
| *pesto* | ground pine nuts, basil, garlic, *pecorino* cheese |
| *pomodoro* | plain tomato sauce |
| *putanesca* | tomatoes, capers, red peppers, anchovies, garlic |
| *quattro formaggi* | with four cheeses |
| *ragù* | tomato-based meat sauce |
| *vongole* | clams or mussels, tomatoes, garlic |

## PLACES

| | |
|---|---|
| *alimentari* | grocery store |
| *caffè* | café |
| *enoteca* | wine shop/bar |
| *gastronomia* | grocery store |
| *gelateria* | ice cream shop |
| *il forno* | bread shop |
| *latteria* | cheese and dairy store |
| *osteria* | blue-collar wine bar |
| *paninoteca* | sandwich bar |
| *pasticceria* | pastry shop |
| *salumeria* | grocery store |
| *tabaccheria* | tobacconist, a place to get newspapers, bus tickets, lottery tickets, pens, etc. |

## OTHER MENU AND FOOD TERMS

### A

| | |
|---|---|
| *abbacchio* | milk-fed spring lamb |
| *acciughe* | anchovies |
| *aceto* | vinegar |
| *acqua cotta* | thick vegetable soup poured over bread |
| *acqua minerale (gassata, naturale)* | mineral water (sparkling, still) |
| *affettai misti* | assorted cold cuts |
| *affettato* | sliced |
| *affumicato* | smoked |
| *aglio* | garlic |
| *agnello* | lamb |
| *agrume* | citrus fruit |
| *albicocca* | apricot |
| *al carbone* | charcoal grilled |
| *al forno* | baked |
| *alici* | anchovies |
| *alla, all'* | in the style of, with |
| *alla brace, alla griglia* | charcoal grilled, grilled |
| *ananas* | pineapple |
| *anatra* | duck |
| *aneto* | dill |
| *anguilla (Veneziana)* | eel (cooked with lemon & tuna) |
| *antipasto* | appetizer |
| *antipasti misto* | assorted appetizers |
| *a piacere* | as you like it |
| *aperitivo* | apéritif |
| *aragosta* | lobster, crayfish |
| *arancia* | orange |
| *aringa* | herring |

| | |
|---|---|
| *arista* | roast pork |
| *arrosto* | roast |
| *asciutto* | dry |
| *asparagi* | asparagus |
| *assaggio* | a taste |
| *assagi* | a series of small portions |
| *astaco (astice)* | lobster |

**B**

| | |
|---|---|
| *baccalà* | dried salt cod |
| *bacelli* | fava beans (Tuscan) |
| *barbabietola* | beet |
| *Bel Paese* | soft, mild cheese |
| *bietole* | Swiss chard |
| *birra* | beer |
| *biscotti* | cookies |
| *bistecca* | beefsteak |
| *bistecca alla fiorentina* | T-bone steak, grilled over coals, served very rare |
| *bollito misto* | mixed boiled meats |
| *braciola* | steak, chop, slice of meat |
| *branzino* | sea bass |
| *bresaola* | air-cured beef, thinly sliced |
| *briosca* | croissant (also called *cornetto*) |
| *brodetto* | fish soup |
| *brodo* | broth |
| *bruschetta* | toasted garlic bread topped with tomatoes |
| *bue* | beef, ox |
| *burro* | butter |

**C**

| | |
|---|---|
| *cacciagione* | game |
| *caffè* | coffee, café |

| | |
|---|---|
| *calamaro (calamaretto)* | squid (baby squid) |
| *caldo* | hot/warm |
| *calzone* | stuffed pizza |
| *camomilla* | chamomile tea |
| *cannellini* | white beans |
| *cannoli (Siciliana)* | custard-filled pastry with pieces of candied fruit (pastry shells filled with ricotta cheese and dusted with sugar) |
| *caponata* | eggplant salad |
| *cappa santa* | scallops |
| *capperi* | capers |
| *capra (capretto)* | goat (baby goat) |
| *capriolo* | venison |
| *carbonade* | beef stewed with red wine |
| *carciofo (alla giudia)* | artichoke (deep fried) |
| *carne* | meat |
| *carpaccio* | thinly sliced raw beef |
| *casalinga* | homestyle |
| *cassata* | ice cream with candied fruit |
| *castagne* | chestnuts |
| *cavolfiore* | cauliflower |
| *cavolo (nero)* | cabbage (dark) |
| *ceci* | chickpeas |
| *cervella* | brains |
| *cicchetti* | snacks (Venice) |
| *ciliegia* | cherry |
| *cinghiale* | wild boar |
| *cioccolato* | chocolate |
| *cioccolato caldo* | hot chocolate |
| *cipolla* | onion |
| *concomero* | watermelon |
| *coda di bue alla vaccinara* | oxtail stew |

| | |
|---|---|
| *coda di roposso* | monkfish |
| *congelato* | frozen |
| *coniglio* | rabbit |
| *contorni* | side dishes (vegetables, salads, potatoes) |
| *coperto* | cover charge added per person to bill |
| *cornetto* | croissant (also called *briosca*) |
| *cotoletta* | chop or cutlet |
| *cozze* | mussels |
| *crema* | custard |
| *crespelle* | crêpes |
| *crostata* | open-faced fruit tart |
| *crostini* | toasted bread spread with pâté |
| *crudo* | raw (as in *prosciutto crudo,* raw ham) |
| *cucina* | kitchen, cooking |
| *cuore* | heart |

**D**

| | |
|---|---|
| *da portare via* | to take out |
| *degustazione* | tasting |
| *di stagione* | of the season |
| *dolce* | dessert |

**E**

| | |
|---|---|
| *erbe* | herbs |

**F**

| | |
|---|---|
| *fagiano* | pheasant |
| *fagioli* | beans |
| *fagiolini* | string beans |
| *fave* | fava beans |
| *fegatelli* | pork livers |
| *fegatini* | chicken livers |

| | |
|---|---|
| *fegato (alla Veneziana)* | calves' liver (with onions) |
| *fettunta* | garlic bread with fresh olive oil (Florence) |
| *fichi* | figs |
| *filetto* | filet |
| *finocchio* | fennel |
| *fior di zucca, fiori di zucchino* | stuffed and fried zucchini flowers |
| *focaccia* | flat bread |
| *Fontina* | delicate, buttery cheese |
| *formaggio* | cheese |
| *fragole* | strawberries |
| *fragoline* | tiny wild strawberries |
| *freddo* | cold |
| *fritelle* | fritters |
| *frittata* | unfolded omelette |
| *fritto* | fried |
| *fritto misto* | assorted deep-fried foods (fish, vegetables) |
| *frutta* | fruit |
| *frutti di mare* | shellfish |
| *funghi* | mushrooms |
| *funghi porcini* | wild boletus mushrooms |

**G**

| | |
|---|---|
| *gamberetti* | shrimp |
| *gelato* | ice cream |
| *gianduia* | chocolate hazelnut ice cream treat |
| *gnocchi, gnocchetti* | small potato dumplings |
| *Gorgonzola* | blue-veined cheese |
| *granchio* | crab |
| *grappa* | alcoholic spirit distilled from grape mash |
| *grissini* | bread sticks |

## H

| | |
|---|---|
| *Hag* | brand name of the most popular decaf coffee; used to mean decaffeinated in general |

## I

| | |
|---|---|
| *imbottito* | stuffed |
| *insalata* | salad |
| *integrale* | whole wheat |
| *involtini* | stuffed meat or fish roles |

## L

| | |
|---|---|
| *lampone* | raspberries |
| *latte* | milk |
| *lenticchie* | lentils |
| *lepre* | wild hare |
| *lesso* | boiled |
| *limone (limonata)* | lemon (lemonade) |
| *lombatine* | veal chop |
| *lumache* | snails |

## M

| | |
|---|---|
| *macedonia di frutta* | dessert of chopped, fresh fruit |
| *maiale* | pork |
| *mandorla* | almond |
| *manzo* | beef |
| *mela* | apple |
| *melanzane* | eggplant |
| *melone* | melon |
| *miele* | honey |
| *mille foglie* | puff pastry |

## N

| | |
|---|---|
| *nazionale* | domestic, meaning made in Italy |
| *noce* | walnut |
| *nocciola* | hazelnut |

## O

| | |
|---|---|
| *oca* | goose |
| *olio di oliva* | olive oil |
| *osso buco* | veal knuckle |
| *ostriche* | oysters |

## P

| | |
|---|---|
| *pancetta* | spicy, salted bacon rolled, eaten raw |
| *pane (tostato)* | bread (toast) |
| *pane e coperto* | bread and cover charge |
| *panettone* | light cake with candied fruit peel |
| *panna (montana)* | cream (whipped) |
| *panino* | sandwich or roll |
| *pasta e fagioli* | pasta and bean soup |
| *patata* | potato |
| *peperonata* | grilled peppers served in olive oil |
| *peperoni* | peppers |
| *pera* | pear |
| *pesca* | peach |
| *pesce* | fish |
| *piselli* | peas |
| *polenta* | cornmeal |
| *pollo* | chicken |
| *polpette* | meatballs |
| *polpo* | octopus |
| *porri* | leeks |
| *primi piatti* | first courses |
| *produzione artiginale* | homemade, usually ice cream |
| *prosciutto* | air-dried, salt-cured ham |
| *prosciutto cotto* | cooked prosciutto |
| *prosciutto crudo* | raw prosciutto |

| | |
|---|---|
| *provolone* | smooth, cow's-milk cheese |
| *prunga* | plum |
| *prunga secca* | prune |
| *puntarelle* | wild chicory greens dressed with oil, vinegar, mashed anchovies |
| *purè di patate* | mashed potatoes |

**R**

| | |
|---|---|
| *radicchio* | red chicory |
| *rape* | turnip greens |
| *ravanello* | radish |
| *ribollita* | bean, bread, cabbage, and vegetable soup (means "reboiled") |
| *ricotta* | soft, mild sheep's cheese |
| *ripieno* | stuffed |
| *risi e bisi* | rice and pea soup |
| *rongnoni* | kidneys |

**S**

| | |
|---|---|
| *salsicca* | sausage |
| *saltimbocca* | veal rolls flavored with sage |
| *sarde (in saor)* | sardines (marinated) |
| *scampi* | prawns |
| *secondi piatti* | main courses |
| *semifreddo* | creamy ice cream |
| *seppie in nero* | squid cooked in its own ink |
| *servizio* | service charge |
| *sógliola* | sole |
| *sorbetto* | sherbert |
| *spezzatino* | stew |
| *spinachi* | spinach |
| *stracciatella* | broth with egg and Parmesan cheese stirred in at the last minute |

## T

| | |
|---|---|
| *tacchino* | turkey |
| *tartufo* | ice cream coated in hard chocolate |
| *tè, thè (con latte, limone)* | tea (with milk, lemon) |
| *tiramisù* | rich, creamy dessert made with Mascarpone cheese, liqueur, espresso, chocolate, and lady fingers (means "pick-me-up") |
| *tisana* | herbal tea |
| *tonno* | tuna |
| *torta* | cake |
| *tostato* | toasted |
| *tramezzino* | sandwich (also called *panino*) |
| *trancia* | slice |
| *trippa* | tripe |
| *trota* | trout |

## U

| | |
|---|---|
| *un'etto* | 100 grams, about 4 ounces |
| *uova* | egg |
| *uva* | grape |

## V

| | |
|---|---|
| *verdure* | vegetables |
| *verza* | cabbage (also called *cavolo*) |
| *vitello* | veal |
| *vino (rosso, rosato, bianco)* | wine (red, rosé, white) |
| *vin santo* | sweet dessert wine, served with *biscotti* |
| *vongole* | clams |

## Z

| | |
|---|---|
| *zucca* | pumpkin |
| *zuppa de pesce* | fish soup |
| *zuppa inglese* | trifle |

# Readers' Comments

In *Cheap Eats in Italy,* I recommend places as they were when this book went to press, but there are no guarantees that they will remain as I found them. While every effort has been made to ensure the accuracy of the information presented, the reader must understand that prices, menu selections, opening and closing times, vacation schedules, and ownership can change overnight. Therefore, the author and publisher cannot accept responsibility for any changes that do occur.

*Cheap Eats in Italy* is updated and revised on a regular basis. If you find that someplace has changed, or make a discovery that you want to pass along, please send me a note stating the name and address of the restaurant, the date of your visit, and a description of your findings. Your comments are extremely important to me, and I read and follow through on every letter I receive. Thank you.

Please send your letters to Sandra A. Gustafson, *Cheap Eats in Italy,* c/o Chronicle Books, 275 Fifth Street, San Francisco, CA 94103.

# Index

## ROME